Contents

atters

Advanced ... and Supply

COURSE BOOK

Risk Management and Supply Chain Vulnerability

© Profex Publishing Limited, 2010

Printed and distributed by the Chartered Institute of Purchasing & Supply

Easton House, Easton on the Hill, Stamford, Lincolnshire PE9 3NZ

Tel: +44 (0) 1780 756 777

Fax: +44 (0) 1780 751 610

Email: info@cips.org

Website: www.cips.org

First edition January 2007
Second edition November 2007
Third edition April 2009
Reprinted with minor amendments October 2010

Preface

Welcome to your new Study Pack.

For each subject you have to study, your Study Pack consists of three elements.

- A **Course Book** (the current volume). This provides detailed coverage of all topics specified in the unit content.

- A small-format volume of **Passnotes**. For each learning objective, these highlight and summarise the key points of knowledge and understanding that should underpin an exam answer. Use your Passnotes in the days and weeks leading up to the exam.

- An extensive range of **online resources**. These include a **Quick Start Guide** (a rapid 40-page overview of the subject), practice questions of exam standard (with full suggested solutions), notes on recent technical developments in the subject area, and recent news items (ideal for enhancing your solutions in the exam). These can all be downloaded from the study resources area at www.cips.org. You will need to log in with your membership details to access this information.

For a full explanation of how to use your new Study Pack, turn now to page xv. And good luck in your exams!

A note on style

Throughout your Study Packs you will find that we use the masculine form of personal pronouns. This convention is adopted purely for the sake of stylistic convenience – we just don't like saying 'he/she' all the time. Please don't think this reflects any kind of bias or prejudice.

October 2010

The Exam

The format of the paper

The time allowed is three hours. The examination is in two sections.

Section A – case study scenario, with two application questions based on the case study, each worth 25 marks.

Section B – questions to test knowledge and understanding. Candidates will be required to answer two questions from a choice of four. As with Section A, questions will be worth 25 marks each.

The unit content

The unit content is reproduced below, together with reference to the chapter in this Course Book where each topic is covered.

Unit characteristics

This unit is designed to enable students to undertake risk analysis and a variety of risk assessments relating to different aspects of purchasing and supply and to implement a range of appropriate risk management tools and techniques.

Students will use a variety of risk assessment tools and techniques designed to provide a detailed analysis of supply chain situations, including legal, corporate social responsibility (CSR), ethical, health and safety, financial, international, innovation and a variety of other potential risk scenarios. The scope covers both the proactive identification and avoidance of risk, as well as provision for post-event recovery initiatives.

By the end of the unit students should be able to:

*   demonstrate a good knowledge and understanding of risk awareness and an effective approach to risk management

*   apply a variety of tools and techniques, in a diverse range of contexts, to proactively establish the level of risk presented and to recommend ways of avoiding, mitigating or managing those risks.

Statements of practice

On completion of this unit, students will be able to:

- Analyse the nature and scope of risks for the organisation

- Assess the sources of risks and the likely impact of those risks upon the organisation

- Plan and implement an appropriate risk management process in order to protect the organisation's interests

- Explain how supplier appraisals, pre-qualification of suppliers and contract monitoring can help to mitigate risks

- Evaluate systems for testing risks and monitoring them accordingly

- Apply risk management principles to various purchasing and supply management scenarios

- Evaluate the application of a range of techniques to mitigate risk proactively and to reduce the consequential losses in the instance of a risk event occurring

- Explain how the use of sound negotiation approaches and techniques help to ensure better business value by reducing risk and vulnerability.

Learning objectives and indicative content

1.0 Understanding the nature of risk in purchasing and supply
(Weighting 25%)

1.1 Define the terminology used in risk assessment and management

• Definition of risk with use of examples	1
• How risk has a direct impact on an organisation's success and how risk can be directly related to cost	1
• Key terms: hazard, risk, risk event, exposure, loss – direct, indirect and consequential – mitigation, avoidance, assessment, management, *force majeure* and acts of God	1
• The differences between risk, vulnerability, exposure and loss, as well as understanding the range of management actions available	1
• What is meant by a risk appetite and use of practical examples to show how this is applied	1

1.2 Distinguish between direct physical loss (eg disrupted supply) and indirect consequential loss (eg reputation)

• Key types of loss that may occur: financial, reputational, environmental, health, safety, welfare and lost opportunities	1

1.3 Analyse potential sources of risk to organisations of both internal and external origin

• Internal and external hazards and risks	2
• Range of risks that might occur within the workplace	2
• Analysis of external environment factors using the PESTLE tool	2
• The likely impact on the organisation and its appetite for risk	2
• Basic quantification methods for measuring	10

1.4 Analyse and explain the use of segmentation and business tools to reduce supply chain vulnerability

• Segmentation tools to help assess and manage supply chain risk appropriately (eg Kraljic, Boston, Pareto, KPIs, spider web or appropriate alternatives)	3
• How you would take a different approach to purchasing from a critical or bottleneck market to that of a leveraged or acquisition market	3
• Management of different products or services within an organisational portfolio	3
• Definition of supply chain vulnerability, supply failure and supplier failure	3
• How to map a typical supply chain and identify potential sources of supply vulnerability	3
• The potential impact of supply and supplier failure	3
• Range of mitigating activities that a purchaser could use when looking to protect against supply or supplier failure	3

3.0   Managing risk and vulnerability
(Weighting 50%)

How to Use Your Study Pack

Familiarisation

At this point you should begin to familiarise yourself with the package of benefits you have purchased.

- Go to www.cips.org and log on. Then go to Study and Qualify/Study Resources. Browse through the free content relating to this subject.

- Download the Quick Start Guide and print it out. Open up a ring binder and make the Quick Start Guide your first item in there.

- Now glance briefly through the Course Book (the text you're reading right now!) and the Passnotes.

Organising your study

'Organising' is the key word: unless you are a very exceptional student, you will find a haphazard approach is insufficient, particularly if you are having to combine study with the demands of a full-time job.

A good starting point is to timetable your studies, in broad terms, between now and the date of the examination. How many subjects are you attempting? How many chapters are there in the Course Book for each subject? Now do the sums: how many days/weeks do you have for each chapter to be studied?

Remember:

- Not every week can be regarded as a study week – you may be going on holiday, for example, or there may be weeks when the demands of your job are particularly heavy. If these can be foreseen, you should allow for them in your timetabling.

- You also need a period leading up to the exam in which you will revise and practise what you have learned.

Once you have done the calculations, make a week-by-week timetable for yourself for each paper, allowing for study and revision of the entire unit content between now and the date of the exams.

Getting started

Aim to find a quiet and undisturbed location for your study, and plan as far as possible to use the same period each day. Getting into a routine helps avoid wasting time. Make sure you have all the materials you need before you begin – keep interruptions to a minimum.

Begin by reading through your Quick Start Guide. This should take no more than a couple of hours, even reading slowly. By the time you have finished this you will have a reasonable grounding in the subject area. You will build on this by working through the Course Book.

Using the Course Book

You should refer to the Course Book to the extent that you need it.

*   If you are a newcomer to the subject, you will probably need to read through the Course Book quite thoroughly. This will be the case for most students.
*   If some areas are already familiar to you – either through earlier studies or through your practical work experience – you may choose to skip sections of the Course Book.

The content of the Course Book

This Course Book has been designed to give detailed coverage of every topic in the unit content. As you will see from pages vii–xiv, each topic mentioned in the unit content is dealt with in a chapter of the Course Book. For the most part the order of the Course Book follows the order of the unit content closely, though departures from this principle have occasionally been made in the interest of a logical learning order.

Each chapter begins with a reference to the learning objectives and unit content to be covered in the chapter. Each chapter is divided into sections, listed in the introduction to the chapter, and for the most part being actual captions from the unit content.

All of this enables you to monitor your progress through the unit content very easily and provides reassurance that you are tackling every subject that is examinable.

Each chapter contains the following features.

*   Introduction, setting out the main topics to be covered
*   Clear coverage of each topic in a concise and approachable format
*   A chapter summary
*   Self-test questions

The study phase

For each chapter you should begin by glancing at the main headings (listed at the start of the chapter). Then read fairly rapidly through the body of the text to absorb the main points. If it's there in the text, you can be sure it's there for a reason, so try not to skip unless the topic is one you are familiar with already.

Then return to the beginning of the chapter to start a more careful reading. You may want to take brief notes as you go along, but bear in mind that you already have your Quick Start Guide and Passnotes – there is no point in duplicating what you can find there.

Test your recall and understanding of the material by attempting the self-test questions. These are accompanied by cross-references to paragraphs where you can check your answers and refresh your memory.

Practising what you have learned

Once you think you have learned enough about the subject, or about a particular topic within the overall subject area, it's good to practise. Access the study resources at www.cips.org, and download a practice question on the relevant area. Alternatively, download a past exam question. Attempt a solution yourself before looking at our suggested solution or the Senior Assessor's comments.

Make notes of any mistakes you made, or any areas where your answer could be improved. If there is anything you can't understand, you are welcome to email us for clarification (course.books@cips.org).

The revision phase

Your approach to revision should be methodical and you should aim to tackle each main area of the unit content in turn. Begin by re-reading your Quick Start Guide. This gives an overview that will help to focus your more detailed study. Then re-read your notes and/or the separate Passnotes accompanying this Course Book. Then return to question practice. Review your own solutions to the practice questions you have had time to attempt. If there are gaps, try to find time to attempt some more questions, or at least to review the suggested solutions.

Additional reading

Your Study Pack provides you with the key information needed for each module but CIPS strongly advocates reading as widely as possible to augment and reinforce your understanding. CIPS produces an official reading list of books, which can be downloaded from the bookshop area of the CIPS website.

To help you, we have identified one essential textbook for each subject. We recommend that you read this for additional information.

The essential textbook for this unit is *The Complete Guide to Business Risk Management* by Kit Sadgrove, published by Gower (ISBN: 0–566–08661–1).

CHAPTER 1

The Nature of Risk in Purchasing and Supply

Learning objectives and indicative content

1.1 Define the terminology used in risk assessment and management

- Definition of risk with use of examples
- How risk has a direct impact on an organisation's success and how risk can be directly related to cost
- Key terms: hazard, risk, risk event, exposure, loss – direct, indirect and consequential – mitigation, avoidance, assessment, management, *force majeure*, and acts of God
- The differences between risk, vulnerability, exposure and loss, as well as understanding the range of management actions available
- What is meant by a risk appetite and use of practical examples to show how this is applied

1.2 Distinguish between direct physical loss (eg disrupted supply) and indirect consequential loss (eg reputation)

- Key types of loss that may occur: financial, reputational, environmental, health, safety, welfare and lost opportunities

Chapter headings

1 Defining risk

2 The impact of risk on organisational success

3 A glossary of key terms relating to risk

4 Differences between risk and vulnerability

5 Risk appetite

6 Direct physical loss and indirect consequential loss

Introduction

The management of risk has developed and come to the fore in business thinking over recent years. In particular, risk in supply chains has attracted attention. Factors such as supplier reduction, closer relationships and the development of lean or agile supply chains have increased dependence within the supply network. Disruption or variability of supply can have severe ramifications on dependent supply chains. In consequence, the considered management of supply chain risk and vulnerability is an increasing requirement and discipline in modern business.

1   *Defining risk*

The historical perspective

1.1   Kit Sadgrove (in *The Complete Guide to Business Risk Management*) identifies three ages of risk management.

- The **first age** covers the period in the 1960s and 1970s where insurance was the main way organisations managed risk. Insurance companies, in turn, sought to reduce the ramifications of risk by encouraging increased security, rewards for not claiming on policies and awareness of safety considerations. Risk awareness focused on these non-entrepreneurial risks and did not extend to areas such as the risks involved in commercial contracts or risk exposure of staff or customers.

- The **second age** during the 1970s and 1980s saw organisations starting to treat risk in a more proactive manner. Quality assurance systems such as BS5750 (released 1979) encouraged organisations to adopt this proactive view. This increasing risk awareness was encouraged by consumer concerns particularly in areas such as product safety and increased governmental involvement and legislation.

- The **third age** arrived in 1995 when Standards Australia produced **AS/NZS 4360:1995**, the world's first risk management standard. Reporting of risk in financial accounts became an issue during the late 1990s driven by the Department of Trade and Industry working to develop a framework for business in the 21st century. Corporate scandals such as Enron, Cendant and Barings demonstrated a clear need for increased risk vigilance. Within the UK the Institute of Chartered Accountants in England and Wales published the Turnbull Report (1999), highlighting the need for better internal financial controls and better monitoring of risk.

Uncertainty and risk

1.2   Any transaction or undertaking with an element of uncertainty as to its future outcome carries an element of risk. As the Greek philosopher Plato long ago pointed out: 'The problem with the future is that more things might happen than will happen'.

1.3   **Uncertainty** has two constituent parts that help explain the quote by Plato.

- **Variability** refers to the situation where one measurable factor can take one of a range of possible values.

- **Ambiguity** is the uncertainty of meaning. It can be used about whether or not a particular event will happen at all, or whether something else unforeseen might occur.

1.4   The minimisation of the possible impacts of uncertainty underpins much of risk management thinking. Some areas of uncertainty can be identified and categorised with scenarios or contingencies developed to minimise the impact. Other areas of uncertainty may be considered as remote or unlikely to occur and, in consequence, may not be fully assessed. Much of effective risk management is about assessing the relative importance of areas of uncertainty and managing those key areas effectively.

1.5 **Risk** is defined by CIPS as 'the probability of an unwanted outcome happening'. Probability is the measure of the likelihood that a given event may occur; it may be measurable using statistical means. In essence, if the unwanted outcome can be identified it may be possible to estimate the probability of the outcome occurring and in consequence guard against it or consider an alternative course of action.

Risk analysis

1.6 Risk analysis is the process of identifying all the potential things that can go wrong with an activity, and then estimating the probability of each happening. For example, when a purchasing need is identified we need to consider commercial issues such as the supply market, finance and quality. A risk analysis system can ensure that all the risks attached to the purchasing decision are identified and assessed within an organisational risk management framework.

1.7 Risk analysis asks: 'What is the worst that can happen?' This approach is often a quick way of getting important information. A more considered approach is to ask: 'What is the probability of something happening?' or 'What is the consequence if something happens?' The outcomes are often scored (eg on a scale of 1–5) and either multiplied or added together. A catastrophic outcome with a low likelihood of occurrence may be of more concern than a minor outcome that is highly likely. This last consideration has never been more relevant than at the time of writing (March 2009). While nobody would have said that a collapse of the financial system in the Western world was at all likely, its overwhelming potential impact should have caused most organisations to place it high on their risk agenda. Few did so.

1.8 There are a number of distinct approaches to risk analysis. In essence, these break down into two types: quantitative and qualitative.

1.9 **Quantitative risk analysis** uses two fundamental elements: the probability of a risk occurring and the likely loss if it does occur. Each element is numerically ranked. Quantitative risk analysis uses a single figure (usually the two figures multiplied together). This is known as the **annual loss expectancy** (ALE) or the **estimated annual cost** (EAC).

1.10 The main problem with quantitative analysis is the unreliability and inaccuracy of the data. It is difficult to assign precise probabilities, and the level of loss is also difficult to estimate as the risk may overlap into other projects. Despite this, many organisations use quantitative risk analysis as the main method of risk analysis.

1.11 **Qualitative risk analysis** is even more widely used. Probability data is not used. Only **estimated potential loss** (EPL) is applied. Qualitative risk analysis uses three main interrelated areas to assess the risk.

   - Threats – things that can go wrong or attack the system such as fire, flood or fraud.
   - Vulnerabilities – things that make a system more prone to attack or more prone to fail if attacked. An example could be the storage of petrol at a filling station. If stored on the surface the risk of fire or explosion would be greater than if the petrol were stored underground. Storing underground lessens the vulnerability.
   - Controls – these are counter-measures to vulnerabilities.

1.12   Controls can be categorised into four types.

- Deterrents designed to reduce the likelihood of deliberate attack
- Preventive controls designed to protect vulnerabilities and to make an attack unsuccessful or of low impact
- Corrective controls designed to reduce the effect of an attack or event
- Detective controls designed to discover attacks and trigger preventive or corrective controls

Risk identification and appraisal

1.13   Risk identification is clearly important in providing the basis for risk analysis. If a risk is not identified it cannot be evaluated and managed. Risk identification is a formal process within risk management that seeks to identify potential problems or uncertain areas. Risk identification is often an inexact discipline, which relies on our past experience of potential risk areas.

1.14   This experience may often prove limited or inappropriate, particularly at the early stages of a risk management programme. Initial risk identification may involve a combination of academic research results, benchmarking, brainstorming or other organisational measures to define and categorise risk. Continuous risk identification is necessary to identify new risks, evaluate changes in existing risks or eliminate risks that may no longer be appropriate. The experience gained over time will help an organisation refine its approach to and understanding of risk identification.

1.15   When a risk has been identified the next stage is to assign a level of probability to it. We may also estimate the costs of controlling or minimising the risk so as to make decisions on whether to accept the risk or to treat it in some other manner (eg by attempting to avoid it, or by insuring against it).

1.16   Risk appraisal takes place as early as possible in the risk management process. Risk control cannot be effective without some prior form of risk appraisal.

1.17   Policies and procedures are crucial in effective risk identification and risk management in general. An organisational structure and process must be established to ensure that risk is being managed in an effective manner.

The risk cycle

1.18   The management of risk is an ongoing process. The risk cycle is a continuous process that evaluates the changing nature of risks facing an organisation and new risks that it may face in future. These risks will come from a combination of internal and external factors that must be understood and constantly monitored as part of the business process.

1.19   The risk cycle requires identification and documentation of the risks at all levels of the organisation that may impact on achieving organisational objectives. The risk cycle provides an ongoing methodology for risk management, based on the following stages.

- Identification of key risks
- Understanding the impact and probability of the risks
- Implementing risk management strategies
- Identifying the organisational level where the risk will be managed
- Identifying influences on the risk outcome and how these outcomes should be managed
- Monitoring, reviewing and improving the processes used

1.20 Effective implementation of the risk cycle requires support at both strategic and functional levels within the organisation.

- **Strategic risk management** requires a risk management strategy to be adopted as a policy across the organisation with support from Board level.

- At a **functional level** the role of risk manager will be introduced with responsibility for facilitating, developing and managing the organisation's approach to risk management and putting in place objectives, organisational structures and methodologies that embed the risk management strategy.

1.21 Risk management has become prominent in recent years as an essential business discipline and is coming to be regarded as a core business function. Risk management covers the activities involved in planning, monitoring and controlling actions that will address the threats and problems identified, so as to improve the likelihood of a project achieving its stated objectives.

1.22 Risk management involves three key elements: risk analysis, risk assessment and risk mitigation within a formal business process. The risk management processes put in place rigorous and auditable procedures to ensure that policy-driven best practice is being applied in key areas across an organisation.

Risk mitigation

1.23 Risk mitigation – lessening the adverse impact of risk – forms a crucial part of effective risk management. If implemented successfully a risk mitigation strategy should reduce the financial exposure to risk in a project. The objectives of risk mitigation are to reduce or eliminate the risk, to transfer the risk to another party, to avoid the risk, or to absorb or pool the risk.

1.24 Risk mitigation forms part of an organisation's risk strategy and the approach to mitigation will form part of strategic policy.

1.25 Risk analysis and risk management are interrelated The risk analysis and risk management phases must be treated separately, to ensure that all decisions are made objectively and based on all the relevant information.

The risk register

1.26 The formal recording of information, usually in a risk register, is an important procedural element. The use of a risk register and the documentary processes that support risk management are crucial to the overall management of risk.

1.27 The risk register lists all the identified risks and the results of their analysis and evaluation together with information on the status of each risk. The recorded details can then be used to track and monitor the perceived risk.

1.28 The risk register will give each item a designated reference, identify an 'owner' of that risk, and identify cost implications. A typical risk register might provide the following items of information in relation to each risk identified.

- Unique risk identification number
- Risk type
- Risk owner
- Date identified
- Date last updated
- Description
- Cost if the risk materialises
- Probability of the risk
- Impact
- Proximity
- Possible response actions
- Chosen action
- Target date
- Closure date

Risk control

1.29 Risk control systems vary across industries and sectors. However, any risk control system will generally involve grouping and assessing risks under five main headings that will be examined further as we progress through the text.

- **Strategic risks**: these arise from being in a particular industry and/or geographic area
- **Operational risks**: these arise from the functional, operational and administrative procedures that underpin organisational strategy
- **Financial risks**: these arise from the financial structure of the business, and financial transactions with third-parties
- **Compliance risks**: these are risks that come from the need to ensure compliance with laws, regulations and organisational policy (such as compliance with an organisation's corporate social responsibility stance)
- **Environmental risks**: these are of increasing importance to many organisations as they adopt a more progressive stance in this area

2 The impact of risk on organisational success

The potential results of uncontrolled risk

2.1 An organisation such as an airline operator faces a number of internal and external risks. Internal risks might include computer viruses, falling quality, workplace accidents, fraud, and loss of key personnel. External risks might include environmental concerns, terrorism, and new competitors. Some of these risk areas are relatively predictable and easy to control, while others are highly unpredictable and difficult to control.

2.2 Sadgrove gives the following table to illustrate the results of uncontrolled risk.

Table 1.1 *The results of uncontrolled risk*

Type of risk	Initial effect	Ultimate effect
Quality problem	Product recall; customer defection	Financial losses
Environmental pollution	Bad publicity; customer dissatisfaction and defection; court action; fines	Financial losses
Health and safety injury	Bad publicity; worker compensation claims; workforce dissatisfaction; statutory fines	Human suffering; financial losses
Fire	Harm to humans; loss of production and assets	Human suffering; financial losses
Computer failure	Inability to take orders, process work or issue invoices; customer defection	Financial losses
Marketing risk	Revenue drops	Financial losses
Fraud	Theft of money	Financial losses
Security	Theft of money, assets or plans	Financial losses
International trading	Foreign exchange losses	Financial losses
Political risks	Foreign government appropriation of assets; prevents repatriation of profits	Financial losses

2.3 Risk can never be eliminated from business but it can be identified and constrained. Risk can be described as a function of uncertainty and constraint. Peter Hunt of ADR (*Supply Management* 6 January 2000) gives the following example: 'Take the debate on rail safety. The cost of new safety systems can be seen as a constraint on their introduction. It is therefore possible to minimise risk by either addressing the constraints, or by finding and reducing uncertainty. In practice, however, few people are able to reduce constraint'.

2.4 Organisations exist for a purpose. This is usually focused around delivery of a product and/or a service. Whatever the focus of the organisation, the successful delivery of its objectives can be severely compromised by the uncertainty surrounding its internal and external environment.

2.5 These areas of uncertainty give rise to risks that the organisation may confront. These risks must be considered, evaluated and managed. The risk should be assessed by consideration of two factors.

- The possibility of the risk occurring
- The effect on the organisation should the risk occur

2.6 Risk management incorporates the consideration of the risk (risk analysis and risk assessment; the **inherent risk**) and the impact on the organisation should the risk materialise (risk mitigation; reducing to an acceptable level the **residual risk**).

2.7 Risk assessment is the process of assessing the likely impact of a risk on the organisation. It involves understanding and analysing the nature of the risk involved, calculating the possibility of the risk occurring (often by looking at the frequency of an event occurring in the past) and developing a number of options to offset the risk.

2.8   Risk is unavoidable and every organisation should take action to manage risk. Resources for managing risk will be limited. As a consequence organisations must use resources in a manner that maximises effective response. This objective can be aided by prioritisation of risks following evaluation in a manner that ensures resources are appropriately allocated.

2.9   The management of risk must be incorporated or embedded into the organisation. Top level recognition and support at board level, the development of a risk management strategy, decisions that transfer responsibility down the hierarchy of the organisation to operational or project areas and a risk management process that ensures strategic objectives are being met, are all essential to the effective delivery of risk management.

2.10   Strategic leadership is crucial. The development of a risk management strategy, with the Board taking ultimate responsibility for the organisational strategy and internal controls, ensures that strategic support will be maintained. The risk strategy should be developed with the objective of embedding risk management within an organisation's systems and processes.

2.11   Managers and staff throughout the organisation should be aware of the relevance of risk to the achievement of their objectives and need to be equipped with the relevant skills that will allow them to manage risk effectively.

2.12   In smaller organisations, the finance director or chief executive will often add the role of risk management to his responsibilities. In larger organisations the role will fall within the remit of a risk management committee, led by senior executives or board members. As the risk management discipline is increasing in prominence the role of a board level chief risk officer is being created in some companies.

A practical illustration

2.13   To illustrate how risk management is already an accepted business discipline in some organisations we reproduce the Balfour Beatty group's published stance on risk management: Figure 1.1.

2.14   The Balfour Beatty policy is an excellent example of a considered approach to risk management. Supported at Board level and with a defined internal organisational structure and processes the systems ensure that relevant risk considerations are analysed and treated in accordance with organisational processes.

2.15   Within the Balfour Beatty text there is reference to the **Turnbull Report.** This will be discussed later in the text. Turnbull put forward guidance on internal controls and the effective management of risk in organisations and has been highly influential in developing risk management thinking.

Figure 1.1 *The Balfour Beatty group's risk management strategy*

The Board takes ultimate responsibility for the Group's systems of risk management and internal control and reviews their effectiveness. The Board has continued to assess the effectiveness of the risk management processes and internal controls during 2005, based on reports made to the Board, the Audit Committee and the Business Practices Committee; including:

- Results of internal audit's reviews of internal financial controls

- A Group-wide certification that effective internal controls had been maintained, or, where any significant non-compliance or breakdown had occurred with or without loss, the status of corrective action

- A paper prepared by management on the nature, extent and mitigation of significant risks and on the systems of internal controls

The Group's systems and controls are designed to ensure that the Group's exposure to significant risk is properly managed, but the Board recognises that any system of internal control is designed to manage rather than eliminate the risk of failure to achieve business objectives and can only provide reasonable and not absolute assurance against material misstatement or loss. In addition, not all the material joint ventures in which the Group is involved are treated, for these purposes, as part of the group. Where they are not, systems of internal control are applied as agreed between the parties to the venture.

Central to the Group's systems of internal control are the processes and framework for risk management. These accord with the Turnbull Guidance on internal controls and were in place throughout the year and up to the date of signing this report.

The Group's systems of internal controls operate through a number of different processes, some of which are interlinked. These include:

- The annual review of the strategy and plans of each operating company and of the Group as a whole in order to identify the risks to the Group's achievement of its overall objectives and, where appropriate, any relevant mitigating actions

- Monthly financial reporting against budgets and the review of results and forecasts by executive Directors and line management, including particular areas of business or project risk. This is used to update both management's understanding of the environment in which the group operates and the methods used to mitigate and control the risks identified

- Individual tender and project review procedures commencing at operating company level and progressing to Board Committee level if value or perceived exposure breaches certain thresholds

- Regular reporting, monitoring and review of health, safety and environmental matters

- The review and authorisation of proposed investment, divestment and capital expenditure through the Board's Committees and the Board itself

- The review of specific material areas of Group worldwide risk and the formulation and monitoring of risk mitigation actions

- The formulation and review of properly documented policies and procedures updated through the free and regular flow of information to address the changing risks of the business

- Specific policies set out in the Group Finance Manual, covering the financial management of the group, including arrangements with the Group's backers and bond providers, controls on foreign exchange dealings and management of currency and interest rate exposures, insurance, capital expenditure processes and application of accounting policies and financial controls

- A Group-wide risk management framework, which is applied to all functions in the Group, whether operational, financial or support. Under it, the key risks facing each part of the Group are regularly reviewed and assessed, together with the steps to avoid or mitigate those risks. The results of those reviews are placed on risk registers and, where necessary, specific actions are developed

- Reviews and tests by the internal audit team of critical business financial processes and controls and spot checks in areas of high business risk

- The Group's whistle-blowing policy

2.16 As we have seen, the impact of risk can have far reaching implications for organisational success. The effective identification and management of risk can mitigate the effects that a risk event would have if not anticipated and managed effectively. Modern business, with its emphasis on core competence, reliance on outsourcing, closer relationships, global reach and increased integration requires a more thorough approach to risk management. External factors such as terrorism, currency volatility, and political uncertainty (among many others) can impact dramatically on vulnerable organisations. Risk management provides a methodology where organisations can plan for the future with an increasing degree of certainty.

3 A glossary of key terms relating to risk

3.1 An **act of God** is a legal term for events outside human control, such as sudden floods and other natural disasters, for which no one can be held responsible.

3.2 **Agility** is the ability of the supply chain to respond rapidly to unpredictable changes in demand

3.3 **Baseline** is the set of assumptions and methods that are used as the base evaluation of risk.

3.4 **Business continuity** is a proactive process that determines the key functions of an organisation and the likely threats to those functions. From this information plans and procedures can be developed which can ensure that key functions can continue whatever the circumstances.

3.5 **Business continuity planning** is the advance planning and preparations necessary to identify the impact of losses and develop viable recovery plans to ensure the continuity of the organisation in the event of a high-risk event occurring.

3.6 **Consequential loss** is indirect loss resulting from a risk event. As an example the recall of a product will incur direct financial costs but the loss of reputation is a consequential loss.

3.7 **Disaster recovery plan** is a plan to resume or recover a specific essential operation, function or process of the organisation.

3.8 **Expected value** measures the overall impact of a risk and is calculated by multiplying the impact of an event with its probability of occurrence.

3.9 **Exposure**: is the consequence, as a combination of the impact and probability, that may be experienced by the organisation if a specific risk is realised.

Exposure is the maximum loss suffered and it can be reduced. The 'residual risk' is the level of risk remaining after internal control has been exercised (to reduce the 'inherent risk'). The objective is that this remaining 'residual risk exposure' should be acceptable to the organisation.

3.10 *Force majeure* means any event deemed beyond control of a company including war, riots, terrorism, natural disasters, explosions, fires, strikes and labour disputes of all kinds and acts of authority whether lawful or unlawful.

3.11 **Hazard**: a dictionary definition shows the following: a risk; a peril; a source of danger. In terms of risk a hazard is the source of the potential danger. Risk identification must highlight the hazard, which can then be evaluated further. Risk is the possibility that a hazard will cause loss or damage.

3.12 **Impact**: the impact of an event is the value of the effect of the risk event and is usually expressed in financial terms.

3.13 **Internal control** is any action, originating in the organisation, taken to manage risk.

3.14 **Links** are the transport and communication infrastructures (such as roads, rail, air) that link together the nodes (eg factories, warehouses, retail outlets) in a supply chain.

3.15 **Mitigation**: action taken to reduce the probability of an adverse event occurring and/or action taken to reduce the adverse consequences if it does occur.

3.16 **Risk event**: the envisaged risk occurring.

3.17 **Physical loss**: the loss of tangible property. This risk will normally be covered by insurance.

3.18 **Probability**: the likelihood or degree of certainty of a particular event to occur in a specified time period.

3.19 **Resilience** is the ability of a system to return to its original (or desired) state after being disturbed.

3.20 **Risk-averse** is the term used to describe individuals or organisations that do not like being exposed to risk. **Risk-enthusiastic** is the opposite.

3.21 **Risk assurance** is an evaluated opinion, based on evidence gained from a risk review, on the organisation's governance, risk management and control framework.

3.22 **Risk evaluation** is the assessment of the significance of risks to an organisation and whether the risk should be tolerated, treated, transferred or terminated.

3.23 **Risk register**: a list of risks identified in the risk review process, including descriptive detail and cross-references.

3.24 **Risk review**: an overall assessment of the risks involved in a project, their possible consequences and their optimal management.

3.25 **Risk strategy** is the overall organisational approach to risk management from Board level. The strategy should be documented and available throughout the organisation.

3.26 **Risk profile** is the documented and prioritised overall assessment of the range of specific risks faced by the organisation.

3.27 **Secondary risks** are risks that arise from actions taken to mitigate risks.

3.28 **Transaction exposure** is the risk to an organisation with known future cashflows in a foreign currency that arises from possible changes in the exchange rate. This definition highlights the origins that modern risk management has in the finance sector.

3.29 **Uncertainty** is a source of risk derived from a lack of sufficient knowledge underlying probabilities of adverse events and/or their consequences.

4 Differences between risk and vulnerability

Supply chain risk

4.1 As we have discussed, organisations are always open to risk. Sound risk management procedures will identify the inherent risk. This is the exposure arising from a specific risk before any action has been taken to manage it to the residual risk stage. The residual risk is the exposure arising from a specific risk after action has been taken to manage it and making assumptions that this action has been effective.

4.2 Supply chain risk refers to uncertain or unpredictable events affecting one or more parties within the supply chain that can negatively influence the achievement of business objectives. An equation often used to measure supply chain risk is: probability of disruption multiplied by impact.

4.3 Recent years have seen a focus on 'lean' supply chains and the efficient linkages between suppliers, logistics and technology. The tighter the supply chain, the more vulnerable it is to common disruptions such as quality issues, late deliveries, poor information etc.

4.4 The concept of agile supply chains takes into account the possibility of supply chain risk and disruption. Although not the basis for an agile supply chain, the ability to be flexible can help to mitigate risk by having considered options and courses of action that may help to reduce the inherent risks in supply chain management.

Supply chain vulnerability

4.5 Vulnerability means being open to attack. In the case of supply chains vulnerability can be seen as disruption to the flow of goods and information that characterise modern supply chain management. Acknowledgement of vulnerable areas ensures that organisations work to minimise the vulnerabilities exposed.

4.6 A report by the Cranfield School of Management (*Supply Chain Vulnerability*, 2002) defines supply chain vulnerability as 'an exposure to serious disturbance, arising from risks within the supply chain as well as risks external to the supply chain'.

4.7 Vulnerabilities are both internal and external. As we will discuss as the text develops it is usually easier to address internal vulnerabilities than external ones. Organisations have greater control over internal than external factors.

4.8 Vulnerability to sudden supply chain disruptions is a major threat to supply chain strategies. Terrorism, theft and natural disasters are only some of the vulnerabilities. To remain in control over the resulting consequences increased emphasis is being placed on developing resilient supply chains.

4.9 Resilience in supply chains describes the ability to recover the original shape following disruption. For organisations it measures their ability and the timeframes in which they can return to their normal level of performance.

4.10 Resilience can be achieved through methods such as increasing safety stocks, developing the ability to move production between production plants, designing products and processes to allow for 'postponement', and matching procurement strategies with appropriate supplier relationships.

4.11 Sourcing strategies and make or buy decisions should be based on a detailed assessment of potential future vulnerability. A vulnerability assessment will address three key issues.

- Is there any business or purchasing vulnerability with this product/service?
- Is any vulnerability containable through commercial controls?
- Is the product/service crucial to strategic capability?

4.12 If the answer to the first question is no then that might suggest a tactical relationship with the supplier(s) concerned. If the vulnerability in the second question can be contained by commercial controls then enter into a contractual relationship. If the product/service is seen as strategically important (the third question), then it may be appropriate (following investment appraisal and analysis) to make/do in-house.

4.13 Professor Martin Christopher of Cranfield University states: 'Potentially the risk of disruption has increased dramatically as the result of too narrow a focus on supply chain efficiency at the expense of effectiveness. Unless management recognises the challenge and acts upon it, the implications for us all could be chilling'.

4.14 The tiering structure of supply chains can often contribute to vulnerability. The number of tiers causes 'distance' between (for example) the first-tier and fourth-tier supplier. The concept where each tier manages the supply chain through the tier underneath them can be questioned, particularly if it leads to vulnerability.

5   *Risk appetite*

What is risk appetite?

5.1 The concept of 'risk appetite' underpins an organisation's approach to achieving effective risk management. Risk appetite can be explained by looking at our own lives. Some people stay in the same area and eat only traditional English food while others scour the world for new tastes and adventures. The first have a low risk appetite, the second a high risk appetite.

5.2 Risk itself is unavoidable. Exposure to risk can be minimised by undertaking a course of action that could be described as 'risk-averse'. Some organisations (such as many local authorities, traditional men's clothiers or small retailers) take a low-risk or risk-averse approach. Other, more entrepreneurial, organisations will take greater risks. 'The greater the risk, the greater the reward' is a phrase often used, but this approach should be balanced against the internal and external factors facing an organisation.

5.3   The concept of risk appetite can also be illustrated by considering whether the risk is viewed as a threat or an opportunity. Risk appetite considers the level of exposure that is acceptable. This is often measured by comparing the potential financial rewards with the cost of the risk becoming a reality and finding a balance. When viewing opportunities the more entrepreneurial approach is to consider how much to risk in order to obtain the envisaged gains.

5.4   Consequently risk appetite is often formalised by means of a series of boundaries that give clear guidance on the amount of exposure an organisation is prepared to undertake. This degree of exposure will vary as time and circumstances change.

Risk appetite at different levels

5.5   As risk management becomes a more accepted discipline there is more discussion of organisations choosing their own risk appetite. Modern approaches to business (such as good communication, a learning environment, lack of blame and analysis of mistakes) are all important to deliver effective risk management.

5.6   The concept of risk appetite can be considered at three distinct levels within an organisation.

   •   **Corporate risk appetite** is the overall amount of risk judged to be appropriate at a strategic level. At strategic level the Board and its members will judge the tolerable range of exposure for the organisation and set policy to ensure that those lower in the organisational hierarchy understand their constraints when taking risks.

   •   **Delegated risk appetite** is the agreed corporate risk appetite that can be passed down the organisational structure, agreeing risk levels for different parts of the organisation. When risk reaches the highest level allowed the risk may not be accepted without reference to a higher organisational level. Risk escalation places boundaries on functional areas (similar to spend levels in purchasing). When the boundary is reached the risk level is referred upwards.

   •   **Project risk appetite**: this falls outside the day-to-day workings of an organisation, often being off-site and having defined objectives and timeframes. Projects may require different risk appetite considerations to reflect the speculative or standardised nature of the project.

Approaches to addressing risk

5.7   The need to address risks at all levels in an organisation gives the ability to turn uncertainty to the organisation's benefit by reducing exposure to risk and by taking advantage of opportunities. There are five key approaches to addressing risk (five Ts): tolerate; treat; transfer; terminate; take.

5.8   **Tolerate**: here the risk has been acknowledged and may be tolerable without any further action required, or managed in such as way as to reduce the risk to an acceptable level.

5.9   **Treat**: the purpose of treating is to manage the risk, recognising the probability of it occurring and minimising the impact it will have on the organisation. A number of controls further define treatment of risk.

- Preventive controls are designed to limit the possibility of a negative outcome being realised. Examples could include division of responsibility (eg more than one person handling a public relations risk) or authority levels (meaning that one person has a defined level of authority in tasks such as invoice authorisation).

- Corrective controls are in place to correct undesirable outcomes that have been realised. Examples could include recourse routes such as legal action and design of contract terms to facilitate ease of correction.

- Directive controls are in place to ensure that a particular outcome is achieved. Examples could include health and safety regulations over staff training, protective equipment or work hours.

- Detective controls arise after the event has been realised and are only appropriate when an event has occurred. They will usually be part of a review process with the objective of ensuring the risk is considered and evaluated in future within the organisational process if appropriate.

5.10 **Transfer**: once a risk has been identified the best response may be to transfer it to someone else. This can be achieved by taking out insurance cover, or by passing the risk to, or sharing the risk with, a third party. One purchasing example is the holding of stock with the risks of capital employed (storage, obsolescence etc). By having the supplier hold the stock the risk can be transferred fully or partly to the supplier.

5.11 **Terminate**: certain risks will only be acceptable up to certain levels. The risk may be too great or the cost of managing the risk may be too high.

5.12 **Take the opportunity**: strictly speaking, this option is not an alternative to the above. It is an option to be considered when tolerating, transferring or treating a risk.

Enterprise risk management

5.13 Enterprise risk management (ERM) is a term that is becoming increasingly accepted as the ideas of risk management become embedded in organisational thinking. The term raises the profile and highlights the increasing recognition and need for effective risk management.

5.14 As risk management achieves acceptance and status, one main consideration is an organisation's risk appetite. Too restrictive an appetite may result in lost opportunities; too open an appetite may result in unacceptable exposure. Organisations should view risk appetite at strategic level and then put in place policies, procedures and guidelines to ensure that the organisation's risk appetite is fully understood and implemented.

6 *Direct physical loss and indirect consequential loss*

Direct physical loss

6.1 Direct physical loss such as disrupted supply, damaged goods, pilferage etc, can cause major disruptions to supply chain schedules and, in consequence, to customer satisfaction.

6.2   Costs such as those arising from damaged goods and pilferage can be covered by insurance. However, as a general rule consequential indirect loss, or damage resulting from loss, or damage caused by a covered peril or risk, will not be covered.

6.3   Taking out insurance is a traditional route of covering against risk but insurance will usually cover only physical or material loss with the aim of placing you back in the same financial situation you would have been in had the loss not occurred. It goes no further. Insurance usually does not take account of any indirect consequential losses deriving from the claim event.

Indirect consequential loss

6.4   Business interruption insurance can be taken out. This extends consequential loss or damage coverage for such items as extra expenses, rental value, profits and commissions but the premiums payable must be rated against the risk.

6.5   Indirect consequential loss can have its most severe impact in the area of company reputation. Failure to deliver to customers as promised may cause those customers to question the ability and commitment of the organisation. The way we handle any issues (eg keeping clients and customers informed, apologising where appropriate, prioritising their next and subsequent orders) can help to reduce the reputational impact and loss of goodwill. However, damage to reputation can take a long time to repair.

6.6   Apart from the financial loss (which is often covered by insurance) and reputational loss other key types of risk loss that may occur are as follows.

- **Environmental**: the increasing interest and legislation in environmental issues places additional risks on organisations. The policy of 'make the polluter pay' is increasingly being embodied in law. Organisations must undertake a full environmental risk analysis of their operation and, as part of the overall risk management programme, ensure that the identified risks are managed effectively.

- **Health**: organisations have both legal and moral obligations to their staff and associated stakeholders in terms of health. Many organisations will put infrastructures in place that go beyond their legal obligations. It is a role of risk management to ensure these obligations are met.

- **Safety**: in the UK much of the regulation surrounding this is included in the Health and Safety at Work Act. Risk management has long been a feature of safety thinking, and structures and methodology serve to underpin the organisational approach.

- **Lost opportunities**: these can be viewed as an outcome of an organisation's risk appetite. Profitable opportunities that are turned down because of the risk approach of organisations represent lost profit. As part of a risk review process the frequency and nature of lost opportunities should be reviewed: is the risk appetite focus still correct for the organisation or is it resulting in too many possibly acceptable lost opportunities?

6.7   The risk management process requires a holistic view of what is at risk. It is important to identify the stakeholders and ascertain their views, concerns and expectations in regard to the need to minimise risk. Risk management requires a long-term perspective. Peter Hunt cites the example of public utilities' focus on savings with their suppliers that yielded significant short-term savings. The risks could be that the suppliers' reduced margins may affect future research expenditure, constraining innovation and creating long-term risks.

6.8   Organisations must take a modern perspective on risk management. There is a need for strategic commitment, an appropriate organisational structure and an embedded understanding of the importance of risk management. The relationship between risk management and supply chain management is of growing importance and will be examined in greater detail later in this text.

Chapter summary

- Any transaction or undertaking with an element of uncertainty as to its future outcome carries an element of risk.

- The management and minimisation of the possible impacts of uncertainty underpins much of risk management thinking.

- Risk can never be eliminated from business but it can be identified and constrained.

- The risk cycle is a continuous process that evaluates the changing nature of risks facing an organisation and new risks that it may face.

- Risk management involves three key elements – risk analysis, risk assessment and risk mitigation – within a formal business process.

- Risk management has gathered pace in recent years as an essential business discipline and is coming to be regarded as a core business function.

- The management of risk should be incorporated or embedded into the organisation.

- Supply chain risk refers to uncertain or unpredictable events affecting one or more parties within the supply chain that can negatively influence the achievement of business objectives.

- Vulnerability means being open to attack.

- Resilience in supply chains describes the ability to recover the original shape following disruption.

- Sourcing strategies and make-or-buy decisions should be based on a detailed assessment of potential future vulnerability.

- Direct physical loss such as disrupted supply, damaged goods, pilferage etc, can cause major disruptions to supply chain schedules and, in consequence, to customer satisfaction.

- Indirect consequential loss can have its most severe impact in the area of company reputation.

Self-test questions

Numbers in brackets refer to the paragraphs where you can check your answers.

1   How do CIPS define risk? (1.5)

2   Define risk analysis (1.6)

3   What are the two elements used in quantitative risk analysis? (1.9)

4   What are the six stages of the risk cycle? (1.19)

5   What is the purpose of risk mitigation? (1.23)

6   What is risk assessment? (2.7)

7   Define and explain 'exposure'. (3.9)

8   What are secondary risks? (3.27)

9   How does the Cranfield School of Management define supply chain vulnerability? (4.6)

10   What three areas will a supply chain vulnerability assessment address? (4.11)

11   What is the difference between corporate risk appetite and delegated risk appetite? (5.6)

12   What are the five key approaches to treating risk? (5.7)

13   List types of loss that may be suffered, other than financial loss and reputational loss. (6.6)

Further reading

•   Kit Sadgrove, *The Complete Guide to Business Risk Management*, Chapters 1–3.

CHAPTER 2

Potential Sources of Risk

Learning objectives and indicative content

1.3   Analyse potential sources of risk to organisations of both internal and external origin.

- Internal and external hazards and risks
- Range of risks that might occur within the workplace
- Analysis of external environment factors using the PESTLE tool
- The likely impact on the organisation and its appetite for risks

1.8   Assess risks involved with using technology, including

- Reliance on technology
- Security
- Hackers
- Fraud
- Storing of vital documents and materials

3.1   Health and safety issues

3.4   Technology failure, impact on supply, use of back-up systems and disaster recovery

Chapter headings

1   Sources of business risk

2   Internal sources of risk

3   External sources of risk

4   Technological risks

5   Risks in the workplace

1   Sources of business risk

Four sources of risk

1.1   No organisation is self-contained, which means that risks can arise from both inside and outside the organisation. The organisation must evaluate the factors that influence its operations at all levels.

1.2   There are four main areas of risk facing organisations.

- **Strategic risks** are those that relate to the vision and direction of an organisation. If the strategic direction is out of alignment with an organisation's risk appetite then this conflict could result in taking unacceptable risks or being too risk-averse and losing opportunities.

- **Operational risks** are those that relate to an organisation's production or operations. Risks could encompass quality issues, operational capacity, location of manufacturing or storage depots or the impact of customers/suppliers going into receivership etc.

- **Compliance risks** are those that relate to the rules and regulations governing an organisation's operations, eg health and safety legislation, compliance with the Turnbull Report etc.

- **Internal and external financial risks** are those that impact on an organisation's ability to trade profitably or meet public service targets. Included in this is the area of 'reputational risk'.

Eight categories of risk

1.3   The **AS/NZS 4360 risk standard** categorises risk under eight risk categories: commercial and legal relationships; economic circumstances; human behaviour; natural events; political circumstances; technology and technical issues; management activities and control; individual activities.

1.4   **Commercial and legal relationships**

- An example of a risk in commercial relationships might be a supply base reduction, with the remaining suppliers attaining a greater proportion of an organisation's business. The commercial relationship must be managed and monitored in such a way as to develop the mutual interests of both parties, over the long term, supported by regular discussions and minuted meetings that allow for risk issues to be discussed

- In a legal contractual relationship the aim will be to provide a framework that enables the relationship to develop while at the same time defining risk responsibilities and obligations.

1.5   **Economic circumstances**: external factors such as growth in the economy, interest rate movements and unemployment affect factors such as house prices, spending power and confidence of consumers. Increasing raw material prices may push up costs. Monitoring of these economic circumstances and how they may impact on the organisation's risk exposure should be integrated into an organisation's risk strategy.

1.6   **Human behaviour**: as an illustration the Health and Safety at Work Act places a joint responsibility on employers and employees to act in a specified manner. Human behaviour can often be irrational. In a business setting there are often legislative procedures that ensure that behaviour is confined within limits thereby reducing risk.

1.7   **Natural events**: these include fire, flood, explosion, tsunami and similar events which are beyond anyone's immediate control.

1.8 **Political circumstances**: these are particularly important in the modern era with the growing threat of terrorism. This category also includes areas such as the implications of a change of national government or (in the UK) changing views from the European Union.

1.9 **Technology and technical issues**: these can have widespread implications for modern business. Vulnerabilities to internet viruses, over-reliance on systems, inadequate back-up procedures and the implications of power failure are just a small number of examples.

1.10 **Management activities and control**: setting limits and constraints on employees so that major problems do not occur. The fall of Barings Bank is a leading example. Policies, procedures, systems and structures must all integrate in a way that allows management to function fully but with limited risk to the organisation.

1.11 **Individual activities**: a major risk consideration can often be an organisation's own employees. Fraud and theft are ongoing risks that organisations face. These risks clearly must be guarded against by putting in place rigorous monitoring procedures. Individual activities and risk management in procurement can be demonstrated by spend limits at organisational levels

Perspectives on risk identification

1.12 The Canadian Human Rights Commission identifies five perspectives that are proposed to help identify sources of risk: Table 2.1.

1.13 The risk issues facing business are wide-ranging and the risk management structures put in place must be thorough and rigorous but must also meet an organisation's individual needs. The Canadian Human Rights Commission report looks at a wide range of risk areas; some will be applicable to certain businesses or sectors, some to others.

1.14 New projects are particularly critical in the area of business risk. Projects, which are examined in greater detail later in the text, are particularly critical during the concept and bidding phases, as the information on which the bid is being placed may be less than desirable. Despite this a project baseline must be decided. The bid manager often faces a dilemma in that risk areas may be traded off against the need to place a competitive bid – with potential repercussions at a later stage.

Reputational risk

1.15 One of the driving factors behind the growth in importance of risk management as a business discipline is reputational risk.

1.16 During the 1950s and 1960s a main concern for companies was the management of their physical assets, eg their plant and equipment. It was considered enough to insure against risks. Through the 1960s and into the 1970s and 1980s the face of business slowly changed; world markets became more mature, marketing techniques developed, and the concept of globalisation slowly became a reality. Marketing became more sophisticated. The contribution of services became an integral aspect of business.

Table 2.1 *Five perspectives on risk identification*

Perspective	Sources of risk
Strategic perspective Sources that can impede the achievement of mandate and objectives	• Policy and strategy • Corporate reputation • Political factors • Public expectations • Stakeholder relations • Media relations • Industry developments • Changing demographics • Globalisation • National security threats • Business continuity • Emergency preparedness
Business perspective Sources that can impede the achievement of business or program objectives	• Business activities • Program activities and delivery • Client services • Service delivery • Alliances, partnerships etc
Corporate management perspective Sources that may not effectively support the achievement of results	• Structure and reporting relationships • Planning and priority setting • Budgeting and resource allocation • Expenditure management • Revenue and cost recovery • Procurement and contracting • Financial management • Performance management • Project management • Change management • Inventory management • Asset management • Human resources • Information and knowledge • Information technology • Communications
Compliance perspective Sources that could embarrass the organisation or cause liabilities for not complying with legal and regulatory frameworks	• Funding and appropriations • Statutory reporting • Compliance to laws and regulations • Agreements and contractual obligations • Workplace health and safety • Environmental protection • Security, privacy and confidentiality • Legal liabilities and litigation
Government perspective Sources that are critical to ensure alignment with government-wide commitments	• Citizen focus • Values and ethics • Accountability • Transparency • Best value spending • Client satisfaction • Improved reporting

1.17 In the latter years of the 20th century the value of intangible assets (eg brands) became a significant part of an organisation's make-up. The total value of organisations could exceed the total value of their physical assets by a factor of 10 or more, based on the potential long-term returns on their brand name and reputation. With this value placed on reputational risk there is a clear need to manage this risk effectively.

1.18 Managing reputational risk is an essential part of the strategic role of risk management. The Board of Directors of an organisation must take into account all stakeholders. The views and perceptions of stakeholders in many ways define the value of an organisation, and will determine its reputation.

1.19 An organisation must be proactive in its management of reputational risk – both good and bad. A sound organisation-wide risk management approach supported with effective scenario planning and contingency management is essential for organisations as they try to maintain or build their reputation.

1.20 In the vast majority of instances business reputations are gained over time. They are hard to gain but can be quick to lose. Reputational risk is often viewed as the most critical risk, as reputation is a key source of competitive advantage as products and services become less differentiated.

1.21 *The Register* (www.theregister.co.uk) quotes a recent respondent programme on risk management by the Economic Intelligence Unit that placed reputational risk (52%) above regulatory risk (41%) and human capital risk (41%).

1.22 Loss of reputation is in consequence a key area of risk management. Re-establishing lost reputation takes a long time and impacts across an organisation.

1.23 Reputational risk management requires a clear focus on the following areas.

- Sound risk management practices with consistent enforcement of controls on governance, business and legal compliance
- Prompt, considered and effective communication with all categories of stakeholders
- Continuous monitoring of threats to reputation
- Ensuring that corporate social responsibility issues are managed and implemented both within the organisation and in external links via supply chain management
- Establishing and regularly updating a crisis management plan defining specific power and authority and supported by a crisis management team.

1.24 Reputational risk is one of the most difficult risk areas to manage. Successful management depends on effective structures, policies and procedures, contingency scenarios and planning. We will examine these areas further as the text develops.

2   *Internal sources of risk*

Internal controls

2.1   Organisations face risks in both their internal and external environments. We will discuss external risk in the following section. However, the main difference between the two is that internal risk can be controlled while external risk factors can only be considered and planned for. Internal risks are controllable, external risks are not.

2.2   An organisation's systems of internal controls are designed to manage internal risk. Internal controls facilitate the effectiveness and efficiency of operations and contribute to delivering risk objectives. Internal controls are put in place to manage both internal sources of risk and the impacts of external sources of risk.

2.3   Internal control systems will vary according to the organisation but should cover the following key areas.

- The nature and extent of the risks facing the organisation
- The extent and categories of risk that it is acceptable to bear
- The likelihood of the risk occurring
- The organisation's ability to reduce the incidence and impact on the business of risks that do materialise

2.4   Internal controls are subject to limitations and these limitations should be considered as part of the risk management process.

- Directors and managers are responsible for the establishment, implementation and continuance of internal controls. Although the processes will be the subject of review and auditing it is effective management that ensures successful delivery.
- Internal controls provide reasonable assurance but are not a total guarantee against risk.
- Within any organisation there will be gaps that can be exploited by individuals. Internal controls must be responsive to potential gaps within the system.

People

2.5   'People are an organisation's biggest asset'; unfortunately they can also be the biggest risk. Organisations are made up of people – as are the markets from which they source labour and supplies and to which they offer products and services. Most organisational functions depend on human knowledge, relationships, decisions or activity. Consequently, people are one of the key resources of any organisation.

2.6   Organisational thinking and structures have undergone considerable change over recent years. The formalised, hierarchical structures of the 1960s and 1970s have given way to a leaner, de-layered management structure that places more emphasis on empowerment and teamworking approaches. These changes themselves create risks that organisations must confront.

The learning organisation

2.7 Pedler, Burgoyne and Boydell (*The Learning Company: A Strategy for Sustainable Development*) are the main proponents in the UK of the concept of continuous organisational learning.

2.8 A learning organisation is one that facilitates the acquisition and sharing of knowledge, and the learning of all its members, in order to continuously and strategically transform itself in response to a rapidly changing and uncertain environment.

2.9 All actions have two purposes.

• To resolve the immediate problem
• To learn from the process

2.10 In terms of risk management the learning organisation approach can help counter the risk that employees will make mistakes and errors because they are not sure what they are doing. The term 'empowerment' involves stretching individuals to maximise their abilities but it can equally stretch individuals beyond their limits and cause them to make mistakes and errors.

Groups and teamworking

2.11 Organisational flexibility is a key issue in human resources. Jobs are being redesigned to allow adaptability and responsiveness to changing task requirements, through multi-skilling, multi-disciplinary teamworking, flexible working hours and so on. Modern commentators such as William Bridges (*Job Shift*) and Tom Peters (*Thriving on Chaos*; *Liberation Management*) have suggested that the 'job' itself is a thing of the past: tasks and teams must be constantly redefined by customer and environmental demands.

2.12 Charles Handy (*Understanding Organisations*) defines a group as 'any collection of people who perceive themselves to be a group'. The purpose of this definition is the distinction it implies between a random collection of individuals and a group of individuals who share a common sense of identity and belonging.

2.13 People in organisations are drawn together into groups by a preference for smaller units where closer relationships can develop; the need to belong and make a contribution that will be noticed and appreciated; shared space, specialisms, objectives and interests; the attractiveness of a particular group activity or resources; and access to power greater than individuals could muster on their own.

2.14 Formal groups are deliberately and rationally designed to achieve objectives assigned to them by the organisation, for which they are responsible. They are task orientated and become teams characterised by:

• Membership and leadership appointed and approved by the organisation
• Compliance of the members with the organisation's goals and requirements
• Structured relationships of authority, responsibility, task allocation and communication

2.15 A team may be defined as a small group of people with complementary skills who are committed to a common purpose, performance goals and approaches for which they hold themselves jointly accountable.

Teams in supply management

2.16   Dobler *et al* (*Purchasing and Materials Management*) note that 'the increasing need in recent years for thorough long-range materials planning has increased the attention given to strategic materials planning activity. A growing number of organisations have … established a new planning group at the corporate level to conduct economic or technical investigations on a continuing basis'.

2.17   One criticism of teamworking is that in many cases teams do not work effectively. Sheryl and Don Grimme (GHR-Training) state that most teams do not work – for one of two reasons.

   •   They are not supported or encouraged by the surrounding organisation and are not recognised or rewarded for their efforts.

   •   They are not real teams but merely groups or at worst a 'pseudo team' (ones that call themselves a team while not functioning as such and whose interactions actually detract from members' individual performance).

2.18   A real team is a small number of people (ideally 5–10) who take the risks of joint action. They have specific goals and a common approach – for which they hold themselves mutually accountable. The output is more than the sum of individual contributions.

2.19   Issues such as ill-defined objectives, lack of trust, personality conflicts, lack of role clarity, poor leadership and poor communication can all work to undermine the successful delivery of team goals.

2.20   In today's more empowered and cross-functional approach to business there is a need for more emphasis on training and a more professional approach to teamworking. Individuals struggling to fulfil their role or teams not working cohesively toward defined objectives can both have a major impact on not achieving organisational success and in opening up the company to serious risk.

Fraud

2.21   Fraud is a major risk to organisations. In the last few years companies such as Enron and Worldcom have highlighted the need for increased risk vigilance particularly against fraud.

2.22   In the USA the **Sarbanes-Oxley** statute and in the UK the **Turnbull Report** (both discussed later in the text) address the issue of corporate governance with the objective of correct management behaviour and putting in place risk safeguards against fraud particularly aimed at senior level in organisations.

2.23   Internally management has the responsibility of providing controls to guard against fraud. This may involve crimes against the organisation, customers, other employees, financial institutions, suppliers and the government. Risk managers have the role of putting in place controls and monitoring them in practice.

2.24   To combat fraud an organisation needs to develop an anti-fraud culture, cultivating risk-awareness and encouraging responsible whistle blowing linked to the establishment of sound internal controls. We will return to the subject of fraud in Chapter 12.

Theft

2.25 Theft is one of the major areas of internal crime in organisations. Business areas such as retailing, warehousing and goods delivery take theft and theft issues seriously, encouraging a positive anti-theft culture and putting in place strong anti-theft measures.

2.26 Theft is a serious issue for organisations. The use of technology, not putting temptation in people's way and encouraging an organisational culture to support effective management in this area is important. Clearly theft is a risk for organisations to include within their risk management strategy.

3 *External sources of risk*

The PESTLE framework

3.1 The macro-environment comprises all those trends and circumstances, organisations and individuals, that affect the way an organisation conducts its operations. It is concerned with the forces in the environment that may at some point affect the organisation, ie be a potential source of risk to an organisation in its micro-environment.

3.2 The micro-environment comprises all those individuals and organisations that affect the operation of a business on a day-to-day basis. To illustrate the difference, suppliers and customers are real individuals and organisations that exist in a company's micro-environment. Trends or developments such as economic cycles, demographics, legal changes, advances in technology etc, will not directly affect an organisation today but may be likely to do so in the future and, in consequence, these changes and developments can be viewed as potential sources of risk in the macro-environment.

3.3 The external macro-environment must be monitored in order to ascertain any potential risks coming from the changing situation.

3.4 One management tool that can be used to illustrate the external factors and/or risks facing an organisation is the PESTLE (Political, Economic, Social, Technological, Legal and Ecological) framework. Table 2.2 shows some of the main factors/risks facing organisations in the external environment.

3.5 The PESTLE factors/risks are outside an organisation's control. Internal factors can be managed; external factors must be monitored, and the changing risk understood and evaluated. Any identified risks should be evaluated in line with an organisation's risk policy.

3.6 Risk evaluation requires continual monitoring of external factors. Risk assessments will often be made applying the existing situation. As external factors develop or change, the original assumptions become outdated or flawed. A process of re-assessment in line with changing external factors should be incorporated into an organisation's risk management strategy.

Table 2.2 *Risks in the PESTLE framework*

PESTLE factor	Risk factors
Political environment	• Change of government
	• Deregulation of markets
	• Moves to introduce private sector practices into the public sector
Economic environment	• Underlying growth and inflation rates
	• Globalisation of markets
	• Regional economies such as the EU and the impact of the euro
Social environment	• Greater emphasis on health and safety
	• Environmental concerns
	• Social equality
	• Demographic changes
	• Values and lifestyle changes
Technological environment	• Reduction in information costs
	• Technological advances
	• Shorter product lifecycles
Legal environment	• Legislation directly affecting an organisation's market, eg Acts of Parliament, directives, regulations
	• Health and safety and associated employee legislation
	• Product liability legislation
Ecological environment	• Opportunities to develop new products and services
	• Environmental product design
	• The increased cost of meeting pollution and other ecological requirements

3.7 The **globalisation of business** has introduced a range of risks. Organisations now need to view risks on different levels.

- Local – the immediate or micro-environment surrounding the company
- Regional – the area where the organisation interfaces with many of its stakeholders
- National – the country in which the organisation operates
- International – where trading introduces a new range of risks (discussed in Chapter 11)
- Global – the wider global environment that requires effective strategies, enhanced cultural awareness and effective communication. The greater the extension of an organisation globally, the greater the need for continual risk monitoring.

3.8 As mentioned above, international trading introduces a new range of risks.

- Country risk – the risk that a country may seize assets or lack currency to make payment
- Buyer risk – the risk that the buyer may not make payment. This risk can be addressed by using more secure methods of payment such as letters of credit and bills of exchange

- Exchange risk – dealing in a range of different currencies in a fluctuating exchange rate environment

- Transit risk – the risk that the goods may become lost or damaged in transit. Taking out insurance cover will traditionally protect this risk.

Competitive forces

3.9   A model originated by Professor Michael Porter suggests that there are five basic competitive forces that influence the state of competition in an industry.

- The rivalry amongst current competitors
- The threat of new entrants
- The threat of substitute products or services
- The bargaining power of customers
- The bargaining power of suppliers

3.10   The application of this model in the external environment illustrates potential areas where risk may come from. The changing nature of the competitive environment requires continual monitoring to guard against unseen risk.

Saunders's model of environmental factors

3.11   A model devised by Malcolm Saunders (Figure 2.1) gives a wider perspective on external factors impacting on the business and looks at a wider range of external factors than PESTLE or Porter's Five Forces. The application of these tools is to direct an organisation's thinking and they are of direct relevance in risk management. The need in external monitoring is to be alert to changes in the environment and to anticipate what those changes may mean. Monitoring in a structured way helps ensure that the unexpected external risk is identified before an unexpected risk event occurs.

Figure 2.1 *Model of environmental factors*

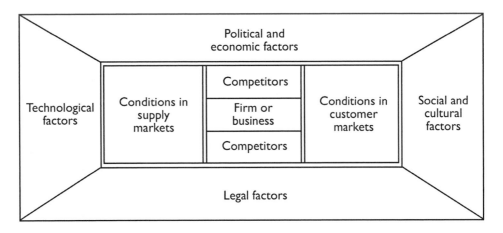

4 Technological risks

Introduction

4.1 The effective application of information technology lies at the heart of organisational management and operations. Information systems offer data management with a global reach that can facilitate trade and information sharing via the internet. Increasingly organisations are reliant on their IT systems and infrastructure. This dependence may also expose an organisation to risk.

4.2 Management of the technological infrastructure of an organisation is a critical function. Any decisions made relating to the supplying company, possible outsourcing, maintenance agreements etc, should be rigorously assessed as part of the risk management process.

4.3 The organisation's ability to use information technology effectively is dependent on the installed computer system, communications, telecommunications and other support systems that comprise the information network. The strategic decisions relating to information systems have long-term ramifications for organisations. They should be considered thoroughly and the potential risks discussed and evaluated.

Theft

4.4 Computers are an attractive proposition to a thief as there is a ready market for the stolen goods. Organisations should put security procedures in place (eg marking, securing or installing an alarm) but should also be aware that if computers are stolen there is an increased risk of the thief returning when new computers have been installed.

Hacking

4.5 Hacking means seeking unauthorised access to the system. This can take two forms.

- A member of staff trying to access confidential areas
- An external hacker trying to access company data and information

4.6 Using a firewall can provide an effective defence against hackers but should not be relied on completely. Firewalls are a combination of hardware and software located between the parts of an organisation's computer system requiring screening and those accessible from outside. Firewalls enable the restriction of access to selected systems and data through a single gateway, enabling password protected access to authorised users.

4.7 If the system detects a hacker they should be locked out by severing links immediately because when discovered the hacker may take extreme action such as deleting company information.

4.8 Hackers often have malicious intent such as industrial espionage, insertion of viruses or retribution against a perceived wrong. The risk they present must be taken seriously.

4.9 Internal and external access should be password protected with passwords changed regularly. Passwords should be unique to the individual and not obvious. Software programs can go through an entire dictionary using all possible words in an attempt to discover a password. The system should allow only a certain number of attempts at password entry before locking the person out of the system. Similarly, the system should insist that a password contains a mix of alphabetical and numerical characters.

Viruses

4.10 A virus is a self-replicating program, usually intended to cause damage to a computer system. Variants include 'worms' that sit in a computer's memory reproducing themselves, 'logic bombs' that lie dormant waiting for a specified date and then 'explode' deleting files, and 'Trojan horses' that start infecting only after the user has interacted with them.

4.11 An integral part of protecting against infection by viruses is the use of anti-virus scanning software that will particularly focus on the interface where emails and the internet enter the system.

4.12 Anti-virus software should also be placed on each individual computer. Many viruses enter the system when employees download programs from the internet or bring in their own CDs or memory sticks. Official organisational policy should discourage this but can be difficult to enforce as staff increasingly work from home, or at least take work home with them in the evenings.

4.13 Spyware, although not as invasive as viruses and related programs, involves collating information about the user's internet activities. Spyware programs capture financial and other details and send them back. All computers are vulnerable, which means that anti-spyware software is as important as anti-virus software. Both software types require constant updating as the threats change over time.

Computer failure and data loss

4.14 Kit Sadgrove (in *The Complete Guide to Business Risk Management*) quotes a statistic from the UK government's Information Security Breaches survey. Two thirds of businesses surveyed had suffered an incident in the last twelve months where they had to restore a significant amount of data from backup.

4.15 An organisation with a high degree of reliance on IT systems can be brought to a total standstill if computer failure occurs.

4.16 Organisations that have a high reliance on real-time processing (organisations such as Amazon, eBay, British Airways etc) are at serious risk in terms of lost business and reputational damage. Other impacts could include: resulting cashflow problems, inability to pay staff, backlog of work and service and quality reduction issues. Computer failure will have different risk ramifications for different organisations but the increasing reliance places IT risk high on the priority list for most organisations.

4.17 Computer failure can often be attributed to a small number of causes: breakdown, mainframe issues, hardware problems and electrical failure are perhaps the most common. The risk management process will consider each of these and the impact the failure will have on the business, and will develop disaster recovery and contingency planning scenarios that can be implemented to minimise or mitigate the impact. We will examine both of these aspects later in the text.

BS 7799 (ISO 17799)

4.18   The organisational management standard that can be applied by companies seeking to manage their IT system is BS 7799 (ISO 17799). This management system helps organisations to achieve the following outcomes.

- Enables organisations to identify the risks facing their information and introduce controls to counter them
- Ensures that personal information is kept secure in line with the Data Protection Act
- Reassures trading partners that the organisation protects and controls their own information and that of their partners

4.19   The BS 7799 (ISO 17799) 'information system security best practice' list provides a thorough and rigorous checklist comprising the following elements.

- Security policy
- Security organisation
- Asset classification and control
- Personnel security
- Physical and environmental security
- Computer and network management
- Systems access controls
- Systems development and maintenance
- Business continuity and disaster recovery
- Compliance

4.20   BS 7799 (ISO 17799) involves putting in place the following actions designed to minimise the impact of IT risk issues.

- Define the organisation's information security policy
- Define the scope of the system
- Assess the risk; identify the threats and vulnerabilities and assess the impacts on the organisation
- Identify the risk management areas
- Select and put in place the controls that will be used
- Document the selected controls

5   Risks in the workplace

The Health and Safety at Work Act 1974

5.1   Management of workplace health and safety is one of the most developed risk disciplines. Supported by law, there is a long history of risk assessment and management related to the minimisation of risks in the workplace. The Health and Safety at Work Act and the Control of Substances Hazardous to Health Regulations 2002 place a duty on employers, employees and others to ensure that the workplace is a safe environment to work in. This duty is supported by a rigorous risk management process ensuring that all relevant parties comply with the legislation

5.2   Acts and regulations on health and safety are both wide-ranging and general in nature. Together they offer a mix of regulations designed to address all relevant issues concerned with health and safety. Like all Acts and regulations they are subject to change and updating. Managers in the area of health and safety require a sound understanding of the Acts and regulations applicable to the work environment together with a positive and proactive attitude towards implementation.

5.3   The Health and Safety at Work Act 1974 (HSWA) was introduced following the Robens Report in 1972, which identified many problems with the health and safety law existing at the time. The Act sought to place general duties on all people involved with work and its associated activities, including employers, employees, contractors, controllers of premises, manufacturers, designers, installers and suppliers.

5.4   The Act set up the Health and Safety Commission and the Health and Safety Executive, and defined their powers and duties. The Act is also an enabling Act and has given rise to many of the regulations, approved codes of practice and guidance notes we know today.

5.5   The Act places duties on employers towards their employees by obliging them to ensure health, safety and welfare at work. The Act extends across all businesses so is equally applicable to employers in transport, vehicle workshops, distribution and warehousing. The Act encompasses delivery vehicles, which are regarded as the workplace of drivers.

5.6   The HSWA imposes a duty of control over the storage and use of explosives, highly flammable substances and dangerous substances both for safety reasons and to outlaw their unlawful acquisition, possession and use.

5.7   The Act also establishes controls relating to the emission into the atmosphere of noxious or offensive fumes or substances from work premises.

5.8   Workplaces must be maintained in such a condition that they are safe and without risks to health, offer adequate means of entry and exit and provide a working environment that has satisfactory facilities and arrangements for the welfare of those employed at the premises.

5.9   The main UK legislation is contained in the Health and Safety at Work Act 1974 which has, along with earlier Factories Acts, made it clear that the law views safety as a responsibility of everyone, not just managers, supervisors or operators. Each individual is legally bound to take responsibility for not only their own safety but also the safety of others around them. The Health and Safety at Work Act is supported by various regulations, the principal ones often being referred to as the 'six-pack'.

- The Workplace (Health, Safety and Welfare) Regulations 1992 (SI 1992/3004)
- Management of Health and Safety at Work Regulations 1999 (SI 1999/3242)
- Manual Handling Operations Regulations 1992 (SI 1992/2793)
- Health and Safety (Display Screen Equipment) Regulations 1992 (SI 1992/2792)
- Provision and Use of Work Equipment Regulations 1998 (SI 1998/2306)
- Personal Protective Equipment at Work Regulations 1992 (SI 1992/2966)

Health and safety inspectors

5.10   To support the HSWA, health and safety inspectors have powers confirmed in the Act:

- to enter premises at any reasonable time (or at any time at all if they consider the situation dangerous), bringing police support if they think they will be obstructed;

- to inspect the premises;

- to bring with them any equipment or materials and any other persons authorised by the enforcing authority;

- to carry out any investigation or examination they consider necessary;

- to take measurements or photographs or make any form of record they consider necessary or appropriate;

- to order that the premises be left undisturbed;

- to take samples of anything found and have it dismantled, tested, rendered harmless or destroyed;

- to demand to see any documents they think necessary;

- to require facilities and assistance – desk, office, phone, etc;

- to interview and take signed statements from anyone they consider appropriate;

- to issue improvement or prohibition notices;

- to prosecute in the Magistrates' Court.

The COSHH requirements

5.11   The Control of Substances Hazardous to Health Regulations 2002, more commonly referred to as COSHH, are regulations published as Statutory Instrument No 2677 to control the storage and use of hazardous chemicals and substances in the workplace. Their purpose is to protect members of the workforce and others from the dangers of exposure to hazardous chemicals and substances through direct contact, inhalation or ingestion, which may jeopardise health. The regulations are available at www.opsi.gov.uk.

5.12   The COSHH regulations provide a legal framework for controlling the exposure of people to hazardous substances relating to work activities. They impose on employers (and self-employed persons) a statutory duty to protect employees and other persons who may be exposed to hazardous substances. They place restrictions and/or prohibitions on the importation, supply and use at work of designated substances that are of a hazardous nature.

5.13   Many substances pose a risk to people. The transit of hazardous material by road, rail, sea and air is highly regulated in order to minimise these risks while allowing business operations to continue. As technology has progressed and science has continued to develop, an ever-increasing range of complex and possibly hazardous materials are being used in the workplace.

5.14   The COSHH regulations seek to impose clear responsibilities on the handling and use of hazardous materials. According to the Health and Safety Executive more people die at work from contact with hazardous substances than from accidents.

Exposure to hazardous material

5.15　The dangers of exposure to hazardous material can result in any number of problems: burns, inhaling or ingesting substances, skin irritation and rashes, and allergic reaction can all cause both long-term and short-term health problems. Biological agents (bacteria, micro-organisms) can cause a variety of infections; carcinogenic substances have cancer-causing potential. All these areas impact on health and should be considered.

5.16　Exposure to hazardous material can relate to:

- substances used in the work environment and work processes including adhesives, paints, thinners and cleaning agents;
- substances generated during the work process such as gases, vapours, fumes and dust;
- naturally occurring substances such as dust and mould on grain or fertiliser used in agricultural work.

5.17　The COSHH regulations place responsibilities on employers to protect employees, and others in the workplace, from exposure to hazardous substances.

5.18　Under the regulations employers are required to make a suitable and sufficient assessment of any health risk created by the work and the measures needed to be taken, as a consequence, to protect people's health. Precautions must be taken to prevent or reduce those risks as far as possible.

5.19　Every employer should ensure that the exposure of their employees to substances that are hazardous to health is either prevented or, where this is not possible, controlled. This could involve closed areas with restricted access, and control measures such as ventilation systems, hygiene regimes, time-exposure limits or protective clothing. All control equipment should be fully maintained with accurate and complete maintenance records kept. The duty of control covers:

- the design and use of appropriate work processes, systems and engineering controls together with the provision and use of suitable work equipment and materials;
- the control of exposure at source, including adequate ventilation systems and appropriate organisational measures;
- where adequate control of exposure cannot be achieved by other means, the provision of suitable personal protective equipment.

5.20　If the risk assessment indicates that it is necessary for adequate control or for protection of the health of employees, the employer must ensure that exposure to substances is monitored in accordance with a suitable procedure. Health surveillance monitoring should be carried out for those who are exposed to materials deemed hazardous. This procedure will only be applicable if:

- an identifiable disease or adverse health effect may be related to the exposure;
- there is a reasonable likelihood that the disease or effect may occur under the particular condition at work;
- there are valid techniques for detecting indications of the disease or effect.

5.21   Every employer undertaking work that is liable to expose an employee to a substance hazardous to health must provide the employee with suitable and sufficient information, instruction and training.

5.22   The employer must also make arrangements to deal with accidents, incidents and emergencies.

- Procedures, including the provision of appropriate first-aid facilities and first-aid evacuation drills, should be in place.

- Information on emergency arrangements relevant to work hazards should be available.

- Suitable warning and other communication systems should be established to enable an appropriate response, including remedial actions and rescue operations, to be made immediately should an event occur.

5.23   The COSHH regulations apply across all sectors of the economy – manufacturing, agriculture or service – and wherever substances hazardous to health are used, processed or manufactured. The regulations are in place to ensure that, in the case of all work involving substances hazardous to health, whether it is in progress or still to be started, the same, thorough, systematic approach is taken, identifying precautions which correctly anticipate and match the risks.

Chapter summary

- An organisation must evaluate the risks that influence its operations at all levels.

- One of the factors behind the growth in importance of risk management as a business discipline is reputational risk.

- The value of intangible assets has become the most important contributor to the value of many companies traded on world stock exchanges. The total value of organisations could exceed the total value of their physical assets by a factor of 10 or more, based on the potential long-term returns on their brand name and reputation. With this value placed on reputational risk there is a clear need to manage this risk effectively.

- Reputational risk is often viewed as the most critical risk, as reputation is a key source of competitive advantage.

- A sound organisation-wide risk management approach, supported with effective scenario planning and contingency management, is essential for organisations as they try to maintain or build their reputation.

- Internal controls facilitate the effectiveness and efficiency of operations and contribute to delivering risk objectives.

- A learning organisation is one that facilitates the acquisition and sharing of knowledge, and the learning of all its members, in order to continuously and strategically transform itself in response to a rapidly changing and uncertain environment.

- In today's more empowered and cross-functional approach to business there is a need for more emphasis on training and a more professional approach to teamworking.

- The macro-environment comprises all those trends and circumstances, organisations and individuals, that affect the way an organisation conducts its operations. The micro-environment comprises all those individuals and organisations that affect the operation of a business on a day-to-day basis.

- The globalisation of business has introduced a range of new risks.

- An organisation's ability to effectively use information technology is dependent on the installed computer system, communications, telecommunications and other support systems that comprise the information network.

- Management of workplace risk is one of the most developed risk disciplines.

Self-test questions

Numbers in brackets refer to the paragraphs where you can check your answers.

1   What are the four main areas of risk facing organisations? (1.2)

2   What are the eight risk categories under the AS/NZS 4360 risk standard? (1.3)

3   Reputational risk management requires a clear focus on what areas? (1.23)

4   Internal control systems will vary according to the organisation but should cover what key areas? (2.3)

5   Define a 'learning organisation'. (2.8)

6   How does Charles Handy define a group? (2.12)

7   The globalisation of business has introduced a wide range of risks. Detail three of these. (3.7)

8   How should an organisation protect itself against 'hacking'? (4.6–4.9)

9   What actions are recommended by BS 7799 to minimise the impact of IT risk issues? (4.20)

10   What powers do health and safety inspectors have under the HSWA? (5.10)

Further reading

•   Kit Sadgrove, *The Complete Guide to Business Risk Management*, Chapter 12.

CHAPTER 3

Segmentation Tools and Supply Chain Vulnerability

Learning objectives and indicative content

1.4   Analyse and explain the use of segmentation and business tools to reduce supply chain vulnerability.

- Segmentation tools to help assess and manage supply chain risk appropriately (eg Kraljic, Boston, Pareto, KPIs, spider web or appropriate alternatives)
- How you would take a different approach to purchasing from a critical or bottleneck market to that of a leveraged or acquisition market
- Management of different products or services within an organisational portfolio
- Definition of supply chain vulnerability, supply failure and supplier failure
- How to map a typical supply chain and identify potential sources of supply vulnerability
- The potential impact of supply and supplier failure
- Range of mitigating activities that a purchaser could use when looking to protect against supply or supplier failure

Chapter headings

1   Segmentation tools

2   Supply chain vulnerability

3   Supply chain mapping

4   Supply chain risk management

5   Supplier failure

1   Segmentation tools

The Boston Consulting Group product/market portfolio matrix

1.1   Risk management requires the effective use of resources. There are a number of selected tools and techniques that enable an organisation to work toward this goal. Many tools may be applied but those described in the first section of this chapter are possibly the most widely accepted tools that can be applied.

1.2   The Boston Consulting Group (BCG) matrix was first established in 1970 and has become one of the most widely accepted tools of analysis. Organisations need to have products that generate positive cashflow to finance operations and to finance the development of new products to take the place of the cashflow generators when they move toward the end of their product lifecycle.

1.3   The BCG matrix is particularly relevant to diversified businesses. The basic logic of the tool is that relative market share is linked directly to cash generation and profitability. The organisation with the largest cumulative sales volume gains the benefits of the experience curve first, so market share is critical.

1.4   The vertical axis in the matrix refers to the growth rate of the market at which each product is targeted. The horizontal axis refers to the relative market share enjoyed by each product. The possible combinations are shown in Figure 3.1.

Figure 3.1 *The BCG product/market portfolio matrix*

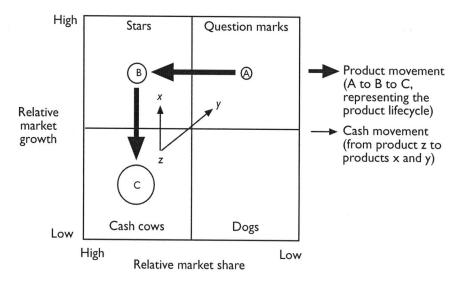

1.5   The four possibilities have been given names that make them reasonably memorable.

- Products with high relative market share in markets with low growth require little investment and generate lots of cash; these are cash cows.

- Dogs have low relative shares in low growth markets, so there is little future in keeping them.

- Question marks (also known as problem children) indicate a follower positioning in a growth market. These products require substantial cash investment to potentially turn them into stars.

- Stars have a leading share in their own market and may at this stage be able to fund their own development to make them into cash cows

1.6   As the diagram indicates, a product's place on the matrix is not fixed forever. Stars tend to move vertically downwards to become cash cows as the market growth rate slows. The cash they generate can be used to turn question marks into stars, and eventually into cash cows. This ideal progression is shown in Figure 3.1.

1.7   The strategies for the overall product portfolio are concerned with balance and risk management. The risk is that the overall portfolio does not generate the cash required to support the organisation and the development of new products. Objectives might include the following.

- Cash cows of sufficient size and/or number that can support other products in the portfolio

- Stars of sufficient size and/or number that will provide sufficient cash generation when the current cash cows can no longer do so

- Question marks that have reasonable prospects of becoming future stars

- No dogs, unless there is a sound reason for supporting them

1.8 A problem with the BCG matrix is that it hinges on a simplistic view of the competitive positioning of individual businesses. Relative market share is indeed important, and so is market growth rate, but there is a wide range of other variables in the business environment, and in the way the organisation is managed, that have a bearing on profitability.

Kraljic's matrix

1.9 An important tool in determining relationships with suppliers is the Kraljic matrix or **procurement positioning grid** developed by Peter Kraljic (1973). Kraljic's matrix is a tool of analysis that seeks to map the importance to the organisation of the item being purchased against the complexity of the market that supplies it. The vertical axis (measuring the importance of the item) is usually related to the amount of the organisation's annual spend on the item in question: high spend implies high importance.

Figure 3.2 *Kraljic's grid*

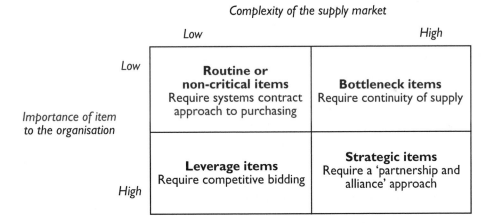

1.10 The approach that the organisation should then take to sourcing an item is decided by where the item is positioned on the grid.

- If an item falls within the low spend/low risk category as a routine item the approach may be to use IT management of the spend. This may be achieved by permitting the supplier to manage the inventory and re-stocking against an annually negotiated agreement, eg as with stationery supplies. Purchasing management is achieved by monitoring the spend against regular reports provided, as agreed with the supplier.

- If an item falls within the high-dependency bottleneck section the objective is one of strategic security. Approaches could be carrying a higher level of stock than would otherwise be the case or developing a closer relationship with suppliers than the value of the item would otherwise indicate. The purchasing objective is to ensure continuity of supply.

- The leverage section indicates a more traditional approach where a number of suppliers exist in a market and can be judged by commercial criteria such as price, quality and delivery. The objective is to secure supply but it is not one where a long-term relationship of importance is envisaged.

- The strategic section of the grid examines the implications of high risk and high value items where the approach could be a more long-term sustainable relationship that will bring benefits through closer supply chain, IT and management processes.

1.11 The horizontal axis demonstrates the risk an organisation is exposing itself to in terms of the degree of difficulty in sourcing a particular product or component or the vulnerability of the supplier to fulfil their obligations. The vertical axis examines profit potential and is used to indicate the extent to which the potential of supply can contribute to profitability.

1.12 Profit potential may be realised by cost reductions, value analysis or efficiency gains. For items in the strategic quadrant we can consider supplier relationships over the longer term by developing supply chain solutions to areas of cost and waste. This can add to profit potential by joint product/service development opportunities and a more integrated approach to information technology and knowledge management.

1.13 Applying the matrix would give different results for different organisations, and even for the same organisation over time. For instance, the sourcing of steel has moved from an adversarial relationship for many organisations when there was a situation of global over supply to a more strategic relationship as organisations react to the impact of Chinese demand on the supply market. In other words, for many organisations steel has moved from being a leverage item to being a strategic item.

1.14 Applying Kraljic's matrix to a particular context is a fairly straightforward process that can prove highly effective. However, it does have some weaknesses.

- It ignores the fact that not all the risk of the supply comes from within the relationship between customer and supplier. External environmental factors, especially competition and the PESTLE factors, can impact greatly.

- It applies to products/services rather than to suppliers. A supplier of non-critical items may also be the supplier of strategic ones, for instance. Applying the grid to suppliers rather than goods or services is often used when contemplating a supplier reduction programme. Treating a strategic supplier as a non-critical one, for instance, simply because it supplies both types of product would be a clear mistake.

- While the buyer may perceive an item to be a leverage one, this is only perceived on the other side of the relationship by the supplier if the buyer's spend is significant. In other words, the relative sizes and perceptions of the parties should also be taken into account. This leads us on to the next tool of analysis: the supplier preferencing model.

Supplier preferencing (or supplier perception)

1.15 The Kraljic matrix of course illustrates the buyer's perspective on the items to be purchased. This will often differ significantly from the supplier's perspective: what is very important to the buyer may be relatively unimportant to a particular supplier.

1.16 Once again, we can approach this issue by reference to a two-by-two matrix. In this case, the vertical axis measures how attractive it is to the supplier to deal with the buyer; while the horizontal axis measures the monetary value of the business that might be available from the buyer.

1.17 The horizontal axis is self-explanatory, but the attractiveness of the buying organisation (measured on the vertical axis) is less obvious. There are various factors that might make a supplier keen to do business with a buying organisation.

  • A buying organisation might be in some way glamorous or high profile. Suppliers will want to deal with such an organisation merely for the sake of boasting to other customers or potential customers about who is on their client list. By contrast, some organisations are inherently unattractive to deal with, and suppliers will give preference to other potential customers unless they are looking to use spare capacity. This might be the case, for example, if the buyer has a poor reputation on corporate social responsibility.

  • A buying organisation with a reputation for fair dealing, or with a record of prompt payment to suppliers, will naturally be attractive. Similarly, a buying organisation will be attractive if it has a reputation of engaging closely with suppliers, keeping them well informed, and perhaps working with them on new product development.

  • Whatever the current attractiveness of a buying organisation, things may change in the future. For example, changes of personnel may lead to changes in the methods of dealing with suppliers. Changes in the competitive environment may make a buying organisation more, or less, successful than it used to be, which can also change its level of attractiveness.

1.18 Once again, we have four quadrants: see Figure 3.3.

Figure 3.3 *The supplier preferencing model*

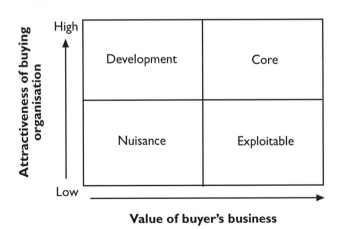

1.19 In the bottom left quadrant, we have buyers who are neither inherently attractive to the supplier, nor particularly valuable in terms of volume business. The model labels these unfortunate organisations as **nuisance customers**. Many suppliers have a policy of reviewing their customer base regularly with a view to terminating contracts with customers who are not 'paying their way'. The situation usually is that the customer takes more effort and cost to service than the value of the business justifies. From the supplier's perspective, the option of termination – or alternatively, hiking prices by a substantial amount – may be the best solution.

1.20 Staying with the relatively unattractive buying organisations, the bottom right quadrant contains **exploitable customers**. They are exploitable in the sense that they offer large volumes of business, which compensates for any lack of inherent attractiveness. It may be this very fact that causes the customer to be unattractive: if the buyers believe they are a major customer, they may exploit this with aggressive behaviour. In such an environment the supplier is grateful enough to do what is required of him under the supply contract, but will not go out of his way to provide extras. And any extras that are demanded will be charged at additional cost.

1.21 In the top left quadrant we have **development customers**. These are customers who do not – or at least do not yet – offer large volumes of business, but who for other reasons are attractive to the supplier. The supplier may see potential for growth in the customer overall, or at least in the volume of business that the customer can offer. It will pay the supplier to court the customer by 'going the extra mile' in fulfilling obligations. This could mean providing extra services for little or no additional cost in order to win favour with the customer, or perhaps accommodating changes in schedules or order levels without complaint. If all goes well, the supplier hopes to push this customer into the top right corner of the grid.

1.22 The top right is occupied by **core customers**. These are the organisations attractive in their own right, and offering valuable levels of business to the supplier. Naturally, the supplier will do all that is possible to stay in favour with these organisations – they are his core business and he will want to maintain close relations. The supplier will want to be aware at the earliest possible stage of any looming threat to the business, and for this reason will keep in regular contact with the customer.

1.23 The supplier preferencing model is not static. The supplier would ideally like to be moving all his customers into the top right quadrant and will work towards doing so. On the other hand, downward progress is possible too. We have already seen that some customers in the bottom left quadrant face possible eviction. Equally, a core customer could move down into the exploitable quadrant if for some reason its inherent attractiveness declined (perhaps because of association with a financial scandal, or because of public concerns over corporate social responsibility issues).

1.24 Buyers can learn a great deal by trying to view relationships from the perspective of their suppliers. It should not be difficult to guess where in the grid a buyer stands: the general attitude of the supplier's sales staff should give plenty of clues. If the sales staff are helpful, and proactive in involving the buyer closely, the signs are good. On the other hand, if sales staff rarely bother to make contact, or show indifference, then a buyer can conclude that he is in the bottom two quadrants.

Pareto analysis (ABC analysis)

1.25 Vilfredo Pareto (1848–1923), an Italian economist and sociologist, made the observation that a large proportion of national wealth tended to be under the control of a relatively small number of individuals. This observation enabled him to formulate the following rule.

In any series of elements to be controlled a selected small factor in terms of number of elements almost always accounts for a large factor in terms of effort.

1.26 The Pareto principle serves as the basis for ABC analysis used in stock management. ABC analysis can be defined as follows.

The application of Pareto's principle to the analysis of supply data. If items in a store are arranged in descending order of usage value and the cumulative number of items is plotted against the cumulative usage value the result would be (expected to) show a curve of the general form associated with Pareto's principle.

1.27 ABC analysis is based on the 80: 20 rule, the Pareto principle that approximately 80 per cent of the total value of material will be accounted for by approximately 20 per cent of the items: see Figure 3.4. This ratio has been evidenced and applied successfully in numerous business situations. The ABC analysis is a refinement of the idea by developing the concept one stage further into three stock categories used extensively in stock control.

Category A items: The 'vital few'. Small in number but high in usage value.

Category B items: 'Normal' items. Medium in number, medium usage value

Category C items: The 'trivial many'. High in number, low usage value.

Figure 3.4 *Pareto analysis of stockholdings*

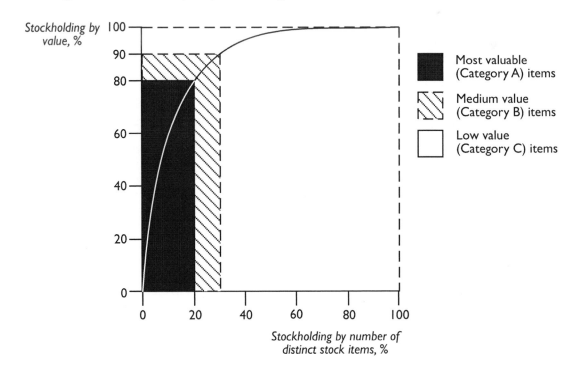

1.28 The application of Pareto in business has developed from the general view that 20 per cent of customers provide 80 per cent of profit. Therefore concentrate management effort on the key 20 per cent. From a purchasing perspective the view would be that 20% of suppliers account for 80% of spend. Time and resources should be allocated appropriately.

Other segmentation tools

1.29 At this point your syllabus mentions key performance indicators (KPIs) and 'spider web'. It is not clear how KPIs can act as a segmentation tool and we defer our discussion to where it is more relevant (see Chapter 11).

1.30 As for 'spider web', it is far from clear what this refers to but CIPS have directed us to a University of Vermont website where such a model is depicted. It seems that the idea is to pick out different possible risks and map the importance of each onto a scale from 1 to 5. The diagram used for this purpose (see Figure 3.5) resembles a spider's web.

Figure 3.5 *A spider web – University of Vermont*

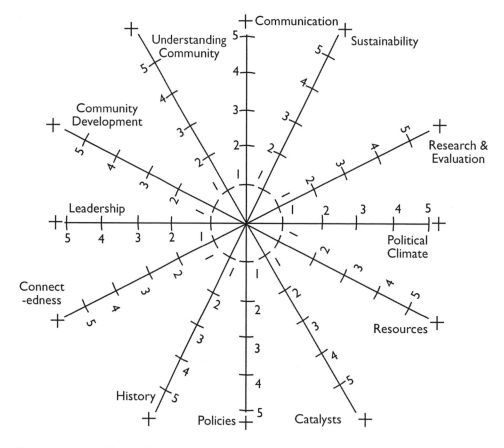

1.31 The example in Figure 3.5 refers to the factors influencing a collaborative process within the University of Vermont. In the context of risk management one might imagine the 'spokes' of the web being labelled with different types of risk: reputational risk, risk of damage to assets etc.

2   *Supply chain vulnerability*

The supply chain concept

2.1   The concept of supply chain management has changed the face of business over recent decades. The move from dealing directly with a high number of suppliers to the tiered approach where reliance is placed on suppliers to manage *their* suppliers to the mutual benefit of all members of the supply chain has been a fundamental shift in business thinking.

2.2   Many companies now focus internal efforts on their core competencies. The goods and services that are not regarded as 'core' are increasingly sourced from outside suppliers. As a consequence the importance of supply chain management has risen.

2.3   Supply chain management can be defined as 'the management of upstream and downstream relationships with suppliers and customers to deliver superior customer value at less cost to the supply chain as a whole'. Because of its customer focused approach, this might arguably be named **demand chain management**.

2.4   When assessing supply chains it is easy to see our own organisation as the focal point. This is not often the case. The objective is to deliver 'superior customer value'. The focal point is the customer. The overall vulnerability is that we let our customer down. That customer is usually a link in the chain, which means that adverse consequences ripple downstream to the customer's customers.

2.5   Another definition of the supply chain is 'a network of connected and interdependent organisations mutually and co-operatively working together to control, manage and improve the flow of materials and information from suppliers to end users' (J Aitken, *Supply Chain Integration within the Context of a Supplier Association*). This definition stresses the mutual reliance in supply chains as well as the flow of information required to make modern supply chains effective.

External factors

2.6   It is this reliance on others within the supply chain that causes vulnerability. For a real-life illustration, see Figure 3.6.

2.7   Port closures due to foot and mouth disease and severe acute respiratory syndrome (SARS), disruption of rubber supplies due to the civil war in Liberia, and EU restrictions imposed on Chinese clothing imports in 2005, are further examples of external factors destabilising supply chains. In October 2002, a 'war game' scenario found that closing US ports for 12 days would create a 60-day container backlog at an estimated cost of $58m.

Figure 3.6 *When the chain breaks …*

It began on a stormy evening in New Mexico in March 2000 when a bolt of lightning hit a power line. The temporary loss of electricity knocked out the cooling fans in a furnace at a Philips semiconductor plant in Albuquerque. A fire started, but was put out by staff within minutes. The damage seemed to be minor: eight trays of wafers containing the miniature circuitry to make several thousand chips for mobile phones had been destroyed. After a good clean up the company expected to resume production within a week.

That is what the plant told its two biggest customers, Sweden's Ericsson and Finland's Nokia, who were vying for leadership of the booming mobile-handset market. Nokia's supply chain managers had realised within two days that there was a problem when their computer systems showed that some shipments were being held up. Nokia immediately put the Philips plant on a watchlist to be closely monitored if things got worse.

They did. Semiconductor fabrication plants have to be kept spotlessly clean. The contamination caused by the fire and the process of extinguishing it had contaminated a large area of the plant. Production could be halted for months. By the time the full extent of the disruption became clear, Nokia had already secured alternative sources of chips.

This left Ericsson with a serious parts shortage. The company had decided earlier to simplify its supply-chain by single sourcing some of its components, including the Philips chips. This severely limited its ability to launch a new generation of handsets and contributed to huge losses. In 2001 Ericsson decided to quit making handsets on its own and entered into a joint venture with Sony.

2.8   Supply chain risks can be categorised under four main headings.

 • Natural disasters such as fire and flood

 • Commodity risk such as the impact of political factors on the price of oil or the growth in demand from countries such as China and India

 • Market risk which includes the direct and ripple effects of strikes and bankruptcies among suppliers

 • Transportation risk including delays and port congestion

2.9   Clearly external factors will impact on the supply chain. We will examine scenario planning later in the text. For now, note that when considering an organisation's vulnerability to disruption, we must pay attention to security (thereby reducing the risk of disruption) and resilience (the ability to bounce back).

Supply chain risk management

2.10   Supply chain intelligence is the process of using knowledge generated and shared by partners in the supply chain. The gathering of supply chain intelligence becomes practical when the supply chain is mapped and understood. The tiering approach of the supply chain provides one way of gathering intelligence, but information needs to travel faster than goods and components.

2.11   The sharing of information should be encouraged throughout the supply chain; for example, fourth-tier suppliers should contact first-tier suppliers directly if the situation warrants. The time delay and uncertainty involved if crucial information is fed back along the tiers of the supply chain may mean that risks and opportunities are not fully appreciated.

2.12 Supply chain risk management is the identification and management of risks within the supply chain through a coordinated approach among supply chain members to reduce supply chain vulnerability and to identify supply chain opportunities.

2.13 The ability to see from one end of the supply chain network to the other is important in this approach. Supply chain visibility implies a clear view of upstream and downstream demand and supply, inventory, logistics and production issues that may impact the ability of the supply chain to deliver.

2.14 Managers must be proactive in their approach to supply chain risk management and must assess their maps and models on an ongoing basis. The proactive approach is directed toward three main goals.

- Constantly monitoring the supply chain for signals that predict problems
- Ensuring timely and precise decision making when problems arise
- Modelling what may happen and planning for the result of outcomes

Changing supply chains

2.15 Supply chain networks continue to increase in complexity as a result of factors such as globalisation, outsourcing and reliance on IT infrastructures. Moves to 'lean thinking' in supply chain management have reduced areas of waste while at the same time they can be criticised for reducing flexibility.

2.16 Much work has been accomplished over the years using such systems as materials requirements planning (MRP) and just in time (JIT). These techniques work towards minimising stockholding in a manner that suits individual operations; supply chains have been configured to meet these needs.

2.17 Lean production and supply was very much the watchword of the 1990s. The concept of lean was to reduce waste. In supply chains this was a philosophy that could be increasingly applied. Lean supply looked at inventory minimisation and cost transparency issues, in particular.

2.18 The lean supply chain concept looked to reduce cost and waste by linking with the logistics of the operation and finding the optimum solutions commensurate with organisational objectives. A critical analysis of lean supply would show that the concept could sometimes be carried too far. Although highly cost effective, lean supply chains were prone to severe disruption as every part of the chain was optimised (as opposed to the whole chain).

2.19 As supply chains get leaner, with less buffer stock, and more inventory being held overseas or 'on the water', there is less ability for the supply chain to soak up and respond to the shocks that occur. The response has been to develop more responsive supply chains that are increasingly resilient to internal and external factors. A development can be charted from just in time, through lean supply, to responsive supply chains: see Table 3.1.

Table 3.1 *Just in time, lean supply and responsive supply chains*

Just in time	Lean production and lean supply	Responsive supply chains
• Pull system	• Focus on waste elimination	• Quick response
• Regular volumes	• Minimised inventory	• Supply flexibility
• Capacity matched to demand	• Cost transparency	• Customised production
• Regular production runs	• Efficient work flow	• Integration with supply partners
• Flexible manufacturing systems	• Low volume of greater variety products	• Optimisation of eTools
• Narrow range of similar items	• Continuous improvement	• Concurrent product development
• Short supplier lead times		

Technology in supply chains

2.20   The impact of technology (especially **radio frequency identification**, RFID) has enabled the realisation of 'perpetual inventory' – the ability to know where stock is held at any time and in any place in the world. **Enterprise resource planning** (ERP) systems work with third party logistic providers to enable real-time tracking of inventory.

2.21   The effective delivery of a supply chain management system is increasingly dependent on the IT infrastructure that underpins it. The management of knowledge and information is a key driver for supply chains, enabling customers to access manufacturing and shipment information, as examples. An integrated approach to IT is increasingly essential.

2.22   The IT-driven supply chain places a high degree of reliance on the integrity and consistency of data. This reliance is also an area of risk. If systems crash or internet connections fail an organisation will find itself in a vulnerable position. Contingency planning scenarios may need to be developed to ensure that if this eventuality occurs then information can still flow.

Resilient supply chains

2.23   The supply chain itself, as we have seen, is susceptible to external risk. The illustrations given are major examples, but even minor local events that would previously have caused little disruption can now have a major impact on supply chains. 'Supply chains are not simply linear chains or processes, they are complex networks.' (*Creating Resilient Supply Chains*, Cranfield School of Management)

2.24   The Massachusetts Institute of Technology has observed that 'the essence of most disruptions is a reduction in capacity and therefore an inability to meet demand'. In consequence most supply chain disruptions create large supply/demand imbalances that could result from an unanticipated spike in demand.

2.25   'Resilience' describes the ability of a supply chain to recover its original shape following disruption. For organisations, it measures their ability and the timeframes in which they can return to their normal level of performance. Resilience is important in risk management as it offers alternatives to the supply chain manager as well as being designed to meet customer needs.

2.26 *Creating Resilient Supply Chains* was produced by Cranfield University School of Management and is one of the leading works in this developing business area. The authors define supply chain risk as 'the identification and management of risks within the supply chain and risks external to it through a co-ordinated approach amongst supply chain members to reduce supply chain vulnerability as a whole'. This definition views the supply chain as an entity and emphasises the need to view supply chain risk from a total supply chain perspective.

2.27 The Cranfield researchers asked supply chain practitioners for their perception of risks in the supply chain. The practitioners identified external and some general risks but focused only on their own area of responsibility. They failed to take a more rounded or holistic view of the supply chain.

2.28 Some of the managers related the problems and risks to critical success factors they were familiar with.

- Cost-focused decisions
- Quality/performance requirements
- Delivery schedule adherence
- Customer-supplier relationships

2.29 Solutions to these often involved 'trade-offs' at an operational level rather than at the wider strategic level. In some cases these 'trade-offs' may trade areas of risk.

2.30 'Critical success factors (CSFs) are those components of strategy where the organisation must excel to outperform competition' (*Johnson and Scholes*). Many CSFs are set at strategic level and managers often felt that decisions taken at a higher level left them with issues they were unable to manage or mitigate resulting in the supply chain not being optimised and being exposed to risk.

2.31 The supply chain network appears prone to the concept of suboptimisation: however effective one or a number of discrete areas of the supply chain are, it will never attain its maximum performance unless it is viewed as a whole.

2.32 The spectrum of supply chain management activity (Figure 3.7) highlights three key supply chain activities and emphasises the overlap between the three areas.

- **Supply chain planning** is based on planning in an ideal world without the legacy of previous decisions and commitments related to factory location, contractual obligations etc. The nearest most supply chain planners will get to this situation is when they are involved in new product development and taking the product into production. Here the supply chain can be designed with limited legacy impacts.
- **Supply chain operations management**. This section illustrates the day-to-day operations undertaken within an existing or mature supply chain. The chain has developed through its early and development stages and can now be viewed as 'mature'.
- **Supply chain change management** occupies the centre of the spectrum. This refers to the times when the supply chain is undergoing modification or seeing new processes implemented. It is this part of the model where vulnerability is considered to be at its highest.

Figure 3.7 *The spectrum of supply chain management activity*

2.33 Three key issues were identified by the Cranfield researchers as being barriers to effective implementation of risk management within supply chains.

- Staff training, with recognition that a wider understanding of risk and of the application of risk management tools is necessary
- Terminology, with a poor understanding of the term 'supply chain' in particular
- Supply chain visibility, with a view that upstream and downstream visibility was poor.

2.34 One approach is similar to that used in placing quality or corporate social responsibility demands on suppliers or partners. The supplier/partner is required to put in place risk management systems to ensure that risk management becomes an integral part of all members in the network. This approach would allow organisations to identify relevant sources of risk within their supply chain remit and control with the assurance that other network members were doing the same.

3 Supply chain mapping

Introduction

3.1 Modern supply chains are designed to enable goods to be produced and delivered in the right quantity, to the right place at the right time in a cost-effective manner.

3.2 Supply chains involve a complex and shifting methodology. They are complex networks of organisations coming together to provide high levels of service and to add value. With the interdependence between organisations and their supply chains there are two risks.

- The organisation is at risk from failure within the supply chain.
- The supply chain is at risk from a business or operational failure.

3.3 With the closer relationships evident in modern supply chain thinking, the biggest risks to business may come from the wider supply chain. The research from Cranfield University stated that 'the current understanding of supply chain risk is under-developed'.

3.4 Supply chain mapping is an approach that provides a time-based representation of the process involved as goods or materials move through the supply chain. The map shows the time taken at the inter-connection and movement points within the chain. In *Creating Resilient Supply Chains* the Cranfield researchers state that the mapping process enables organisations to determine:

- The inter-connecting 'pipeline' of suppliers through which products, components and materials must travel to reach the end-user
- The transport links by which products, components and materials are passed from one node to another in the chain
- The amount of work in progress and inventory stockpiled at each stage in the pipeline
- The time it would take to source replenishment from various points in the pipeline in the event of disruption

3.5 The Cranfield research states that the information gained can assist in identifying areas of risk and taking actions, including:

- Determining alternative sources of supply
- Decisions to hold additional 'just in case' inventory
- The formation of contingency plans regarding alternate transport arrangements in the event of disruption
- Decisions to hold inventory in a form that is most flexible, eg goods in plain packaging permitting later over-wrapping.

The purpose of supply chain mapping

3.6 Supply chain management thinking involves mapping the supply chain back to source. This will involve tiering via a number of suppliers many of whom may be internationally based. The supply chain approach involves most organisations in international sourcing although often indirectly. In consequence, external risks of this nature must be monitored and understood. Continuity of supply is one of the main prerequisites for purchasing.

3.7 The extended enterprise, where closer relationships are formed between organisations with increased inter-dependencies, is also a concern for risk management. As an example, over-reliance on one supplier can cause major disruptions for business continuity.

3.8 Maps assist in our understanding of a situation. The old adage 'a picture is worth a thousand words' can be very true. A network diagram is a form of supply chain mapping. Clearly when an organisation maps its own supply chain/network it will be far more detailed than the illustrations shown in textbooks.

3.9 The benefits of supply chain mapping are given by Gardner and Cooper:

'The benefits of supply chain mapping are to enhance the strategic planning process, facilitate supply chain redesign or modification, clarify channel dynamics, provide a common perspective, enhance communications, enable monitoring of supply chain strategy and provide a basis for supply chain analysis'.

3.10 The purpose of mapping is to create a supply chain that delivers the strategic objectives required by an organisation. It will focus on how goods, information and money flow throughout the supply chain. The level of detail will reflect the time and resources applied.

3.11 The place of supply chain mapping in risk management is in enhancing risk assessment. The clearer the understanding of a situation the more valid a judgement can be made. Often a pictorial or graphic presentation will encourage issues to be raised that might otherwise have been missed in discussion.

3.12 Supply chain mapping can increasingly be accomplished by using IT systems rather than being built by hand. Issues to be considered include the number of tiers involved, the length of the chain, the value of the chain, the criticality of the chain, the viewpoint from which the map is seen; the organisation or the industry, the inclusion of logistics operations, the breadth of product coverage and the implementation processes concerning the detail to be included and the parties the map will be circulated to.

3.13 One criticism of supply chain management is its reliance on managing suppliers down the supply chain through first tier suppliers. This approach may be becoming less acceptable as the impact of issues down the supply chain can expose vulnerabilities further up the chain. Supply chain mapping is an integrated approach by those in the supply chain to increase understanding and help identify and highlight issues of risk management or supply chain improvement.

4 Supply chain risk management

Supply risk and demand risk

4.1 We have seen how events, both internal and external, can impact on an organisation's supply chain strategy. This presents a major challenge for management. However, an understanding of where potential disruption will come from and planning for those eventualities places an organisation in a stronger position.

4.2 Cranfield University School of Management (www.cranfield.ac.uk/som/scr) have produced a useful self-assessment workbook on understanding supply chain risk. A key point is emphasised early in the text: 'research shows that supply chain vulnerability is an area of concern that has not yet been addressed by many organisations'.

4.3 Risk, and in consequence vulnerability, can come from events on the supply or demand side or from within the company itself.

4.4 The Cranfield researchers quote the following considerations in relation to supply chain risk management.

- There are many types of risk in the end-to-end supply chain.
- Their characteristics in terms of probability and severity will vary greatly.
- Risk will be sensitive to the context of the company, its markets and its position in the supply chain.
- The permutations and combinations of risk are such that few generalisations will apply.
- Pinpointing all of the areas that a company may face is likely to be a difficult task, but also a worthwhile one.

4.5 The external risks are the ones most commonly considered. They are often regarded as remote and unlikely to occur. However, unreliable supply, unpredictable demand and business environmental issues, as examples, are common to most organisations.

4.6   **Supply risk** is the risk associated with an organisation's suppliers being unable to supply or supplying goods of inadequate quality. Within a supply chain format that can be extended to include the supplier's suppliers back down the supply chain.

4.7   The supply risk is generally perceived as a failure of suppliers and and of the process that led to their selection. However, that view is too simplistic. The risk may result from a number of reasons: unanticipated demand, materials shortages, quality issues, delivery delays etc. Some of these may be the direct responsibility of an individual supplier or the result of delay further down the chain. In the long term the concept of continually improving the supply chain can apply. Lessons are learned and remedial action put in place. The supply chain gets stronger and more resilient as a result.

4.8   Supply chains vary both within and across organisations. Some run lean, some are more flexible, some are longer and some are global. But however the supply chain is configured, there is a need to understand the supply chain and the strengths and weaknesses within it. Supply chains are a work in progress with the aim of addressing weaknesses and making the chain fit for purpose.

4.9   **Demand risk** is the risk of a company experiencing demand for its products that it has not anticipated. Demand risk can refer to unexpectedly high or unexpectedly low demand and is often a result of poor or inaccurate forecasting.

4.10   For demand risk to be managed it requires better forecasting linked to a late manufacturing or customising production system. If variations are a feature of a particular supply chain this can be built into to the design of the chain.

4.11   Here are some of the consequences of demand risk.

   •   Demand exceeding supply could result in price increases that will either have to be absorbed by the organisation or passed on to customers.

   •   The inability to meet demand may be perceived by customers as a failure of commitment and may affect both future business and reputation.

   •   Demand that is consistently below projections will be a major threat, as investments would have been made on the projected figures throughout the specific areas of the supply chain.

4.12   The increasing emphasis in business on 'demand management' rather than 'forecasting' is a direct consequence of demand side risk. Increasingly sophisticated software programs are being used alongside specialist demand managers to ensure that projections are as accurate as possible.

Environmental risks

4.13   Environmental risks are those that emanate from external sources and are often viewed as uncontrollable. Examples would include terrorism, earthquakes and volcanic activity. In most cases the organisation will be unable to mitigate these risks as they are usually not able to be insured against or may be considered too remote to be a realistic risk requiring assessment.

4.14 Some environmental risks can be monitored and mitigated against. Economic and political trends can be monitored and regularly assessed. If the organisation is involved in international supply chains regular country risk monitoring is carried out by organisations such as Dun & Bradstreet. These reports can be subscribed to or tailor-made to suit individual requirements. The better informed the organisation is the more realistic an appraisal it can make of the risks it faces.

Process risks

4.15 Internal processes are the sequence of value-adding activities undertaken by an organisation. Included in this are the management processes and policies that drive the operation. Process risk is the risk of disruption to these processes.

4.16 Organisations face decisions regarding process and process management. A key decision surrounds the concept of 'core competence' – the core business the organisation is in. This decision in turn determines whether things are accomplished in-house, or outsourced or subcontracted. Make or buy decisions will often relate to the strategic objectives of the company.

4.17 If the decision in some areas of business is to outsource or subcontract the process then the operational role is to manage and monitor the outsourced or subcontracted business with the aim of meeting specified objectives.

4.18 If the company retains full control and retains the operational processes in-house then it accepts the process risk. The organisation's process risk can be seen in a number of areas.

- Variation in manufacturing output
- Poor equipment utilisation
- Quality issues
- Warehouse operating issues
- Supply chain issues
- Transport issues

4.19 The cost of process risk is evident in the under-utilisation of equipment. Quality issues can have a direct impact on reputational risk etc. One method of control is to put in place procedures that ensure that investment decisions are soundly made, that forecasting is as accurate as possible and that equipment and support areas are 'fit for purpose'.

4.20 Process risk can be further controlled by the introduction and establishment of industry recognised standards such as the ISO9000 group of standards, or by benchmarking against similar companies.

4.21 The Cranfield researchers associate the greatest process risks with introduction of new products, technology and customers as well as changes to facilities and operating methods. They state that a common maxim of risk management is not to undertake too many risk initiatives at one time.

Control risk

4.22   Controls must be put in place to ensure that processes operate within defined and considered parameters. Controls are the assumptions, rules, systems and procedures that govern the workings of an organisation.

4.23   Control risk is the risk arising from application or misapplication of these rules. Control risk is a broad category of risk and issues arising from it are usually internal failures of omission or commission.

4.24   Controls that are applied to the supply chain will cover relationship issues with suppliers/partners, capacity, inventory management, demand management and logistics issues. Controls will be monitored by sound management supported by effective measures, often in the form of key performance indicators (KPIs) that serve to monitor performance.

Creating a supply chain risk management culture

4.25   As with the introduction and establishment of total quality management (TQM) into an organisation a crucial prerequisite is commitment from top management to lead and support the process. The Turnbull Report (to be discussed in a later chapter) has placed risk management on the agenda of senior management. The understanding of supply chain risk and its impact on the profitability and continuity of the business may need to be better understood.

4.26   Supply chain risk is a serious threat to business continuity but is often not considered at Board level. This is a developing business area and frequently senior managers do not fully appreciate the role of supply chain management in today's changing business environment.

4.27   A supply chain risk management cross-functional team should be established. The role is to develop a risk register, maintain and update it, and provide regular updates to Board level. A full series of supply risk worksheets is available at www.cranfield.ac.uk/som/scr.

5   *Supplier failure*

Guarding against supplier failure

5.1   Guarding against the possibility of supplier risk, in particular supplier failure, starts at the beginning of the relationship with supplier appraisals. These form part of a risk assessment strategy but assessment is ongoing and must continue during a business relationship with a particular supplier.

5.2   Supplier appraisal procedures form an important part of modern purchasing. Supplier appraisal is a formal process where the supplier will usually complete a detailed questionnaire giving data on its financial position, years in business, leading customers, stance on corporate social responsibility etc, with the aim of providing the purchasing organisation with reassurance that this company will be a suitable and secure supplier.

5.3   The supplier appraisal process is not adequate on its own and will be supported by checking the organisation's reputation and standing, taking up references and making visits as required.

5.4   Assurance can also be requested in the form of third party certification such as ISO standards or other industry specific standards.

5.5   If supplier selection is part of a tendering process, the tender document must request full and detailed information from the supplier. This information will then be validated as part of the tender process before any contract is awarded.

The financial status of suppliers

5.6   Supply side failure may come as a result of financial factors. This can often come without prior warning and can cause considerable disruption. Market intelligence may provide advance warning if such a system is in place.

5.7   Monitoring the financial health of suppliers is a well-established discipline in many purchasing organisations. Many suppliers are charged with providing regular financial updates, often on an annual basis. This forms an integral part of their business relationship with the buying organisation.

5.8   The purchasing department, often linking with the finance department, should put in place regular monitoring procedures on the financial and business status of suppliers. With the dependence on fewer suppliers this is an increasingly important consideration.

5.9   Published and industry figures will often indicate trends in companies. Ratio analysis, share price monitoring, and change of ownership should all be included in the market intelligence system. With IT integration, records and monitoring of suppliers can be part of an organisation's processes.

5.10 Supplier failure, at any point of the supply chain, will have repercussions throughout the chain. In consequence, the need to monitor suppliers throughout the chain is evident. Procedures should be put in place to ensure that each tier puts in place monitoring procedures on their first tier suppliers.

5.11 Supplier failure can have severe consequences, particularly if the organisation is tied into a single-sourcing agreement. The conclusion is obvious: if our organisation is involved in a single sourcing agreement we are increasing the level of risk, as we are dependent on one supplier. To minimise the risk, that supplier should be monitored closely and highlighted in the supply chain risk management process.

5.12 Effective contingency planning can mitigate the impact of supplier failure. Alternative suppliers should be appraised and accredited where possible. Existing suppliers should be encouraged to offer flexibility if possible. In purchasing it is difficult to keep a supplier interested if no business is being offered but many suppliers are aware that being considered as a contingency is better than not being considered at all. The experience of Toyota is relevant here: see Figure 3.8.

Figure 3.8 *Toyota*

When a fire at the Aisin Seiki factory in Kariya, Japan destroyed most of the 500 precision tools used to make proportioning valves (P-valves) for brakes, Toyota quickly ran out of valves and had to shut down two-thirds of its assembly lines.

Purchasing and setting up replacement machinery would have taken months, so Aisin and Toyota worked with their supplier networks to come up with a solution. More than 50 companies worked with engineers to find ways to make P-valves using alternative equipment and machining practices. Within a few days Toyota was able to start re-opening plants.

5.13   Partnerships and closer relationships between customer and supplier will often involve a free flow of agreed financial and other relevant information as part of the commercial agreement underpinning the relationship. This approach is likely to develop to partners further along the supply chain.

Due diligence and credit risk

5.14   When a buyer contemplates doing significant business with a supplier he should analyse the supplier's financial position to the full extent possible from available information. This process is often referred to as **due diligence**.

5.15   As we have mentioned already, the risk of **supplier insolvency** has potential for huge disruption throughout the supply chain. As an example, suppose that a publishing company sends master copies of a series of textbooks to a printer for manufacturing bulk copies. If the printer becomes insolvent, and is unable to deliver, the publisher will face huge embarrassment and customer dissatisfaction.

5.16   This suggests that we should try to assess the likelihood of a supplier becoming insolvent. A number of models have been developed for this purpose. One of these – the Springate model – is cited by Sadgrove (*The Complete Guide to Business Risk Management*).

5.17   Springate identifies four important financial criteria.

- A: the ratio of working capital to total assets. We would like this ratio to be high: this would mean that a good proportion of the supplier's assets are in liquid form rather than being tied up in the form of fixed assets (premises, machinery etc).

- B: the ratio of net profit before interest and taxes to total assets. We would like this to be high: this would mean that the supplier makes a healthy profit from the assets he employs in his business.

- C: the ratio of net profit before taxes to current liabilities. We would like this to be high: again, it suggests that the supplier is making sufficient profits to enable payment of his creditors.

- D: the ratio of sales to total assets. We would like this to be high: it indicates that the supplier's assets are working hard to generate sales output.

5.18   Springate attaches 'weights' to each of these ratios, and derives a Z-score calculated as follows:

$$Z = 1.03A + 3.07B + 0.66C + 0.4D$$

5.19 From what we have already said, it is clear that we want this score to be as high as possible. A low Z-score indicates a risk of supplier insolvency. 'Where Z is less than 0.862, the firm is classified as failed' (Sadgrove). Dun and Bradstreet and similar **credit reference** agencies offer a service based on analysis of statistics such as these; this can help a buyer to predict possible problems of supplier failure.

Chapter summary

*   Kraljic's matrix is a tool of analysis that seeks to map the importance to the organisation of the item being purchased against the complexity of the market that supplies it.

*   The supplier preferencing matrix is a segmentation tool recognising that suppliers may have a different view of the relationship from the buyer.

*   It is reliance on others within the supply chain that causes most areas of vulnerability.

*   As supply chains get leaner, with less buffer stock, and more inventory being held overseas or 'on the water', there is less ability for the supply chain to soak up and respond to the shocks that occur.

*   The effective delivery of a supply chain management system is increasingly dependent on the IT infrastructure that underpins it.

*   'Supply chains are not simply linear chains or processes; they are complex networks.'

*   However effective one or a number of discrete areas of the supply chain are, unless the supply chain is viewed as a whole it will never attain its maximum performance.

*   Risk, and in consequence vulnerability, can come from events on the supply or demand side or from within the company itself.

*   The supply risk is the risk associated with an organisation's suppliers being unable to supply or supplying goods of inadequate quality.

*   Demand risk is the risk of a company facing demand that it has not anticipated.

*   Guarding against the possibility of supplier risk, in particular supplier failure, starts at the beginning of the relationship and is ongoing thereafter.

Self-test questions

Numbers in brackets refer to the paragraphs where you can check your answers.

1 What are the names of the four quadrants of the Boston Consulting Group matrix? (1.5)

2 Describe the 80/20 rule. (1.27)

3 Define supply chain management. (2.3, 2.5)

4 Supply chain risks can be categorised under what four main headings? (2.8)

5 What is resilience in the context of supply chains? (2.9, 2.25)

6 What three issues were identified by the Cranfield School of Management as being barriers to effective implementation of risk management within supply chains? (2.33)

7 What benefits of supply chain mapping were given by Gardner and Cooper? (3.9)

8 What are the consequences of an organisation being open to demand risk? (4.11)

9 What are internal processes? (4.15)

Further reading

• Martin Christopher, *Logistics and Supply Chain Management*.

• www.cranfield.ac.uk/som/scr

CHAPTER 4

The Different Levels of Risk

Learning objectives and indicative content

1.5   Distinguish between strategic, operational and project based areas of risk.

- Examples of how to define risk at the strategic, operational and/or project based level
- Range of risk mitigation methods at each level
- How risk can be bounded and also how, if unmanaged, it can have knock-on consequential impacts on other areas of the organisation

Chapter headings

1   Strategic risk

2   Operational risk

3   Project risk

1   Strategic risk

Defining 'strategy'

1.1   Strategy has many definitions. Strategies will emerge from a mix of business competencies, environmental business appraisals and structured planning to ensure that an organisation remains competitive to meet future needs.

'Strategy is the direction and scope of an organisation over the long term; ideally, which matches its resources to its changing environment, and in particular its markets, customers and clients so as to meet stakeholder expectations'. (Johnson, Scholes and Whittington)

1.2   A further definition of strategy (by Coulter) is 'a series of steps in which organisational members analyse the current situation, decide on strategies, put those strategies into action, and evaluate, modify or change strategies as needed'. This definition requires that the operations of an organisation are flexible to allow for modification or change.

Formulating strategy

1.3   Decisions will be made at corporate level within organisations, based on many factors such as future growth plans, the competitive environment the organisation operates in, and internal constraints such as manpower, money and machinery. Strategic thinking at corporate level involves developing the future direction of the business. Consideration should be given to the future vision of the organisation. What is it about? Where does it want to be? Often, managers draw up a mission statement that people can associate with, setting down values that will help shape the culture of the organisation.

1.4 The **strategic vision** and **mission statement** will clarify what business an organisation is in. The strategic vision involves 'envisioning' where you want the company to be in (for example) five years in the future. This process helps the strategist to plan a course of action to achieve the appropriate vision.

1.5 The mission statement serves to define the nature and business of the company and to give focus to key business areas. Examples of both vision and mission statements can be found at www.missionstatements.com.

1.6 Within the field of risk management, consideration should be given by organisational strategists to both the vision and mission statements. They need to be demanding but not out of reach. Strategic statements that are too aspirational may push management into taking risks beyond the abilities of the organisation.

1.7 The method of strategy development will vary between organisations. There are three principal approaches to strategy development: planned (or deliberate) strategies; emergent strategies; logical incrementalism.

1.8 **Planned strategies** evolve from gaining a detailed and thorough understanding of environmental factors such as competitors and market trends. This knowledge is interlinked with current organisational strengths and weaknesses such as resources, location and customer base. From these external and internal considerations a strategy is deliberately developed that will drive the business forward over the future.

1.9 A planned approach will not always happen in practice. Defined patterns of behaviour will already exist in any organisation, which means that superimposing a new strategy is not a simple matter. Existing patterns of behaviour will often help to shape strategies adopted. If new strategies conflict with existing patterns, the strategies may be modified in practice. This process is described as **emergent strategy**: 'one idea leads to another until a new pattern forms. Action has driven thinking and a new strategy has emerged' (Mintzberg).

1.10 JB Quinn argued that there are good reasons why managers proceed by means of short steps, building on strategies already in place, and making only limited changes (**logical incrementalism**). Quinn's view was that strategies emerge from the organisational periphery following political processes. The political strength behind each new idea is a signal to top management about the feasibility of implementing it. Top management sits above the political activity, but is able to make rational judgements about what should be tried and when.

Strategic planning

1.11 Strategic planning involves setting objectives, quantifying targets for achievement and communicating these targets to others. This incorporates selecting strategies, tactics, policies, programmes and procedures for achieving the objective. Planning involves decisions about the following issues.

- What to do in future?
- How to do it?
- When to do it?
- Who is to do it?

1.12 Good planning is increasingly essential as business becomes more complex and competition increases. Good planning offers the following benefits.

- It involves those concerned.
- It informs those concerned.
- It improves communications.
- It provides better co-ordination of activities.
- It identifies expected developments.
- It considers the risk elements of plans.
- It increases organisational preparedness to change.
- It reduces conflicts regarding the direction of the company.
- It forces management to think ahead systematically and realistically.
- Available resources can be better matched to opportunities.
- The plan provides a framework for the continuing review of operations.

1.13 Implementation of strategic directions will involve an audit of all business areas such as marketing, production, finance, purchasing etc. The audit will help address the 'where are we now?' scenario by appraising the current position of the organisation. This audit will examine current resources and measure them against how they will meet the future needs of the organisation.

1.14 The second stage ('where do we want to be?') looks at the current situation and compares it with the intended path of the organisation. It may become apparent at this stage that (for example) the investment in our manufacturing capability may be too low or that warehouses are poorly located to meet future needs. With issues being identified we can consider various options in order to meet company needs.

1.15 The third stage ('how are we going to get there?') puts in place decisions at a tactical level that will enable us to reach the stated objectives. These could involve more consideration being given to subcontracting or outsourcing or relocation of warehouses in order to meet these objectives. These are major operational decisions that must be well considered, discussed and costed. The impact on the current workforce and how that should be handled could be an important area of consideration.

1.16 The final stage ('how do we ensure arrival?') involves putting in place the changes and making them happen. Key personnel are given defined roles. Project management structures and timetables are developed and put into action. Projects are seen through to successful completion.

1.17 Decisions are passed down to organisational departments to implement (eg finance, production, marketing, purchasing). These departments, working together, devise tactical plans as to how the desired decision can be best achieved. These tactical plans then become implemented at an operational level.

1.18 Decisions made at a strategic level in an organisation have the greatest impact on the future direction and success of the organisation. Strategic decisions are influenced by many factors (competitor actions, pressure on share prices, investment needs etc), and it is the need to balance all these business and environmental risks while at the same time maximising resources and moving the organisation forward and the 'trade-offs' involved that may open the organisation to risk.

1.19   As an example, an organisation may consider a rival company as a takeover target. To raise funds it may need to consider ways of financing. All funding decisions carry risk (share price fluctuation, interest rate rises, short-term vulnerability to competitor actions etc). Decisions made should be considered within a wider framework than commercial decision-making. Risk management methodology puts in place a formal and structured approach that ensures strategic decisions are rigorously evaluated.

1.20   Change management situations present issues as organisations seek to embed new processes and roles. Change risks are created by decisions to pursue new strategies beyond current and existing capability. The risk is that the change process will not be successful and this must be considered within the risk management framework. The additional point is that risk management involves both 'hard' and 'soft' areas of the organisation, as appropriate.

1.21   Strategy requires the matching of resources to requirements and it is here that strategy and operations interface. Effective and efficient operations management is reliant on an appropriate operations strategy. The development of an operational strategy should involve consultation and feedback between the operational and strategic levels of the business to ensure that when corporate plans are raised they are taking into account the resource implications that may constrain proposed developments.

The impact of strategic decisions on supply chain activities

1.22   Strategic decisions are taken at Board level in organisations. They take into account a wide range of factors, as discussed, and are passed down through the management hierarchy to be implemented by operational areas.

1.23   The development of the supply chain management philosophy, linked to modern ideas on closer supplier relationships and partnering approaches, places restrictions on strategic planning. Supply chains take time to establish and refine. Strategic changes must take into account the time, contractual links and re-establishment requirement of new supply chains.

1.24   Modern business practice favours a different structure where specialist outsource providers and subcontractors are used where appropriate. The move to outsourcing can be a high-risk area for organisations. After contract award, the key is effective contract management to maintain the contract and the standards defined within it. Even in a non-core business area the failure of an outsource provider to deliver reflects on the organisation in terms of possible damage to reputational risk. Outsource contracts should be managed with regard to the risk they represent.

The impact of strategic decisions on human resources

1.25   Strategic decisions are about change. The organisation does not remain the same but takes a new and different direction. It is the role of the human resources function to manage this change in a manner that ensures the organisation can successfully deliver the new strategic objectives.

1.26 The remit of human resources is wide ranging: recruitment and selection, managing redundancies, pay, promotion, welfare and disciplinary activities etc. These areas all carry a degree of risk and should be managed in a manner in line with an organisation's risk policy.

1.27 Effective human resource management is about planning for the future. It is here that risks may be higher. Training and development, career planning and succession planning are about the future of the organisation and ensuring the right people with the right skills are available when required.

The impact of strategic decisions on the finance function

1.28 As you will see in the following section, the area of finance at strategic level has come in for close scrutiny following a number of high profile corporate scandals and the publication of the **Turnbull Report** in the UK. The management of financial risk is one of the highest priority areas in risk management.

1.29 Financial risk involves ensuring the long-term success of the business while meeting the needs of stakeholders over the short term. To achieve this, organisations need a financial strategy that meets strategic objectives while enabling the financing of operations in the short term.

1.30 Key considerations are as follows.

- Liquidity: the ability to have cash available either immediately or by means of converting assets to cash as quickly as possible.

- Interest rates: these are controlled by central government and are an important aspect of currency management governing the value of one currency in regard to another (money will move out of one currency to another with a higher interest rate to gain a better return) and in slowing down spending (if interest rates increase organisations and people have less money to spend).

- Credit: business exists on credit periods. The effective management of credit can enhance the liquidity of a company, but this must be balanced with suppliers' requirements.

- Foreign exchange: most organisations operate across borders and will be involved in foreign currency transactions. This gives rise to 'exchange risk': the risk that the currency will move up or down to the detriment of the company. Many companies will have specialist departments to manage this risk and to ensure that money is moved between currencies in such a way as to minimise risk. Banks also provide services such as forward exchange contracts and currency options that can aid organisations in minimising their exchange risk.

- The future: an organisation requires cash cows to provide the funds for the development of new products or services. It is the remit of finance to provide these funds but it will only be able to do so if organisational strategy has ensured that cash generating products are producing the cash.

1.31 During the latter part of the 20th century and the start of the 21st century there have been a number of financial scandals that have caused international concern. Steps have been taken to ensure that such financial scandals will not occur again. These are looked at in the following section.

The Turnbull Report

1.32   Concern regarding the ethics of business practice, business controls and financial reporting became a major issue in the United States following the scandals surrounding WorldCom and Enron in the late 1990s and early 2000s. The US **Sarbanes-Oxley Act** **(2002)** was introduced as a response with an emphasis on financial controls and public reporting by companies. It was felt that governance at Board level should be monitored more closely and in a more structured manner.

1.33   In many respects, Sarbanes-Oxley represents the end of one era and the beginning of another. The legislation's intent is no less than to change American corporate culture by drawing a direct enforceable relationship between senior corporate management and the integrity and quality of their companies' financial statements.

1.34   Alongside this, the UK government commissioned the Turnbull Report to examine and report on good business practice in the 21st century. Clearly a concern of Turnbull was to ensure that the US example was not repeated in the UK and the Turnbull Report puts in place a series of risk management processes which, when implemented, reduce the risk of corporate fraud or poor governance.

1.35   The Turnbull Report on organisations' internal control and risk management was first published in 1999 (revised 2005). The report is not about the avoidance of risk; rather it is about effective risk management; determining the appropriate level of risk, being aware of the risks being taken and putting in place methods to manage those risks.

1.36   The Turnbull Report seeks to outline good business practice. Organisations should be implementing the necessary changes in a way that meets their business needs and objectives. The guidance provided by Turnbull is intended to:

- Reflect sound business practice whereby internal control is embedded in the business processes by which the company pursues its objectives
- Remain relevant over time
- Enable each company to apply it in a manner that takes account of its particular circumstances

1.37   For an organisation to be able to identify its risk appetite, it must first strategically identify its long-term objectives. At strategic level the Board should identify what they regard as the main business risks to be managed and monitored at group level.

1.38   Turnbull stresses the importance of internal control and risk management.

- A company's system of internal controls has a key role in the management of risks that are significant to the fulfilment of its business objectives. A sound system of internal controls contributes to safeguarding the shareholders' investment and the company's assets.
- Internal control facilitates the effectiveness and efficiency of operations, helps to ensure the reliability of internal and external reporting and assists compliance with laws and regulations.

- Effective financial controls, including maintenance of proper accounting records, are an important element of internal control. They help ensure that the company is not unnecessarily exposed to avoidable financial risk and that financial information used within the business and for publication is reliable. They also contribute to the safeguarding of assets, including the prevention and detection of fraud.

1.39   A company's objectives, its internal organisation and the environment in which it operates are continually evolving and, as a result, the risks it faces are continually changing. A sound system of internal control therefore depends on a thorough and regular evaluation of the nature and extent of the risks to which the company is exposed.

1.40   The Turnbull guidance is based on the adoption by a company's board of a risk-based approach to establishing a sound system of internal control and reviewing its effectiveness within the normal organisational management and governance processes.

Responsibilities

1.41   Under Turnbull the Board of Directors are responsible for the company's system of internal control and should set appropriate policies and seek regular assurance to satisfy themselves that the system is working effectively and in the manner it has approved.

1.42   It is the role of management to implement the Board's policies on risk and control. Turnbull states that in fulfilling its responsibilities management should identify and evaluate the risks faced by the company for consideration by the board and design, operate and monitor a suitable system of internal control which implements the policies adopted by the Board.

1.43   The Board should ensure that the risk management process is continually and effectively monitored. It should regularly receive and review reports on internal control.

1.44   When reviewing reports the Board should take the following steps.

- Consider what are the significant risks and assess how they have been identified, evaluated and managed

- Assess the effectiveness of the internal control system in managing the significant risks, having regard in particular to any significant failings or weaknesses in internal control that were reported

- Consider whether necessary actions are being taken promptly to remedy any significant failings or weaknesses

- Consider whether the findings indicate a need for more extensive monitoring of the system of internal control

1.45   The risk management approach developed by Turnbull is equally appropriate to multinationals, public sector bodies and medium-sized enterprises. The theme of Turnbull is relevant across all businesses. The focus should be on fulfilling business objectives through improved risk management.

1.46 Andrew Hiles give the following keys to success with Turnbull.

- Make Turnbull an integral part of the way the business works.
- Define clear business objectives – identify specific performance markers.
- Continuously monitor actual performance against the performance markers.
- Keep Board reports short and simple.
- Implement a risk approach as a project.
- Create a documented project plan.
- Keep things simple.
- Once the initial project is over, the Turnbull programme must be maintained, continued and developed.

Mitigation of strategic risks

1.47 Any organisation that adopts an inappropriate strategic direction runs the risk of seriously damaging the business. The importance of risk management has increasingly become an issue on the agenda of strategic business thinking. Strategic decisions are being made and evaluated using risk management criteria with the aim of ensuring that any decisions taken fall within the organisation's risk appetite.

1.48 Strategies must be checked against the risk appetite of the organisation by a formal risk assessment. The direction and scope of strategic plans must fall within the agreed remit.

1.49 Areas that are considered too great a risk may be able to be handled in other ways. It may be that launching a new product in France is considered too great a risk but by entering a joint venture with a French partner we can mitigate the risk to an acceptable level. Partnering, strategic alliances, joint distribution arrangements etc, all allow a risk mitigation strategy to be introduced.

1.50 Bringing in another partner is in itself a risk that must be evaluated but the gains that can often be made with two or more organisations working together are very much a feature of modern business at the strategic level.

2 Operational risk

Introduction

2.1 Operations strategy involves maximising the capabilities of resources in specific markets in a way that meets the aims and objectives given in strategic plans. Operational objectives revolve around the ability to deliver what is being promised or is expected. If these delivery parameters or expectations are not met then both commercial and reputational risks result.

2.2 Within an organisational hierarchy the strategic goals and objectives are implemented at operational level. If operational and business goals are not aligned to strategic goals successfully there is potential for failure. The application of risk management methodology puts in place the structures, policies and procedures to ensure that both strategic and operational goals remain in alignment.

2.3   Operational strategies (ie those strategies that give direction and purpose to the operations management role) should be developed to ensure that they meet corporate objectives. Underlying correct strategic alignment, the operational and commercial activities of an organisation are required to deliver the goods/services that comprise the core of the business.

2.4   An organisation can be involved in the entire (vertical) chain encompassing:

- Raw material extraction
- Design
- Manufacture
- Assembly
- Distribution

2.5   Any of these stages can be contracted out. It is a matter of corporate policy to determine the core business area and the amount of vertical integration required. Vertical integration (control of all the factors listed under the bullet points above) offers two main advantages.

- By having everything under central control the objective is to improve reliability and responsiveness. Systems that cover full vertical integration often prove to be too cumbersome and bureaucratic to be effectively managed and are rarely used. The absence of competition can also lead to deterioration in service and quality.
- As subcontractors or outsource providers require to make a profit it is assumed they will be more expensive. Cost savings can be made but the assumption is that a large general operation can be as efficient and flexible as a small specialised one.

2.6   The operational capacity and capability to deliver organisational objectives is imperative to ensure success. In order to meet strategic objectives resources must be in place. Failure to correctly configure and optimise resources may result in failure to deliver the promised end result. Product/service failure within agreed time and quality standards can cause severe reputational and commercial loss considerations.

2.7   Operational risks will vary with each organisation. Some of the more common cross-organisational risk areas are listed here.

- Inability to reduce the cost base
- Loss of key people
- Failure of new products or services
- Lack of orders
- Ineffective use of technology
- Failure of outsource provider to deliver
- Inefficient management and operational processes
- Poor succession planning
- Skills shortages
- Poor industrial relations

2.8   All the above and others relevant to the organisation will feature in the initial risk assessment.

Outsourcing

2.9　Outsourcing is a strategic decision that should be managed at operational level. As a consequence organisations need to develop a suitable contract management structure to ensure outsource providers are delivering and continually improving on their contractual obligations.

2.10　Figures indicate that up to 50 per cent of outsourcing arrangements break down in the first three years. This clearly is a concern for organisations as the impact of outsourcing risk is both internal and external.

2.11　Effective contract negotiation and management is an essential part of ensuring outsourcing success. Measurement against key performance indicators, regular meetings and defined contacts are vital. From a risk perspective, outsource deals require careful and ongoing monitoring with concerns logged in the risk register.

2.12　One difficulty with outsourcing is that if the contract breaks down the fallback is either to award the contract to another party (whom you may have rejected initially) or to bring the work back in-house. Contingency plans should be developed for this eventuality. Outsourcing often means selling or losing plant, equipment and skills, which means that recovery by bringing the work back in-house can be difficult. Outsourcing does however need a full ongoing risk assessment supported with developed contingency plans.

2.13　Management of the outsource provider or subcontractor is a major operational role. In many organisations this role may be carried out with the Purchasing Department as they can bring a range of applicable skills to this business area.

Identifying risks

2.14　Within operations the major risk areas are often common across organisations, but this is not always the case. Each company will have its own issues and criteria; identifying risk must be handled in a structured manner applicable to the organisation.

2.15　Common approaches involve risk identification and assessment workshops, brainstorming sessions or questionnaires where views can be put forward, developed where appropriate and discussed further.

2.16　More formal approaches (such as the examination and re-evaluation of business processes, benchmarking, health and safety inspections, quality standards such as ISO9000 and audits) all have a purpose in not only keeping a business 'fit for purpose' but in highlighting areas of risk that can be developed further.

Mitigation of operational risks

2.17　The role of operations is to take the inputs into an organisation and to transform them into the end product or service as outputs. The inputs can be stock or components in the case of production or concepts or people in the case of services.

2.18　Table 4.1 shows some of the operational problem areas identified earlier, with suggestions for mitigation.

Table 4.1 *Mitigating operational problems*

Operational problem	How to mitigate
Inability to reduce the cost base	The risk could be mitigated by subcontracting or outsourcing work to a third party supplier, allowing for the selling of machinery, freeing of space and reducing the cost of staff.
Loss of key people	Mitigate by making the job more attractive or by a more formal and robust succession planning approach.
Failure of new products or services	Undertake better customer research and involvement in the development process; use cross-functional teams during the development and launch phase; benchmark against other companies to learn from their approach.
Lack of orders	Analyse the product/service range; improve customer feedback and demand management.
Ineffective use of technology	Undertake a detailed audit and appraisal of the IT infrastructure.
Failure of outsource provider to deliver	Refer above to the previous section of the chapter.
Inefficient management and operational processes	Carry out a process audit, benchmarking against similar organisations, or introduce a business process re-engineering approach.
Skills shortages	Use education and training as part of a formal process with the human resources team. Attract new and qualified workers with a suitable package.
Poor industrial relations	Improve the quality of discussion, enabling parties to see all sides of an issue. Value good industrial relations.

2.19   There are a wide range of operational risks, many of which (as above) have fairly clear paths for reducing or mitigating the risk. The use of third parties – as in outsourcing or subcontracting and getting suppliers to hold stock at their risk until it is called off – are just two examples of reducing the organisational risk. Appreciate that risk management in this sense is not a new discipline. In many business areas it has been practised for a long time but has not necessarily been viewed from this perspective.

3   *Project risk*

The particular difficulties of projects

3.1   Projects vary in size and complexity from office relocation to large capital projects such as the building of the new Wembley Stadium, the Scottish Parliament and Terminal 5 at Heathrow. Capital projects require a wide mix of skills, abilities and knowledge blended with effective costing and IT project support.

3.2   Of the three examples above, two have been beset with problems: changes in design, changes in specifications and contractual disputes have arisen. The Terminal 5 project, however, is cited as an example of a well managed and developed project.

3.3   Projects require a mix of skills to be effectively delivered. As the project progresses different skills are required. Timelines and milestones are set, as are budgetary constraints. If these are missed the financial and reputational repercussions can be severe.

3.4   It is the role of the Project Manager to bring the project in on time and on budget but this is often a difficult task for both internal and external reasons. Risk management is consequently a high priority. Effective risk management can evaluate risks and put in place contingency actions that can mitigate the risks, often in a time-critical environment.

The concept and bidding phase

3.5   The most critical phases in the project lifecycle are the conceptual phase and the bidding process. At this point only scarce information is available. It is at this time however that a baseline figure and time period must be established that, in effect, becomes a constraint for the project in terms of time, cost and performance.

3.6   The more competitive the bid in terms of price and non-price factors, the greater the possibility of winning but the higher the possibility of deviating from the planned project baseline.

3.7   The value of the bid is assessed using competitive factors such as price, technical assistance, delivery times, safety, training etc, which must be assessed and defined before the bid is submitted.

3.8   Three issues must be assessed.

   •   How to estimate the bid's competitive value and assess the probability of winning
   •   How to estimate the project baseline and measure the probability of meeting the related constraints
   •   How to assess the risk involved

3.9   Competitive bidding is a one-of-a-kind process and the bid itself is faced with uncertainty concerning judgements made, because of the imprecise knowledge of the competing context. The degree of uncertainty is generally at its highest at the start of the bidding preparation process and will reduce as new information becomes available.

3.10   Past experience of similar projects, coupled with the availability of external information on competitors, the client and the state of the market, all serve to reduce the risk. Advanced tools such as the **multi-attribute decision making model** can bring a mathematical application to the bidding process.

3.11   Assessment of the bid's competitive value gives rise to two main areas of uncertainty.

   •   The appraisal or evaluation scheme of the owner
   •   The profile of competitors' bids

The project risk management cycle

3.12 With every project subject to constant change and a business environment that is also constantly changing the management of risk is a crucial component of the overall project. The risk management cycle is a six-stage process that enables a structured approach to be taken to risk evaluation, monitoring and reporting. The six stages are as follows.

- Risk identification
- Risk evaluation
- Identification of responses to risk
- Risk control actions
- Planning and resourcing
- Monitoring and reporting

Risk identification

3.13 The first step identifies the potential risks (or opportunities) facing the project. It is too early to make a refined risk judgement at this stage, but group consideration, brainstorming and discussion will enable more considered responses.

3.14 When risks have been identified they will be entered onto a risk register. This contains details of all the risks, with their current assessment and status. The register provides a ready reference of the risks facing the project.

Risk evaluation

3.15 This is concerned with making an assessment of the probability of an individual risk occurring and estimating the impact that it might have. The estimation should take into account any relevant factors outside the immediate scope of the project. The impact would normally be evaluated in respect to time, quality, benefit, people and finance. Financial risk can be evaluated in numerical terms. Reputational risk cannot.

3.16 When evaluating the probability of risks occurring, some will be further away in time than others. It is usual to focus on the more immediate risks, though risks with a high potential impact should be evaluated no matter how distant in time.

Identification of responses to risk

3.17 Possible responses to project risk are similar to the responses introduced in Chapter 1. They are just applied in a different situation.

- Tolerate the risk
- Treat the risk
- Transfer the risk
- Terminate the risk
- Plan contingency actions

Risk control actions

3.18 The next step will be the preparation of risk management plans. Risk management controls should be developed and put in place. It is important that the control action put in place is proportional to the risk. The control action must offer value for money in relation to the risk being controlled.

3.19 There may be effects on other parts of the project. For example, a delay in one critical area may cause a series of delays further down the project timeline. Any control actions should consider the consequential risk.

Planning and resourcing

3.20 Planning, from a risk perspective, will involve the development of scenarios, new timescales and contingency measures. Countermeasures would involve:

- Identifying the resources required to carry out the actions
- Developing plans of action
- Updating plans of action as new information becomes available
- Obtaining management approval for the suggested actions

Monitoring and reporting

3.21 As part of the risk management process the project manager should appoint an 'owner' of each risk. It is their responsibility to monitor the risk and update the risk management team regularly. Details of any changes to an existing situation should be formally recorded in the risk register with updates in control activity as required. The project manager has overall responsibility to monitor the risks and to ensure that procedures are being followed.

3.22 The following checklist on assignment of risk ownership should be used.

- Have owners been allocated to all the various parts of the complete risk process and the future risks been catered for? For example, suppliers may be tasked with ownership of assessing risk as part of their contracts.
- Are the various roles and responsibilities associated with ownership well defined?
- Do the individuals who have been allocated ownership actually have the authority?
- Have the various roles been communicated and understood?
- Are the nominated owners appropriate?
- In the event of change, can ownership be quickly and effectively reallocated?
- Are the differences between benefit and delivery risks understood?

3.23 Risks are frequently common across projects and benefit from a centralised control. Costs of corrective action can be reduced if effective risk management is in place.

Mitigation of project risks

3.24 Risk mitigation forms an important part of project risk management. There are many opportunities in projects for risks to come to fruition. Contingency planning is an important mitigation tool in that having options available at short notice can often reduce the impact of a risk event.

3.25 Placing the responsibility to deliver a particular aspect of the project with a particular supplier frequently mitigates risk. This is supported by liquidated damages if the supplier fails to deliver in accordance with the contract. This does not however mean that the risk no longer applies.

3.26 The consequential impacts of risk should be considered in strategic, operational and project risk areas. They can be best illustrated in the project environment where the failure to deliver on one part of the project can cause delays elsewhere. It is possible that the liquidated damages would not cover the costs of these delays and that damage to reputational risk might arise if the project overran.

3.27 In all areas of an organisation's business risk, management not only needs to consider how to mitigate a potential risk event but also needs to evaluate the consequential impact if such an event occurs.

Reasons why projects fail

3.28 Slack *et al* give a detailed list of 'critical success factors' (CSFs) for successful project management.

- Clearly defined goals (and commitment to them from the project team and stakeholders)
- Top-management support or sponsorship
- Competent (appropriately skilled) project manager and project team members
- Sufficient resource allocation, available when required, to complete the project
- Effective communication channels and mechanisms
- Effective control mechanisms to monitor progress and recognise schedule/cost/output deviations which must be dealt with
- Feedback capabilities, so that relevant stakeholders are able to review project status and make necessary corrections
- Troubleshooting mechanisms, to highlight, diagnose and trigger action on problems as they arise
- Project staff continuity through the project lifecycle.

3.29 Because of their complexity, projects are inherently at risk of overrunning on time and/or cost, and/or failing to deliver their stated outcomes, and/or having to be abandoned because of external disruption or resource depletion.

- As suggested by the CSFs listed above, such failures may be traced to some or all of the following shortcomings.
- Poor project definition by the project's owner (perhaps because of insufficient consultation with stakeholders or their failure to be specific about desired outcomes/deliverables)
- Lack of ownership and personal accountability
- Inadequately skilled or experienced project personnel
- Inconsistent understanding of required project activities, roles and responsibilities
- Inadequate reporting arrangements and feedback for decision-making
- Inadequate risk assessment in regard to disruption by contingencies and external factors

Chapter summary

- 'Strategy is the direction and scope of an organisation over the long term; ideally, which matches its resources to its changing environment, and in particular its markets, customers and clients so as to meet stakeholder expectations.'

- Strategic thinking at corporate level involves developing the future direction of the business.

- Strategic planning involves setting objectives, quantifying targets for achievement and communicating these targets to others.

- Change risks are created by decisions to pursue new strategies beyond current and existing capability.

- The Turnbull Report is not about the avoidance of risk; rather it is about effective risk management; determining the appropriate level of risk, being aware of the risks being taken and putting in place methods to manage those risks.

- Strategies must be checked against the risk appetite of the organisation by a formal risk assessment.

- Operations strategy involves maximising the capabilities of resources in specific markets in a way that meets the aims and objectives given in strategic plans.

- Competitive bidding is a one-of-a-kind process and the bid itself is faced with uncertainty concerning judgements made, because of the imprecise knowledge of the competing context.

- Risk mitigation forms an important part of project risk management. Placing the responsibility to deliver a particular aspect of the project with a particular supplier frequently mitigates risk.

- The consequential impacts of risk need to be considered in strategic, operational and project risk areas.

Self-test questions

Numbers in brackets refer to the paragraphs where you can check your answers.

1   What is the purpose of a mission statement? (1.5)

2   What are the three principal approaches to strategic development? (1.7)

3   List key considerations in the area of financial risk. (1.30)

4   What is the Turnbull Report concerned with? (1.35)

5   What factors does Andrew Hiles give as the keys to success with Turnbull? (1.46)

6   How do operational objectives contrast with operational strategy? (2.1–2.3)

7   Give five examples of common cross-organisational risk areas. (2.7)

8   Give six examples of methods used for risk identification. (2.15, 2.16)

9   Why are the most critical phases in the project lifecycle the conceptual phase and the bidding process? (3.5)

10   What are the six stages of the project risk management cycle? (3.12)

CHAPTER 5

The Role of Stakeholders

Learning objectives and indicative content

1.6   Evaluate the role of an organisation's stakeholders in risk management.

- The roles and responsibilities of an organisation's risk function in relation to other functional areas
- The impact of a risk event at the functional level
- The benefits of a cross-functional team when assessing, preventing and minimising risk
- The role of purchasing to mitigate potential losses to the whole organisation from risk events
- The merits of taking a consistent approach across the organisation to the assessment of risk

Chapter headings

1   Stakeholders

2   The role of stakeholders in private sector risk management

3   The role of stakeholders in public sector risk management

4   The role of purchasing

1   Stakeholders

Defining 'stakeholders'

1.1   Stakeholders are individuals and groups who have an interest or 'stake' in the organisation. At the extreme they can be understood as anyone who is affected by the decisions made by an organisation. They are an important interface between an organisation and its environment.

1.2   Stakeholders are often categorised as simply internal and external stakeholders. However, in risk management it is particularly relevant to identify a third category: connected stakeholders.

- Internal stakeholders exist within the boundaries of the organisation.
- Connected stakeholders are those outside the organisation – such as suppliers, partners, customers and shareholders – who have a direct interest in the organisation's activities.
- External stakeholders include national and local government, the public and pressure groups.

Internal stakeholders

1.3   Management and employees are regarded as the key internal stakeholders as they have a close, personal interest in an organisation's growth, expectations and goals. The organisation is where management and employees spend a great deal of their time and energy and where they gain an income. In consequence they have an interest in the organisation's continuing existence.

1.4   Within this, individuals have certain expectations and goals that they are looking to fulfil. These can include security of income, fulfilling work and career development.

1.5   In the private sector the key stakeholders are often those who own the business, in particular the shareholders. Public sector organisations are 'owned' by the state. In essence this means that all citizens 'own' the organisation. Private sector organisations largely exist to make profit, whereas public sector organisations exist to provide a service. Stakeholders in public sector organisations (and that includes all of us) are looking for an organisation that is accountable for its management and accountable for spend.

Connected stakeholders

1.6   Connected stakeholders are those who have an interest in an organisation so far as its continuation and profitability affects their own business or returns. They are an extension of external stakeholders, the difference being their greater degree of involvement. For consumers their interest lies in their experience of dealing with the organisation, increasingly with regard to the organisational stance on corporate social responsibility (CSR) issues.

1.7   Shareholders are looking for a return on their investment. Increasing shareholder concern has focused on CSR issues and more recently on corporate governance issues.

1.8   Major suppliers will often be key stakeholders particularly if they are partners or part of a supply chain. All suppliers will be looking to be paid by the organisation.

External stakeholders

1.9   External stakeholders – such as the government, local authorities, pressure groups, professional bodies, the community at large – are likely to have quite diverse objectives and have a varying ability to ensure that that the organisation meets them.

1.10   The government at national and local level is an important stakeholder to all organisations but to public sector bodies in particular. Government has an indirect involvement in areas such as employment, spending patterns and tax collection. It may be a direct employer or employ indirectly as with public authorities where funding comes from a variety of sources with a core funding from government.

Stakeholder management

1.11   Identifying an organisation's stakeholders, and their expectations, is part of the strategic analysis process, often termed **stakeholder analysis**. The result of stakeholder analysis is often a set of conflicting demands or expectations, most often between the demands for return on investment and employees' expectations of job security in the private sector or demand for quality service and financial constraints in the public sector.

1.12   An organisation will seek to achieve an acceptable balance between the various conflicting demands placed upon it. Some will try to balance the expectations of their stakeholders, so that profit maximisation will be sacrificed, to a degree, in favour of job security. Some will accept cost savings in selected areas so as to be able to deliver a higher level of service in other areas.

1.13   Stakeholder expectations are fluid, as is the degree to which stakeholders have an interest in the organisation. Over time, the balance that the organisation is trying to achieve with its stakeholders will move. This means that stakeholder analysis is an ongoing process.

1.14   An organisation will look to:

- Identify who their stakeholders are
- Identify their respective importance
- Identify their power
- Assess how the business affects stakeholders and how stakeholders affect the business
- Identify stakeholders' interests

1.15   The way in which stakeholders relate to the organisation is largely dependent on what type of stakeholder they are and on the level of management hierarchy at which they are able to apply pressure. The relative bargaining strength of stakeholders is an important consideration when management decide on the type of relationship that is applicable.

Stakeholder mapping

1.16   Stakeholder mapping is a management tool used to assess and manage each stakeholder group. **Mendelow** devised a grid showing the two key aspects of stakeholders: their level of power, and their interest in exercising that power. This is shown in Figure 5.1.

Figure 5.1 *Satisfying stakeholder groups*

Stakeholder group's interest/aspirations

	High	Low
Strong	**1** Keep close	**2** Keep satisfied
Weak	**3** Keep informed	**4** Minimal effort

Stakeholder group's power/influence

1.17 The terms within the quadrants describe the approach to managing stakeholders.

- Quadrant 1: the stakeholders have strong power and influence over the organisation and are clearly interested in the activities of the organisation. Shareholders are often located in this quadrant. Key players are found in this quadrant and strategies must be acceptable to them and gain their support.

- Quadrant 2: stakeholders in this quadrant must be treated with respect because of their power. They are often passive in approach but are capable of moving into Quadrant 1 if their interest is aroused. They should be kept satisfied.

- Quadrant 3: these do not have great ability to influence strategy but their views can be important in influencing more powerful stakeholders. Groups such as community representatives and charities often fall into this grouping. They should be kept informed.

- Quadrant 4: these are considered at the periphery of stakeholder influence, Private organisations will often use minimal effort with this group. With the public sector this group are usually customers or users and can feel strongly on specific issues. More effort in terms of advice, reasons for spend and initiatives etc should be given.

1.18 There are two main reasons why managers must consider the influence of stakeholders when setting organisational objectives.

- Managers must accept that stakeholders can affect the success of a strategy. For example customers may not purchase products, staff may leave or shareholders may sell their shares.

- Managers must ensure that they take into account the interests of stakeholders when making decisions. For example staff may not want to be relocated to another town or may be demotivated if a centralised management structure is adopted.

2 The role of stakeholders in private sector risk management

Introduction

2.1 Stakeholder mapping plays a crucial role in understanding stakeholders and for prioritising them in a structured manner. To date the view of stakeholder mapping described in this chapter is largely from a strategic viewpoint. The grid might well be different if viewed from an operational or project perspective where different issues are relevant. At all levels it is important that the organisation realises that any decisions relating to stakeholders are subject to legal and ethical constraints.

The Board of Directors

2.2 The Board of Directors is charged with managing the organisation on behalf of shareholders or investors. They hold the responsibility to ensure that risk management procedures are being enforced in line with organisational policy. They must also be aware of changes in stakeholder views and take these into account when reviewing strategy.

2.3 One good example of this is the growing awareness and integration of corporate social responsibility issues. Much of the pressure to adopt this more rounded and ethical approach developed from stakeholder concerns in areas such as environmental issues, use of child labour and international health and safety obligations.

2.4 The increasing prominence of corporate governance, as we have seen, came about through concern following corporate failures. In the US, this trend is supported by legislation, most notably the **Sarbanes-Oxley Act**, and in the UK by the **Combined Code** of the London Stock exchange.

2.5 Issued in June 1998 the Combined Code places responsibility on the Board to conduct a review of all material controls – including financial, operational and compliance controls – and risk management systems. The Combined Code was a consolidation of work of the previous Cadbury, Greenbury and Hampel committees. While in theory the Code is voluntary, it is a requirement of the London Stock Exchange that all listed companies make a disclosure statement in their Annual Report and Accounts to report on how the Code's principles are applied and to confirm compliance or explain non-compliance with the Code's provisions.

Shareholders

2.6 Shareholder power is now acknowledged as a major influence on an organisation's strategic direction. Shareholders have challenged directors on issues such as going public (particularly Building Societies), corporate social responsibility issues and directors' salaries. Their influence was so great that John Major set up the Greenbury committee in 1995 to identify and report on what should be considered good practice in relation to directors' salaries.

2.7   Shareholders are looking for a return on their investment over the short or long term. Institutional shareholders, in particular, are looking for regular returns from a well-managed company. Companies complying with the Combined Code give an assurance that recognised policies on compliance are enforced and that the organisation is being run in the correct and proper manner.

2.8   The shareholder risk is the risk that shareholders will remove their funds from the organisation. To ensure this does not happen the company must provide an acceptable return on investment to the shareholders and must be managed in compliance with the Combined Code.

Management

2.9   The role of management is to fulfil the strategic direction of the organisation by optimising resources to meet corporate goals in compliance with company policy.

2.10 Failure to deliver against the strategic plan will cause concern for many stakeholders, most notably the shareholders. Checks and balances – in the form of financial or **balanced scorecard** controls – aid in ensuring that delivery objectives are being met. Underpinning the traditional strategic approach is the formal process of risk management that provides for a rigorous appraisal of management decisions and actions to ensure that any risks taken fall within the organisation's risk appetite or are mitigated until they do.

2.11 One major change in management thinking over the past decade has been the development of **cross-functional working** in many organisations. This approach (which will be discussed further below) gives management a wider vision and perspective on the organisation. This wider perspective has clear benefits for risk management thinking as management and staff gain an appreciation of the ramifications of their decisions across the organisation. If the cross-functional teamworking extends outside the company then clearly there are benefits for the wider organisation.

Suppliers

2.12 The role of suppliers in modern business is central to the operations of most companies. Trends in supplier reduction, quality improvement, inventory management and supply chain thinking have all led to a greater reliance on fewer, but better suppliers.

2.13 The move to concentrating on core competencies can ensure that an organisation excels in its business area. This move to excellence is supported by a network of suppliers who operate outside the core competence area, providing opportunity for an organisation to excel.

2.14 Modern business is far more reliant on suppliers than in previous years. Organisations have decided to give away expertise in non-core areas, relying on specialist suppliers to fulfil that role. The role of purchasing is increasingly viewed as one of 'relationship management' as there is now greater impact if a supplier-principal or partnering agreement breaks down.

2.15 This increased reliance on fewer suppliers and modern relationship management issues brings new risks.

- • Over reliance on one supplier can cause major disruption if the supplier fails.
- • The supplier may become over reliant on the principal, causing problems if risk management highlights concern.
- • Purchasing management methodology can change the role of purchasing to a wider contract management role.
- • Contingency plans must be put in place.

2.16 Communication with suppliers is clearly of the utmost importance. Apart from closer business relations, the need to remain updated on suppliers' actions, schedules and deliveries is common throughout the purchasing discipline.

2.17 The purchasing team, using accepted methods such as supplier appraisal, auditing, financial and company updates, and site visits, must ensure that supplier information is regularly updated and any concerns discussed and placed on the risk register if appropriate.

Customers

2.18 Customer focus is not just a phrase; it is a reality of modern business. The product or service organisations are providing is designed to meet customer requirements.

2.19 Customers' views are consequently of immense importance. Customers' views should be sought throughout the concept and development phase of new products and services through focus groups, questionnaires, testing etc. The objective is to ensure that when a new product or service is released, relevant research to ensure a successful launch has been carried out to minimise risk.

2.20 Feedback from customers should be ongoing through a marketing information system (MkIS) or similar approach. Delivering what customers want is paramount.

Auditors

2.21 The role of auditors within risk management has increased since the introduction of the Combined Code. This relatively new formal discipline should be subject to internal and external auditing.

2.22 An in-house team, tasked with the auditing role, will carry out internal auditing. The team will ensure that risk procedures are being carried out in the designated manner and that all relevant detail is being documented in the appropriate manner. They will provide assurance that mitigating strategies are effective and comply with the organisation's risk appetite.

2.23 Internal audit teams will report to the board and audit committee on a regular basis with the purpose of confirming that the system is working effectively or that issues have been identified that need to be taken further.

2.24   External auditors can be used by any size of organisation but are of particular relevance to listed companies affected by the Combined Code. Their role is to assess and report on the risk management process – its effectiveness and efficacy – and to ensure that risk management and control procedures meet the requirements laid down in the Combined Code.

2.25   We say more about the role of auditors in Chapter 10.

3   The role of stakeholders in public sector risk management

Differences compared with the private sector

3.1   The public sector has a wide remit encompassing organisations ranging from national and local government, the Environment Agency, the constituent parts of the National Health Service and HM Revenue and Customs. Alongside these bodies are government owned organisations such as Royal Mail and autonomous organisations such as Transport for London and the College and University sectors that are reliant to a large degree on central government funding to provide their service.

3.2   The public sector has undergone substantial change and updating over recent decades and has evolved a more forward thinking and progressive culture with greater awareness of stakeholders and of the need to meet stakeholder needs.

3.3   The public sector requires a different perspective on stakeholders than the private sector. The difference stems from accountability. The private sector has a responsibility to make money and consequently focuses on key stakeholders such as shareholders and banks. The public sector is accountable for providing a range of services that underpin our society.

3.4   This fundamental difference places stakeholders at the heart of many public sector decisions and in consequence there is a greater need to engage with stakeholders and listen and respond to their views and concerns. The Transforming Public Sector Performance initiative highlights this awareness.

Transforming Public Sector Performance

3.5   Stakeholders are at the centre of the public performance agenda. More information in terms of ranking and league tables allows for comparing and contrasting public sector bodies across a range of services.

3.6   This requirement has been driven by government over the past ten to twenty years as part of an attempt to bring competitive thinking into the public sector. By placing schools, hospitals and local authorities within a ranking structure it provides the public at large with performance indications that allow them to compare and contrast the services on offer and make choices where appropriate.

3.7 The need to focus on providing information to stakeholders in this manner is not without its critics. Most criticism focuses on the time and effort spent on gathering and producing the information and the relevance of the figures being produced. It is important for public sector bodies, as stakeholders in these processes, to make their views known to central government.

3.8 The New Public Sector Performance Agenda places stakeholders at the start of the thinking in transforming public sector performance management. A seven-stage guide is given for delivering strategic performance improvement.

- Take a stakeholder view of performance: understanding that government and citizens are increasingly demanding and that these stakeholders are the main drivers for change. The need to prioritise stakeholders and understand stakeholder needs is paramount in this thinking.

- Define strategic performance goals: develop an understanding of strategic thinking within the public sector. Define strategy and strategy formulation, develop vision and mission statements and move away from short-term thinking. The roles of partnershipping and public/private partnerships play an increasingly important role at both strategic and operational level.

- Choose a strategic measurement framework: using appropriate key performance indicators but adapting financial indicators and approaches such as the **balanced scorecard** to give a wider and more realistic approach. (The balanced scorecard approach is based on a wide range of performance indicators, not just financial ones.)

- Selecting the most effective performance measures: understanding the benefits of measurement and selecting targets and measures that stretch the organisation towards continuous improvement. Audit within the organisation and use appropriate research techniques, such as questionnaires, to obtain stakeholder opinions. Benchmark against leading public sector bodies to improve identified weak areas, learning from others.

- Assign responsibility and accountability: by leading from the top while cascading strategic objectives throughout the organisation. Develop self-assessment capabilities and pass 'ownership' down to lower organisational levels.

- Build a high performance culture and service delivery: by encouraging leadership, incentivising managers and ensuring sound and consistent management practice across the organisation.

- Provide feedback for continuous performance improvement: ensure quality processes, audit and review procedures are in place and monitored effectively.

Stakeholder mapping

3.9 The Mendelow grid (stakeholder analysis matrix) remains applicable to the public sector but greater consideration must be given to the positioning of stakeholders in the quadrants.

- Quadrant 1: these stakeholders have the most power and influence over the organisation and are clearly interested in its activities. This quadrant may include the Office of the Deputy Prime Minister, the Audit Commission, and The Office of Government Commerce, as well as more specialist organisations focusing on the area of public service

- Quadrant 2: stakeholders in this quadrant must be treated with respect because of their power. They are often passive in approach but are capable of moving into Quadrant 1 if their interest is aroused. They should be kept satisfied. This could include national charities and concern groups and the press.

- Quadrant 3: these do not have great ability to influence strategy but their views can be important in influencing more powerful stakeholders. Groups such as community representatives and charities often fall into this grouping. They should be kept informed.

- Quadrant 4: these are considered at the periphery of stakeholder influence. These form a complex and more influential group in the public sector. The public sector has a greater responsibility to minority groups and individuals than the private sector. There are many examples of people coming together over local issues such as hospital closures, bypass schemes etc. This group should receive good communications and be treated with respect.

3.10 When developing a stakeholder strategy the starting point is often to ask the question 'what are we trying to achieve?' Consider a decision to close a hospital casualty department. One view of the objective might be 'to save money'; another might be 'to gain economies of scale by merging with a similar, better resourced operation'. It is never easy to respond to two diametrically opposed stakeholder views.

3.11 The Civil Contingencies Secretariat suggest the following, more detailed approach.

- What are the potential issues?

- Who will be affected by the risk and consequences of any management decision?

- Which parties or individuals have knowledge and expertise that may be useful to inform any discussion?

- Which parties or individuals have expressed an interest in this particular, or a similar, risk problem?

- Which stakeholders will be prepared to listen to and respect different viewpoints, and might be prepared to negotiate?

3.12 A 'fitness for purpose checklist' will often be applied at this point, asking the following questions.

- Have all the stakeholders and their interests been identified?

- Is there agreement from all interested parties about content, frequency and method?

- Has a common standard been considered?

- Has time to carry out the identified communications been allowed for in the stage plans?

3.13 It is important to determine the interests of stakeholders, who may represent different groups, and to resolve conflicting requirements. Further information is available at www.ogc.gov.uk.

Communications

3.14 A communications strategy should be developed to document how information will be disseminated to, and received from, all stakeholders in the activity. It identifies the means and medium as well as the frequency of communication between the different parties and is used to establish and manage ongoing communications throughout a programme or project.

3.15 A communications 'fitness for purpose checklist' would include the following items.

- A list of all stakeholders and their information requirements
- Communication mechanisms to be used (such as written reports, seminars, workshops, email and newsletters)
- Key elements of information to be distributed by the different mechanisms
- Roles and responsibilities of key individuals ensuring that communication is adequate, appropriate and timely
- Identification of how unexpected information from other parties (including stakeholders) will be handled within the scope of the activity

The influence of government bodies

3.16 Public sector bodies have made great strides in governance and risk management. A succession of papers and reports has been issued by HM Treasury, The Strategy Unit, The National Audit Office, the Office of Government Commerce and others, each containing guidelines and best practice principles for ensuring that the business of government is delivered in the best interests of all its stakeholders.

3.17 The most influential review bodies or support organisations are listed below.

- **The Office of the Deputy Prime Minister (now Communities and Local Government)** provides direction and advice for local authorities and encourages 'best practice' across the public sector.
- **HM Treasury**. The Treasury is responsible for formulating and implementing the Government's financial and economic policy. Its aim is to raise the rate of sustainable growth, and achieve rising prosperity and a better quality of life with economic and employment opportunities for all. It issues advice and guidance to public sector organisations on expectations and the principles of sound governance and the effective governance of risk.
- **The Audit Commission**. Their role is stated as follows: 'We ensure that public services deliver value for money'. They audit public sector bodies to ensure they are delivering value. Their role encompasses auditing risk management policies, procedures and effectiveness.
- **The Office of Government Commerce**. The OGC's role is to provide procurement as well as programme and project support to public sector organisations. It works in a number of areas but places risk management high on the agenda, developing training tools and assisting public sector employees to do their job better. 'Acquisition programmes and procurement projects in the central civil Government are subject to OGC Gateway reviews. The process examines a programme or project at critical stages in its lifecycle to provide assurance that it can progress successfully to the next stage.' (www.ogc.gov.uk)

Stakeholder influence

3.18 Public sector bodies and organisations operate in a different sphere from private sector companies. They may be subject to a range of external factors that need stakeholder evaluation. These can include political changes, a wide range of funding providers and local community or charitable groups.

3.19 The stakeholder groups are either providing funding or influencing the spending of the funds available. Their needs and desires must be understood in order to effectively meet their needs. A stakeholder needs analysis enables a better understanding and evaluation of stakeholder needs to be made.

3.20 The analysis provides a means to investigate, learn, understand and form considered opinions of issues relevant to stakeholders. Gathering stakeholder information is frequently undertaken in a formal manner. Stakeholders must be defined and categorised in terms of the stakeholder analysis matrix. Stakeholder meetings should be held, or at the very least a questionnaire issued and evaluated on its return.

3.21 From the meetings and questionnaire it is possible to elicit the problems and issues and rank these in an order of priority. For each stakeholder it is possible to elicit specific requirements. This information will then lead to the publication of a stakeholder needs list that can then be circulated as appropriate.

Stakeholder risk information needs analysis

3.22 Communication is a key element of risk management, but it is often a weak area in terms of both personal skills and organisational structures. A stakeholder risk information needs analysis can help to ensure that the risk process is communicated specifically and precisely, so that each stakeholder gets the information they need, at the time they need it.

3.23 The process is twofold.

- Identify all stakeholders, including their involvement, level of commitment and degree of influence.

- Determine the type and level of risk information they require, the purpose for which they require it, the required timing and frequency of delivery and the preferred medium or format for delivery.

3.24 A range of outputs from the risk process should then be designed, with the following considerations.

- Content: a range of risk outputs can be produced at different levels of detail, designed in a hierarchical manner, so that high-level outputs can be produced as summaries of more detailed reports, in order to avoid the overheads of producing multiple outputs and of providing excessive, complex information when it is not required.

- Delivery method: which should be appropriate for each stakeholder group (as already discussed).

- Responsibilities: each output needs an owner responsible for its production, and approval authority. It may be helpful to identify whose contributions will be required, and who will receive the output of the information. A RACI chart (Responsible, Approver, Contributor, Informed) may be useful.

3.25   The various outputs from the risk process should then be mapped to the stakeholder information needs, in order to ensure that all the needs can be met by the planned outputs. This makes it possible to decide which stakeholder requires which outputs.

3.26   Some stakeholders may only require a copy of the risk register, or a relevant extract, summary report or narrative from it. Each stakeholder has a different requirement for risk-related information, and the risk process should recognise this and deliver timely and accurate information at an appropriate level of detail to support the needs of each stakeholder. When all stakeholders get the information they need, they will be able to play their part in ensuring the risk is properly managed.

3.27   The challenge of risk management in the public sector is not about the identification and quantification of risk as this has largely been addressed. This is an area where the public sector leads the private sector although the influence of the Combined Code, in particular, will mean that the gap is narrowing.

3.28   The challenge in both the public and private sectors is about consistently embedding risk management across the organisation and with external stakeholders.

4   *The role of purchasing*

Dealing with risk

4.1   Possibly the most accepted statement of objectives for a purchasing function is: to acquire the right quality of material, at the right time, in the right quantity, from the right source, at the right price.

4.2   We could add 'with the minimum risk', if we are applying risk management thinking. In this context minimum risk does not mean no risk, but the minimum acceptable risk.

4.3   The concept of risk has long been accepted in purchasing. Placing business with a supplier who has a poor track record of on-time delivery, but whose product quality is high, as opposed to placing business with an indifferent supplier who will deliver on time, involves purchasing in considering the risks involved.

4.4   The decision is made by weighing up the factors surrounding the purchasing decision. Purchasing decisions are not necessarily about taking the easy, most secure option. They can be about weighing up all the factors and then deciding on the one that may turn out to be more of a risk, usually for justifiable reasons.

4.5   The difference is that these were decisions made as part of the job. The modern perspective of risk management asks purchasing to weigh up the factors, where applicable document the factors, and assess the risk.

4.6   At its simplest, this may be a straightforward traffic light system: green for little risk, amber for some risk and red for high risk. Such a scheme is used in some computer systems as a tool to enable a quick visual assessment of risk. As the purchasing cycle progresses and if the situation changes those authorised can update the categorisation.

4.7   The system places an onus on purchasing to make a risk assessment with every order placed. This is not a complex or particularly onerous process but starts to formalise risk thinking within the purchasing discipline.

4.8   The purpose is not to be critical of an individual but to place risk thinking on the purchasing agenda. The 'traffic light' system encourages joint discussion as part of a formal process and demonstrates an awareness of the risks. The reasons behind the thinking can also be documented.

4.9   The system is also auditable and can be used to evaluate the purchasing department's 'risk appetite'. An analysis of the decisions made will show, over time, the types of decisions made and whether they are in line with an organisation's risk appetite.

4.10   In its own way this approach creates a purchasing risk register that adds little to the existing workload but enables a better risk management evaluation of the purchasing function. With the increased spend now made by most purchasing departments it is appropriate that purchasing should be evaluated as part of the risk process.

Stakeholder satisfaction and the role of purchasing

4.11   The starting point in discussing stakeholder satisfaction is to define who the stakeholders are and then determine what they require from purchasing.

4.12   As an example, the Gershon Report in the public sector focuses on reducing total cost in order to provide funding to frontline services. From a purchasing perspective the stakeholder objective of 'reducing total cost' drives the process.

4.13   By understanding the stakeholder viewpoint at the start of the process it is possible to take a wider purchasing viewpoint. 'Reducing total cost' enables us to take a whole life costing (WLC) perspective examining such items as:

- The running costs of the purchase item
- The disposal costs of the purchase item
- Value for money
- Evaluation of alternatives
- Examination of possible savings and improvements by adopting a supply chain approach
- Lean thinking
- Service levels
- Payment terms
- Customer needs

4.14   With the greater application of **cross-functional teamwork** purchasing gains a wider perspective of the requirement of internal stakeholders. The wider thinking gained by working with internal stakeholder groups cannot but help to influence for the better any decision where purchasing has gained a better understanding. The same will apply if purchasing is involved in external cross-functional teamwork or simultaneous engineering projects where the needs of external stakeholders can be better understood.

4.15   With the move to closer supplier relationships, the role of purchasing changes to one of relationship management. At this more strategic level it is important to understand stakeholder needs. The time and investment in the relationship is greater and so is the understanding of the partnering organisation.

4.16   Clarity on stakeholders must be achieved between partner organisations. This ensures that the relationship is working to satisfy stakeholders in the appropriate manner. Stakeholder mapping should form an integral part of relationship management.

4.17   The joint understanding of stakeholder and stakeholder needs ensures that both organisations are focusing on achieving the optimum outcome to meet the various stakeholder needs.

Purchasing stakeholders

4.18   Purchasing stakeholders are both internal and external. As with all stakeholders they should be kept informed. Their importance will vary according to the particular issue being handled. However, there is a responsibility placed on purchasing to ensure communication is suitable and adequate.

4.19   Internal stakeholders will have established formal and informal links with purchasing. There is a need to realise the importance of these internal stakeholders and rate them accordingly.

4.20   The cross-functional team approach widens the influence and knowledge of purchasing within the organisation. It also gives the opportunity to interact and understand the needs of others who have a stake in the purchasing process.

4.21   External stakeholders such as suppliers and partners have seen their role as stakeholders change over recent years. This is particularly true of strategic suppliers or partners who may form a close business relationship. There is a need to inform all stakeholders but the more strategic ones will feature more highly when considering stakeholder mapping.

4.22   These more strategic suppliers work in a closer and more integrated manner. However, it is a criticism levelled by the Cranfield School of Management that managers with supply chain responsibility generally focus on internal operational risks. They are not explicitly asked to address supply chain vulnerability and resilience.

4.23   The focus of current supply chain issues is currently on closer integration, sharing of knowledge, reducing waste and cost. Stakeholder supply chain management needs to address, with increasing seriousness, the risk implications of the supply chain.

4.24   Supply chain vulnerability requires a change management approach examining culture, structures and business drivers that dominate a particular industry. Cranfield School of Management identified four issues that foster success in supply chain continuity management.

- Risk awareness among top managers
- Risk awareness as an integrated part of supply chain management
- An understanding by each employee of their role in risk awareness
- An understanding that changes in business strategies change supply chain risk profiles.

4.25 Suppliers/partners are also connected stakeholders in the true sense of the term. Their closeness and the inter-reliance of the supply chain approach make the connection very close. The management of these suppliers/partners also requires the management skills associated with stakeholder management.

Chapter summary

* Stakeholders are individuals and groups who have an interest or 'stake' in the organisation.

* In the private sector the key stakeholders are often those who own the business, in particular the shareholders. Public sector organisations are 'owned' by the state.

* Identifying an organisation's stakeholders, and their expectations, is part of the strategic analysis process, often termed stakeholder analysis.

* Stakeholder mapping is a management tool used to assess and manage each stakeholder group.

* The Board of Directors is charged with managing the organisation on behalf of shareholders or investors. They hold the responsibility to ensure that risk management procedures are being enforced in line with organisational policy.

* An increased reliance on fewer suppliers and modern relationship management issues brings new risks.

* The public sector requires a different perspective on stakeholders than the private sector. The difference stems from accountability.

* 'To acquire the right quality of material, at the right time, in the right quantity, from the right source, at the right price with the minimum risk': a traditional definition of purchasing's objectives.

* The starting point in discussing purchasing stakeholder satisfaction is to define who the stakeholders are and then determine what they require from purchasing.

Self-test questions

Numbers in brackets refer to the paragraphs where you can check your answers.

1   Define internal, connected and external stakeholders. (1.2)

2   What is stakeholder analysis? (1.11)

3   The relative bargaining strength of stakeholders is an important consideration when management decide on the type of relationship that is applicable. Whose matrix aids this process? (1.16)

4   When was the Combined Code of the London Stock exchange first issued? (2.5)

5   Define 'shareholder risk'. (2.8)

6   What new risks do the increased reliance on fewer suppliers and modern relationship management issues bring? (2.15)

7   What is the role of an auditor? (2.21–2.24)

8   What questions would a 'fitness for purpose checklist' ask in relation to stakeholder mapping? (3.13)

9   What questions would a 'fitness for purpose checklist' ask in relation to a stakeholder communications strategy? (3.15)

10   What responsibility does the 'traffic light system' place on purchasing? (4.7)

Further reading

•   Kit Sadgrove, *The Complete Guide to Business Risk Management*, Chapter 5.

CHAPTER 6

Benefits of Effective Risk Management

Learning objectives and indicative content

1.7   Evaluate how effective risk management can have positive benefits for organisations.

- Reduction in levels of threat
- Reduced exposure to uncertainty
- Higher risk opportunities being successfully pursued or mitigated
- Successful anticipation of shocks or other risk events
- Crises being avoided or mitigated
- Successful application of contingency or business continuity plans
- Disaster recovery planning and implementation
- Limited or no reputational or public relations damage
- Securing supply and mitigation of supply chain vulnerability
- Improved decision and policy making
- Increased customer and stakeholder satisfaction
- Improved organisational coordination with service and delivery partners

Chapter headings

1   Increasing organisational success

2   Mitigating losses

3   The effects of planning

1   *Increasing organisational success*

Strategic benefits of risk management

1.1   The purpose of risk management is to identify potential problems before they occur so that risk-handling activities may be planned and invoked as needed to mitigate adverse impacts on achieving objectives. In other words, it helps a company avoid additional costs, disruption and in some cases closure.

1.2   At a strategic level, risk management ensures that the directors of an organisation are acting in a correct and proper manner and that this can be verified by audit. Strategic plans are developed in line with an organisation's stated risk appetite and the risk management process will assure this.

1.3 The strategic ownership of the risk management approach ensures that support from the top of the organisation is given to the effective use of resources. It is an organisation's resources – its people, its factories, its location, its equipment and even its brand name – that come together to give a competitive edge or an ability to deliver a superior service.

Improving decision and policy making

1.4 Effective risk management is expected by stakeholders, in particular government bodies and shareholders who are looking for evidence of a well-managed organisation with high standards of corporate governance. Following a number of corporate scandals in both the USA and the UK higher standards are now applied to the governance of companies and stakeholders expect these standards to be delivered in an auditable manner.

1.5 The role of auditors, both internal and external, imposes rigour on the risk management process. Internal systems can be self-regulated or open to spot audits. The main consideration is that an auditor can ensure policies and procedures are being followed and can advise on areas of concern or areas where improvements might be made. External audits ensure that all systems are in compliance with governance criteria and will highlight areas of concern.

1.6 The risk management process imposes rigour on organisational activities such as the recruitment and training of staff, the purchase of capital equipment etc. This ensures that resources are appropriate, that they are required and that they will 'add value' to the organisation. It is the organisation that delivers its product and/or service in the most effective way that usually proves successful in today's marketplace.

1.7 Risk management forces managers to examine and justify decisions relating to resources across the organisation and to define their efficient and effective use in terms of meeting the stated strategic objectives.

Continuous improvement

1.8 Risk management has a focus on continuous improvement. This influential approach is embedded in many organisations. Risk management champions the approach by driving the company forward in a consistent and considered manner. The need to identify and challenge areas of risk gradually improves an organisation's confidence and fitness in its business area.

1.9 The risk management process ensures that fewer shocks and unwelcome surprises should occur. The system allows for a considered assessment and approach to be taken to risk, ensuring that risks are foreseen and treated as appropriate before becoming major incidents or embarrassments.

1.10 The risk management process has an important role to play in offering new opportunities to companies. The identification of a risk, threat or vulnerability may also provide the opportunity to put in place future potential or opportunities. The solving of risk issues will often call for creative thinking away from the mainstream business processes and this approach, if suitably encouraged, can add value to organisational thinking.

Communications

1.11 There has been a major change and rethink in the way organisations are structured and operate in recent years. Organisations are less internally focused and more customer focused. Structures have been changed to accommodate this approach, in particular by use of **cross-functional teams**.

1.12 The cross-functional approach enables departments to interact in a proactive and collaborative manner with other parts of the organisation. This has the benefit of increasing the organisational and product knowledge of individuals who are members of the teams.

1.13 Risk management encourages an organisation-wide approach with the realisation that many risks will cross organisational boundaries into a number of departments. Within the risk management structure these cross-boundary issues should be identified and discussed as part of the risk framework.

1.14 Risk management, particularly in purchasing, will involve discussions with external suppliers and partners as a matter of course. With risk management criteria increasingly being agreed with suppliers/partners there is pressure to improve communications between companies, particularly in relation to supply chain issues.

Quality

1.15 Quality plays a central role for many companies. The quality system has developed over the last fifty years to deliver quality products and services designed to meet customer needs consistently. Quality systems and approaches continue to develop. We will look at Six Sigma, one of the latest approaches, later in the text.

1.16 The risk of quality not being delivered impacts on an organisation, its reputation and its customers. The question being asked is 'Will risk management integrate quality within it?' The logical answer is yes, for two main reasons.

- Quality is embedded in organisations. Risk thinking places a new perspective on a widely accepted and successful approach.
- Risk management takes a wider view of an organisation's strategies and operations and it makes sense to place quality within the risk framework.

Focus on outcomes, not processes

1.17 Risk management is about continuing to deliver the goods and services customers require on a consistent and regular basis. This customer-focused approach looks at successful outcomes. The processes that deliver and meet customer demands should be designed to meet those needs. The customer does not usually need to know the processes; they are interested only in the outcomes. This focus of risk management is very much in line with modern management thinking.

Safeguarding and improving image and reputation

1.18 The value of reputational risk has already been discussed. Risk management helps to safeguard against the damage that may be caused by reputational risk and, through scenario planning and contingency planning approaches, considers in advance potential areas of reputational risk and how they might be handled, mitigated or contained.

1.19 Kit Sadgrove in *The Complete Guide to Business Risk Management* lists advantages of managing risk proactively: see Table 6.1.

Table 6.1 *The benefits of proactive risk management*

Type of risk	Benefits of proactive management
Marketing	Maintain market share
Health and safety	Avoid worker litigation, reduce insurance premiums
Environmental	Avoid litigation from regulatory authorities, reduced premiums
Fire	Avoid loss of production, avoid going out of business, reduced premiums
Bomb threats	Avoid loss of life or destruction of a building
Computer risks	Prevent inability to invoice, lack of access to information
Theft, fraud and industrial espionage	Prevent loss of money, assets or concepts. Loss of market share
Technical risks	Avoid being left behind with obsolete manufacturing methods or technologies, avoid production stoppage
Kidnap and ransom, extortion	Safeguard managers abroad or at home, prevent payment to criminals
Product contamination	Avoid harming customers and prevent litigation

Higher-risk opportunities

1.20 Risk management provides an assurance of stability for organisations. The process gives confidence to stakeholders and enables decisions to be made in a formal, considered way. However, it is important not to equate stability with being risk-averse.

1.21 An organisation will define its risk appetite to reflect the nature of the company. Where there is risk, there is profit. Organisations need to consider their 'risk appetite', ie the level of risks they are prepared to take.

1.22 Risk appetite, at the organisational level, is the amount of risk exposure, or potential adverse impact from an event, that the organisation is willing to accept or retain. Once the risk appetite threshold has been exceeded, risk management treatments and business controls are implemented to bring the exposure level back within the accepted range.

1.23 Having too restrictive a risk appetite can lead to organisations missing potentially profitable opportunities. At a strategic level it is essential to define the level of risk an organisation is willing to take.

1.24   Defining the level of risk an organisation is comfortable with will help in:

- Making better informed business decisions
- Focusing on the risks that exceed the defined appetite level
- Developing a business culture with a high awareness of risk
- Striking a balance between daring and prudence.

1.25   An organisation has to determine whether it is 'risk-taking' or 'risk-averse'. This assists in identifying risk thresholds, the trigger points where a risk moves from one category to another (eg from the category of not being monitored to the category of being monitored).

1.26   The amount of risk an organisation is prepared to tolerate before action is required is known as 'risk appetite' or 'risk tolerance'. It is advisable to have a risk tolerance for each risk identified but it is also useful to determine a 'global risk tolerance'. If a risk goes through this threshold, immediate attention would be required.

Securing supply

1.27   Securing supply is the basic function of purchasing. The purchasing discipline has been applying risk management thinking for many years in delivering this basic requirement. We have already seen how tools such as the Kraljic matrix can help with this task.

1.28   How does risk management benefit purchasing?

- It provides a documented and auditable decision making trail.
- The 'traffic light' risk assessment method is compatible with operational workloads.
- It ensures that supplier relationships are considered and developed as appropriate.
- It makes purchasing aware of the importance of their decisions and the ramifications for the company as a whole if they get it wrong.
- The cross-functional approach engendered by risk management increases the knowledge of purchasing both internally and externally. Equally other parts of the organisation gain an increasing awareness of purchasing issues.

1.29   Risk management is a reality in business today and in the future. Purchasing has the opportunity to be involved at an early stage and 'champion' risk throughout the organisation. Purchasing is already involved in many of the benefit areas displayed above. There is an opportunity to maximise purchasing involvement.

Improved organisational coordination

1.30   The structure of many organisations is undergoing a fundamental shift. The traditional management structure is based on functional divisions. This leads to a focused concentration of knowledge within specific functional areas. However, modern business needs to take a wider view, integrating its business areas and spreading knowledge across the organisation.

1.31 One of the risks of modern business is 'suboptimisation': no matter how good or efficient one function or part of a business is, unless the component parts of the organisation work together it will never optimise its potential. Optimising the outcome for a subsystem will in general not optimise the outcome for the system as a whole.

1.32 Lack of organisational integration makes it difficult to put the customer first. A mix of functional strategies that seek to optimise individual business processes supports the supply chain. Decisions made are made primarily with the individual business process area in mind. It would be preferable if decisions could reflect overall objectives of the organisation as a whole, or even the entire supply chain.

1.33 The answer may be to concentrate on meeting the needs of customers. A genuine organisation commitment with a common focus should enable functional strategies to be developed that, over time, come more into line with each other.

1.34 Risk management encourages an organisation-wide rather than a functional perspective. This approach will enable risk evaluation and decision making to be seen in a wider perspective, to the benefit of the organisation as a whole.

Increasing stakeholder and customer satisfaction

1.35 As we have discussed, the benefits of the risk management approach and methodology are wide-ranging.

- Viewed from a strategic viewpoint, the process ensures good governance, considered and planned strategic development, and assurance to stakeholders that a rigour is being applied to the organisational processes.

- Viewed from a stakeholder perspective, there is clarity of purpose and an assurance that processes are in place to ensure that an organisation is acting in a correct and proper manner.

- Viewed from the perspective of customers, they can have confidence that the company will deliver its promises in the manner they expect. For example if a company has a strong stance on corporate social responsibility issues this will be evidenced and supported by a rigorous risk assessment and management process.

1.36 There are clearly many benefits to be gained from effective risk management. The benefits must be weighed against the cost implications involved to get an acceptable balance for the organisation.

2   *Mitigating losses*

Options for handling risks

2.1 To mitigate is to lessen the impact should a risk event occur. Here are some of the options for handling risks. Often, especially for high risks, more than one approach to handling a risk should be generated.

- Risk avoidance: changing or lowering requirements while still meeting the user's needs
- Risk control: taking active steps to minimise risks
- Risk transfer: reallocating design requirements to lower the risks

- Risk monitoring: watching and periodically re-evaluating the risk for changes to the assigned risk parameters
- Risk acceptance: acknowledgment of risk without taking any action.

2.2 In many cases, risks will be accepted or monitored. Risk acceptance is usually implemented when the risk is judged too low for formal mitigation, or when there appears to be no viable way to reduce the risk. If a risk is accepted, the rationale for this decision should be documented.

2.3 Risks are monitored when there is an objectively defined, verifiable, and documented threshold of performance, time, or risk exposure (the combination of likelihood and consequence) that will trigger risk mitigation planning or invoke a contingency plan if it is needed.

Risk mitigation planning

2.4 Risk mitigation planning is the activity that identifies, evaluates, and selects options to set risk at acceptable levels given program constraints and objectives. Risk mitigation planning is intended to enable program success. It includes the specifics of **what** should be done, **when** it should be accomplished, **who** is responsible, and the **funding** required to implement the risk mitigation plan. The most appropriate program approach is selected from the mitigation options listed above and documented in a risk mitigation plan.

2.5 The intent of risk mitigation planning is to answer the question 'What is the approach for addressing this potential unfavourable consequence?' One or more of the following mitigation options may apply.

- Avoiding risk by eliminating the root cause and/or the consequence
- Controlling the cause or consequence
- Transferring the risk
- Assuming the level of risk and continuing on the current program plan

2.6 Once the mitigation approach has been selected, it must be implemented. This will involve the following actions.

- Determine what planning, budget, and contractual changes are needed
- Pursue coordination with management and other stakeholders
- Direct the risk teams to execute the defined and approved risk mitigation plans
- Outline the risk reporting requirements for ongoing monitoring
- Document the change history

2.7 A critical component of a risk mitigation plan is to develop alternative courses of action, workarounds, and fallback positions, with a recommended course of action for each critical risk.

2.8 The risk mitigation plan for a given risk includes techniques and methods used to avoid the risk, and also estimates the extent of damage incurred should the risk occur. Risks are monitored and when they exceed the established thresholds, the risk mitigation plans are deployed to restore the situation to an acceptable risk level.

2.9   If the risk cannot be mitigated, a contingency plan may be invoked. Usually, risk mitigation and contingency plans are generated only for selected risks where the potential consequences are determined to be high or unacceptable. Other risks may be accepted and simply monitored.

Reduction in levels of threat

2.10   The process of mitigation is designed to reduce the threat to an acceptable level. If the desired level cannot be achieved, then the option of terminating the risk or threat remains if practical.

2.11   Threats can be reduced in a number of ways.

- Monitor the external environment. The better informed an organisation is, the better it can respond. Formal market monitoring processes, designed to meet organisational needs, can provide relevant information both for a management information system and specifically for risk management.

- Insure against the risk. The traditional method of protecting against risk has been to insure. Insurance restores us to the same financial position we would have been in had the loss not occurred. This is relevant when applied to tangible items such as buildings and equipment but less applicable to intangibles such as reputational risk.

- Use third parties to mitigate the risk. One of the ways in which a purchasing department can mitigate risk is to have the supplier carry the risk instead. For example, a buyer can use call-off orders. The product remains in the supplier's ownership and at the supplier's risk until called forward. Another option is to place the onus on suppliers to complete the delivery by a specified time, as often happens in project management. If they fail to meet the specified date, damages may be payable. We return to this subject in Chapter 9.

- Hedge the risk. If buying or selling goods or services in currencies other than their own, importers and exporters open themselves to the 'currency risk' or 'exchange risk', the risk that the currency will fluctuate in value in the period between prices being agreed and payment being received. Management of this exposure is essential to minimise the potential risks and to maximise the profit from the underlying transaction. The technique of protecting against future exchange rate movements is usually referred to as 'hedging'; this is carried out by use of various financial products such as futures contracts. Again, this is discussed further in Chapter 9.

Anticipation of shocks and other risk events

2.12   Kit Sadgrove in *The Complete Guide to Business Risk Management* gives the following diagram assessing risk severity and probability. Items analysed as serious or catastrophic, or in the categories of improbable or very unlikely, can cause shocks to an organisation.

Figure 6.1 *Risk severity and probability*

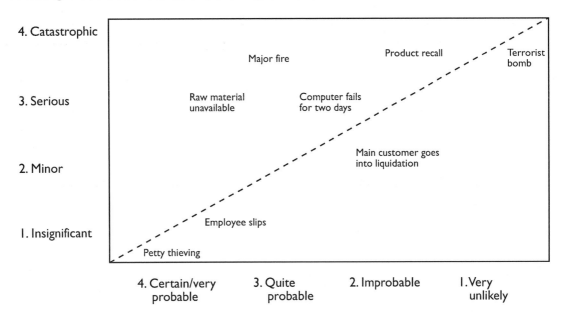

2.13 Catastrophic events are improbable (terrorist attack, earthquake, aircraft crashes etc) but still need to be considered. Many of the world's leading organisations do not permit their senior board members to travel together in case of an air or rail disaster. If basing employees in an area known for terrorism, the safeguards would be employed.

2.14 If the risk, however unlikely, is seen as catastrophic for an organisation then it makes sense to take steps to reduce or eliminate that risk. The loss of the entire Board in an air crash would have a major impact on the organisation. It makes sense to acknowledge the risk, assess the risk and find some way of reducing the risk.

Avoiding crises

2.15 Crisis management is a relatively new field. Typically, proactive crisis management activities include forecasting potential crises and planning how to deal with them, for example, how to recover if your computer system completely fails.

2.16 Organisations have time and resources to complete a crisis management plan before they experience a crisis. Crisis management in the face of a current, real crisis includes identifying the nature of the crisis, intervening to minimise damage and recovering from the crisis.

2.17 Crisis management often includes strong focus on public relations to recover any damage to public image and assure stakeholders that recovery is underway.

2.18 In business there are three main types of crisis.

- **Financial crisis** – short-term liquidity or cashflow problems; and long-term bankruptcy problems
- **Public relations crisis** – more commonly called 'communications crisis', ie negative publicity that could adversely affect the success of the company
- **Strategic crisis** – changes in the business environment that call the viability of the company into question

2.19 Certain preliminary measures should be taken to prevent a crisis. Companies should always plan ahead and project likely outcomes. They should avoid decisions that have the potential to turn into a crisis. They should be aware of their worst case scenarios and have a contingency plan to cope with them. We will examine these issues later in the text.

2.20 If prevention has not been successful, then the following six steps should be undertaken immediately.

- Do an objective assessment of the cause(s) of the crisis.
- Determine whether the cause(s) will have a long-term effect or whether it will be short-term.
- Project the most likely course of events.
- Focus all the most capable people on activities that will mitigate or eliminate the problem.
- Look for opportunities.
- Immediately act to guard cashflow.

2.21 If it is a cashflow crisis, do not wait for further evidence before acting. Immediately take actions to maintain or increase cashflow.

2.22 If it is a public relations crisis, act immediately to prevent or counter the spread of the negative information. Containment may require intense media activities. Use every medium available to provide a counter argument or to question the credibility of the original negative publicity.

2.23 Business continuity management aims to ensure that crises do not occur, but should the worst come to the worst, effective crisis management can make the difference between business-as-usual or disaster.

Avoiding reputational problems

2.24 As discussed in Chapter 2, corporate reputation is a key determinant of future business success. Indeed corporate reputation can form much of the added value of an organisation, particularly in the eyes of consumers and shareholders.

2.25 The impact of recent corporate governance and regulatory changes, combined with growing investor engagement and greater stakeholder awareness, is making transparency and accountability the norm. A good reputation is a critical asset to any organisation; it should be protected and nurtured.

2.26 The risks to reputation can arise from many sources.

- Financial performance and profitability
- Corporate governance and quality of management
- Social, ethical and environmental performance
- Employees and corporate culture
- Marketing, innovation and customer relations
- Regulatory compliance and litigation

2.27 Effective management of risk can result in reputation being not only protected, but enhanced.

2.28 Figure 6.2 contains an article from *The Scotsman* giving an illustration of some of the key reputational issues that have faced leading organisations over recent years.

Figure 6.2 *Dell product recall*

Four million laptops recalled amid Dell fire hazard fears

More than four million laptops are at the centre of a global alert over batteries that can overheat and catch fire. Dell issued the biggest product recall in computer history after video footage showed a laptop bursting into flames during a conference in Osaka, Japan.

Similar incidents have been reported across the world. Dell said it had been told of six instances of batteries overheating, causing damage to furniture and belongings but no personal injuries. Consumers are being urged to stop using the batteries immediately and to get in touch to obtain replacements.

The company said yesterday it was recalling 4.1 million batteries for use in Latitude, Inspiron and Precision laptops. The batteries are also used by other companies including Apple.

Dell blames the problem on the lithium-ion batteries made by Sony Energy Devices. This type of battery has been in use since the mid-nineties and is often found in devices such as mobile phones and digital music players.

It is estimated the recall could cost Dell more than £157million, without taking into account damage to the firm's reputation. Spokesman Ira Williams said: 'In rare cases, a short-circuit could cause the battery to overheat, causing a risk of smoke and fire. It happens in rare cases, but we opted to take this broad action immediately.'

Fears surrounding laptops emerged this month as pictures of some of the charred machines circulated on the internet. One man from Singapore told an Australian newspaper how his laptop caught fire as he was working late in his office. He said: 'White smoke began to pour out of the machine, completely filling up the room, and there were flames coming up the sides of the laptop.'

The recall involves 18 per cent of Dell's 22 million notebook computers sold between April 2004 and last month. This is the third recall of Dell notebook batteries in the past five years. In December it recalled 22,000 notebook computer batteries over similar fears. The company also recalled 284,000 batteries in 2001.

It comes as a major blow to Dell, which has recently lost ground to its leading rival Hewlett-Packard.

The words Dell and 'Made in Japan' or 'Made in China' or 'Battery cell made in Japan, assembled in China' are printed on the back of the batteries. Dell stressed that the short-circuiting problem was rare.

A Sony spokesman said the two companies had studied problems with the battery packs for more than a month, after getting reports of about half-a-dozen fires or smoking laptops in the US.

Dell is urging customers to check via its website if their batteries are subject to the recall. Customers whose battery identification numbers match those being recalled will be automatically connected to a replacement order form.

2.29 High-profile product recall alerts to consumers in recent years have ranged from foodstuffs to cars.

- In 1990 Perrier was involved in a massive worldwide recall of its products after traces of the poisonous chemical benzene were discovered in its water.

- Millions of products were taken off supermarket shelves in February 2006 after the contaminated Sudan I dye was used in a batch of Crosse & Blackwell Worcester sauce.

- General Motors recalled nearly 200,000 pick-ups, vans and sports utility vehicles after a possible problem was discovered in the braking system.

- In June 2006 Cadbury Schweppes, the confectionery giant, withdrew more than one million of its products after traces of salmonella were discovered.

2.30 The loss to reputation can be substantial. The way the company responds is critical as it can mean the difference between continuing in business and ceasing to exist.

Managing reputational risk

2.31 All employees bear some responsibility for the identification and management of risks to reputation. However, members of the Board play a crucial role in setting the tone.

2.32 Leaders in reputation risk management have put the following components at the heart of their approach.

- A clear vision: 'what we stand for and are prepared to be held responsible for'
- Clear values, supported by a code of conduct, setting out expected standards of behaviour
- Policies clearly stating performance expectations and 'risk tolerance' in key areas
- Understanding of stakeholders' expectations, information requirements and perceptions of the organisation
- An open, trusting, supportive culture
- A robust and dynamic risk management system which provides early warning of developing issues
- Organisational learning leading to corrective action where necessary
- Reward and recognition systems which support organisational goals and values
- Extension of vision and values to major partners and suppliers
- Open and honest communications tailored to meet the needs of specific stakeholders

2.33 There is increasing evidence that a good reputation enhances profitability and contributes positively to longer-term success. It does this by supporting the recruitment and retention of high quality personnel, maintaining customer and supplier loyalty, attracting investment and bolstering competitiveness.

2.34 There is no 'one size fits all' solution to managing reputation risk. Reputation can be regarded as a source of risk in its own right and/or as a consequence of other risks occurring. The critical issue is to ensure that all major risks are comprehensively identified and prioritised and that appropriate action is taken to manage them.

2.35 The ability to manage reputation and its associated risks effectively is a key competence in an increasingly competitive world. In consequence, reputational risk is a key focus, particularly of organisations whose brand or image is their main differentiating factor.

2.36 The management of reputational risk is underpinned by effective contingency planning, scenario building and disaster recovery plans. For many organisations reputational risk is of crucial importance.

The risk scoring matrix

2.37 A quantitative tool for assessing risk is the risk scoring matrix. This considers two factors in relation to each identified risk: the likelihood of the event occurring, and the impact it will have if it does occur.

2.38 Likelihood ranges from very low (1) to very high (5). Impact ranges from insignificant (1) to very serious (5). The combined scores on a 5 x 5 matrix produce scores ranging from 1 to 25. The scoring will be on the basis of the risk owner's view of the risk before and after taking into account their judgement of the effectiveness of the existing management controls.

2.39 The following monitoring regime is recommended according to the risk score.

- A risk score of 6 or less (low level of risk) should require no mitigating action. However, risk owners should review controls for low-risk areas to ensure they are effective and not disproportionate. The risk score should be reviewed annually.

- A risk score of 8 to 12 (medium level of risk – a score of 7 is impossible) should trigger a review of the existing controls, if a new risk, and may require the implementation of additional controls for existing risks. Risks with this score should be reviewed annually or twice a year if necessary.

- A risk score of 14 to 20 (high level of risk – a score of 13 is impossible) should trigger a review of the existing controls and is likely to require the implementation of additional controls. The problem may need to be escalated to the relevant committee for consultation. Risks with this score should be reviewed at least quarterly or six-monthly.

- A residual risk score of 21 or above (top level of risk) should trigger a review of the existing controls and is likely to require the implementation of additional controls. The problem should definitely be escalated to the relevant committee for consultation. Risks with this score should be reviewed continuously.

2.40 Should the top risks be avoided? It depends on the stated 'risk appetite' of the organisation. As with other risks it may be possible to treat them in some way. Joint ventures, consortiums and partnerships are all established business practices. They also enable an organisation to spread the risk between like-minded companies.

2.41 The consortium approach enables companies in a particular sector to come together by offering a range of complementary skills. By coming together in this way they are also dividing the project between themselves – lessening the potential profitability but also lessening the risk.

2.42 For any remaining risks, contingency plans should be developed. Contingency plans should be appropriate and commensurate to the impact of the original risk. In many cases it is more cost effective to allocate a certain amount of resources to mitigate a risk rather than start by developing a contingency plan which, if necessary to implement, is likely to be more expensive. The number of scenarios likely to require a full contingency plan depends upon the project. Contingency planning should not be confused with the normal re-planning necessary to react to minor changes in the developing project plan.

3   *The effects of planning*

Introduction

3.1   Good planning is increasingly essential as business becomes more complex and competition increases. Good planning offers the following benefits.

- It involves those concerned.
- It informs those concerned.
- It improves communications.
- It provides better coordination of activities.
- It identifies expected developments.
- It considers the risk elements of plans.
- It increases organisational preparedness to change.
- It reduces conflicts regarding the direction of the company.
- It forces management to think ahead systematically and realistically.
- Available resources can be better matched to opportunities.
- The plan provides a framework for the continuing review of operations.

3.2   Risk planning will also force organisations to look ahead and examine the implication of the major, if less likely, risks that can seriously damage or destroy a company.

Contingency and business continuity plans

3.3   Every business and organisation can experience a serious incident that can prevent it from continuing normal operations. This can range from a flood or fire to a serious computer malfunction or information security incident. We introduce this topic briefly at this point, but business continuity, disaster recovery and contingency plans will be developed further in Chapter 15.

3.4   Business continuity management (BCM) is a process that can be applied to help manage the risks that threaten survival. The objective of BCM is to identify hazards that may affect critical activities and ensure that these can be reduced or responded to in an effective manner.

3.5   The management of the organisation have a responsibility to recover from such incidents in the minimum amount of time, with minimum disruption and at minimum cost. This requires careful preparation and planning. Business continuity planning is the process of planning for the unexpected. An effective plan provides procedures to minimise the effects of unexpected disruptions.

3.6   The plan should enable the organisation to recover quickly and efficiently with minimum disruption to day-to-day activities.

3.7   It is vital that the organisation takes the development and maintenance of the disaster recovery or business continuity plan seriously. It is not a task that can just be left until someone has time to deal with it. A serious incident can happen at any time.

3.8   The contingency plan should be developed by a team representing all functional areas of the organisation. If the organisation is large enough, a formal project should be established, which must have approval and support from the very top of the enterprise.

3.9   One of the first contingency planning tasks to be undertaken is to prepare a comprehensive list of the potentially serious incidents that could affect the normal operations of the business. This list should include all possible incidents no matter how remote the likelihood of their occurrence.

3.10   Against each item listed the project team or manager should note a probability rating. Each incident should also be rated for potential impact severity level. From this information, it will become much easier to frame the plan in the context of the real needs of the organisation. This is the procedure described earlier in the context of the risk scoring matrix.

3.11   Once the assessment stage has been completed, the structure of the plan can be established. The plan will contain a range of milestones to move the organisation from its disrupted status towards a return to normal operations.

3.12   The first important milestone is the process that deals with the immediate aftermath of the disaster. This may involve the emergency services or other specialists who are trained to deal with extreme situations.

3.13   The next stage is to determine which critical business functions should be resumed and in what order. The plan will of necessity be detailed, and will identify key individuals who should be familiar with their duties under the plan.

3.14   Once this plan has been developed it must be subjected to rigorous testing. The testing process itself must be properly planned and should be carried out in a suitable environment to reproduce authentic conditions in so far as this is feasible.

3.15   The plan must be tested by those persons who would be involved in reality. The test procedures should be documented and the results recorded. This is important to ensure that feedback is obtained for fine-tuning the plan.

3.16   Equally, it is important to audit both the plan itself, and the contingency and back-up arrangements supporting it.

3.17   Once a business continuity plan has been agreed, as with the development of contingency plans and disaster recovery scenarios, it is the start of an ongoing commitment. As organisations constantly evolve, plans must evolve with them.

3.18   Business continuity, disaster recovery and contingency plans are now accepted as requirements for organisations. It is widely accepted that a detailed business continuity/disaster recovery plan should not only exist but should be up to date.

Chapter summary

- Risk management helps a company avoid additional costs, disruption and, in some cases closure.

- The risk process is expected by stakeholders, in particular government bodies and shareholders who are looking for evidence of a well-managed organisation with high standards of corporate governance.

- The role of auditors, both internal and external, imposes rigour on the risk management process.

- The focus of risk management is in line with modern management thinking.

- The process of mitigation is designed to reduce the threat to the organisation to an acceptable level.

- A critical component of a risk mitigation plan is to develop alternative courses of action, workarounds, and fallback positions, with a recommended course of action for each critical risk.

- If a risk, however unlikely, is seen as catastrophic for an organisation then it makes sense to take steps to reduce or eliminate that risk.

- A good reputation is a critical asset to any organisation; it should be protected and nurtured.

- The management of reputational risk is underpinned by effective contingency planning, scenario building and disaster recovery plans.

- Modern business needs to take a wider view integrating its business areas and spreading knowledge across the organisation.

- The objective of business continuity management is to identify hazards that may affect critical activities and ensure that these can be reduced or responded to in an effective manner.

Self-test questions

Numbers in brackets refer to the paragraphs where you can check your answers.

1   What are the benefits of cross-functional working? (1.12)

2   Give five advantages of managing risk proactively. (1.19)

3   When are risks monitored? (2.3)

4   The intent of risk mitigation planning is to answer what question? (2.5)

5   In business there are three main types of crisis risks. What are they? (2.18)

6   If crisis prevention has not been successful what six steps should be undertaken immediately? (2.20)

7   The risks to reputation can arise from many sources. Give five of them. (2.26)

8   Give three examples of organisations that have had reputational risk problems. (2.28, 2.29)

9   What is the objective of business continuity management? (3.4)

Further reading

*   Kit Sadgrove, *The Complete Guide to Business Risk Management*, Chapter 14.

CHAPTER 7

Risk Management Processes and Structures

Learning objectives and indicative content

2.1   Develop a risk management strategy.

- Example of appropriate supply chain risk policy
- How to define objectives and content for a risk management strategy
- Describe an appropriate risk policy
- How an organisation's appetite for risk may affect the risk policy
- The purpose of a risk management strategy and a risk management framework
- The key components of a risk management strategy
- The key implications of the Turnbull Report

2.2   Formulate an effective risk management process in the context of an organisation's strategic objectives and a dynamic external environment.

- Key stages of a risk management process: risk identification, risk analysis, risk evaluation, risk treatment and risk reporting
- Methods for identifying, assessing and quantifying risks
- Classification of risk within the organisational context
- A risk report and the role of a Board risk committee
- How identified risks should be monitored and reviewed

Chapter headings

1   The purpose of a risk management strategy

2   Formulating a risk management strategy

3   Internal risk management systems

4   Stages in the risk management process

1   The purpose of a risk management strategy

What is a risk management strategy?

1.1   Risk management is the sum of all proactive management-directed activities within an organisation that are intended to acceptably accommodate the possibility of failures in elements of the organisation. 'Acceptably' is as judged by the customer in the final analysis, but from an organisation's perspective a failure is anything accomplished in less than a professional manner.

1.2 The purpose of risk management is to identify potential problems before they occur so that risk-handling activities may be planned and invoked as needed in order to mitigate adverse impacts on achieving objectives.

1.3 When risk management goes well it often remains unnoticed. When it fails, however, the consequences can be dramatic.

1.4 Risk management is a process for defining, analysing, controlling and mitigating risk, with a view to providing assurance that:

- Objectives are more likely to be achieved
- Damaging outcomes will either not happen or will become less likely to happen
- Beneficial outcomes will either be achieved or will be more likely to happen

1.5 Risk management makes a major contribution in helping an organisation to achieve its objectives.

- It improves strategic planning, business planning, project management and best value reviews – as well as day-to-day operations.
- It provides clear responsibility and accountability lines.
- It provides critical success factors and key performance indicators.
- It provides clear pictures of risks and their management at every level of the organisation.

1.6 Risk management is a continuous, forward-looking activity that is an important part of organisational, business and technical management processes. Risk management should address issues that could endanger achievement of critical objectives. A continuous risk management approach is applied to effectively anticipate and mitigate the risks that have critical impact on a project.

1.7 Effective risk management helps an organisation to achieve its wider aims such as: understanding and delivering change management, the efficient use of objectives, better project management, minimising waste and fraud and supporting development and innovation.

1.8 Effective risk management includes early and aggressive risk identification through the collaboration and involvement of relevant stakeholders. Strong leadership across all relevant stakeholders is needed to establish an environment for the free and open disclosure and discussion of risk.

The aims of risk management

1.9 A key aim of a risk management strategy is summed up in the phrase 'no surprises'. By managing threats effectively an organisation will be in a stronger position to ensure business continuity, provide better services and offer value for money.

1.10 Risk management involves putting in place processes, methods and tools to deal with potential threats that have been identified. This can be as simple as setting financial reserves aside to ease cashflow problems. Similarly, it can refer to ensuring the effective back-up of IT systems. In more extreme cases, it can refer to planning for eventualities such as a terrorist attack.

1.11   Risk management is a wide-ranging process and involves the following elements.

- Integrated management of an organisation's full spectrum of risk
- Dealing with risk as a strategic issue, from a high-level corporate perspective
- Recognising that strategic success usually depends upon taking risks
- Engaging all functions and line management levels in the process
- Bridging the traditional gap between risk disciplines (eg financial, physical)
- Cutting across traditional boundaries

2   *Formulating a risk management strategy*

Introduction

2.1   As we have seen, the drivers for developing an effective risk management strategy have increased at a rapid pace over recent years. It is increasingly regarded as good practice across all business and public sectors and requires effective implementation at the strategic level.

2.2   The risk management strategy forms part of an organisation's strategic plan. In modern business, risk thinking is becoming an integral aspect of organisational management. No strategic plan should fail to incorporate the role and contribution of risk management in effective organisational development.

2.3   The risk management strategy comprises the processes that will be put in place and link together to identify, assess, address, review and report on organisational risk.

2.4   The strategy should go further than the mechanics of risk management. It should aim to embed the principles of risk management within the organisation over the long term. This requires consistent strategic support linked to building awareness among managers and staff.

2.5   There is no specific set of standards for risk management. There is however guidance and good practice, as we have seen that organisations and public bodies need to implement.

Corporate governance

2.6   Corporate governance is the system by which an organisation is directed and controlled at its most senior levels, in order to achieve its objectives and meet the necessary standards of accountability, probity and openness. The requirement for improved corporate governance has increased significantly over recent years following the publication of the Turnbull Report and other reports.

2.7   Governance involves defining policies and setting objectives, allocating resources, appointing senior staff sufficient to meet the objectives, and monitoring progress towards meeting those objectives.

2.8   Members of the Board need to be satisfied that processes and procedures are in place that are sufficient, necessary and effective in the running of an organisation. They will do this by putting in place and operating a risk management programme and appointing managers and auditors to deliver the objectives and verify that the system is working as envisaged. They will ask probing; searching questions and ensure that responses are sound, confident and consistent, rather than doing direct checking themselves.

Roles and responsibilities

2.9   Roles and responsibilities differ between organisations but follow a similar pattern. The names and roles will vary, particularly between the public and private sector, but in the UK governance is based on the **Combined Code** and the **Turnbull Report**. (You should refer back to Chapter 4 for detailed explanation.) There needs to be clear allocation of responsibility; otherwise an organisation will be exposed to risks being unmanaged, causing damage or loss that could otherwise be influenced, controlled or avoided.

The Accounting Officer

2.10   The Accounting Officer is appointed by the Board as the person ultimately responsible for the organisation and management of risk. He must:

   •   Have a clear understanding and assessment of the risks that could prevent delivery of objectives

   •   Ensure that the organisation has effective risk management and control processes

   •   Be provided with assurance that the process and key strategic roles are being effectively managed

2.11   He will require assurances in order to sign off the statement of internal control.

The Board

2.12   The Board has a fundamental role in the management of risk. The role includes:

   •   Receipt of an annual opinion from the Audit and Scrutiny Committee that will include its review of the process of risk management and internal control

   •   Consideration of risk issues as they affect Board decisions

   •   Reviewing key strategic risks that will be analysed alongside the corporate plan

   •   Periodically reviewing risks as part of the monitoring of the annual operating plans

2.13   The Board is corporately responsible for owning the organisation's risk management strategy, implementing the approach to managing risk and strategically reviewing the organisation's top risks. The 'top ten' risks should be agreed, owned and addressed by Board members.

The Risk Management Committee

2.14   The Risk Management Committee's remit will include consideration of policy in respect of issues or activities that are organisation-wide. The committee is responsible for reviewing and agreeing the process of managing risk in the organisation. It is responsible for advising the Board on the performance of the key processes (identifying, assessing, addressing, reviewing and reporting risks) and on how effectively the principles of good risk management are embedded across the organisation.

The Audit and Scrutiny Committee

2.15   The main purpose of the Audit and Scrutiny Committee is to give advice to the Board on the adequacy of audit arrangements and on the implications of assurances provided in respect of risk and control in the organisation. They have the responsibility for internal audit and will bring in external auditors at the request of the Board, usually annually.

Directors

2.16   Each director is responsible for ensuring that risks have been properly identified and assessed across their departmental and cross-functional areas. They are responsible for agreeing the risk register return and taking identified risk issues higher if concerns warrant. Each director should have the expectation of owning some of the main risks in their area and personally addressing them. This will also help to set the tone for risk management across their areas of responsibility.

Contents of the strategic risk plan

2.17   The risk strategy and supporting plan must acknowledge the actual and potential threats facing the organisation and determine the structures and reporting mechanisms for risk management. Publication of the risk management strategy will normally be on an annual basis. Because of the financial input and auditing requirements it is common to publish alongside the annual accounts.

2.18   A published risk management strategy might include the following six sections.

Section 1: Introduction and purpose

The risk strategy will usually define what risk is to the organisation. This definition may be placed in an organisation context. An illustration is *'The threat that an action or event will adversely affect the organisation's ability to achieve its current and future objectives'*.

Section 2: Aim, principles and implementation

The aim (eg *'becoming one of the leading organisations in the management of risk and the innovative management of threats'*) sets the scene. Becoming an exemplar of best practice, together with comment regarding attaining a balance between risk and opportunity, would be appropriate.

A principles statement is well illustrated in a public sector context at www.defra.gov.uk. The key terms – transparency, co-ordinated, publicly credible and effective – reflect the public service ethos within a positive statement of the need to embed risk management within the organisation.

An implementation plan will be prepared. Implementation will take place under the structure established by the Board and individual roles will be defined.

Section 3: Risk identification

The statement might begin with an overview of the organisation's strategic objectives and the role of risk management in ensuring the objectives will be met. The statement will define and detail the main types of risk facing the organisation and state how the organisation will manage these risks.

Activities such as gathering market intelligence (eg through a management information system), horizon-scanning (identifying future developments that may introduce new opportunities and risk) and surveillance programs (ensuring regular feedback throughout the organisation) may be appropriate.

Once risks have been identified they should be included in the risk register, which forms a central register of identified risks.

Section 4: Assessing risks (risk analysis and evaluation)

Risks will be assessed in terms of their likelihood and the scale of their potential impact.

To assess risk adequately is a difficult area and one that requires a consistent approach. The need is to identify the consequences of a risk event occurring and to give each risk a score or risk rating. The initial assessment will then be refined and a risk owner identified who will then be responsible for reviewing and accepting the assessment that will then feed into the risk register.

Risk assessment will be emphasised requiring all risks to be managed and monitored at the appropriate organisational level. The risk assessment statement will stress the need to have robust systems in place to ensure that a thorough view can be taken on risk identification and management that ensures that nothing has been missed or duplicated.

Section 5: Addressing risks (risk treatment)

Having properly identified and assessed risk, reference might be made to the five Ts (as explained in Chapter 1: tolerate, treat, transfer, terminate, take). The appropriate approach must be selected from these five for each risk identified.

A statement relating to contingency planning and the importance of business continuity plans and disaster recovery plans will also form part of the risk management strategy at this stage.

Section 6: Reviewing and reporting risk

The strategy must ensure that appropriate and effective review and reporting arrangements are in place to reinforce and support risk management activities. The role and responsibilities of the Board will be highlighted and the information they require defined.

Timeframes and review periods will be put in place to ensure that all systems are working correctly and that any required changes can be incorporated into the process.

2.19 There are a number of accepted criteria that should be applied as appropriate to ensure successful implementation of a risk management strategy.

- The initial implementation of a risk strategy requires time. The concept is increasingly accepted by businesses of all kinds but requires organisational strategists to appreciate the benefits and implications to an organisation and then to establish structures and effectively disseminate information throughout the company.

- Top-level commitment is essential. This level of commitment is not just paying lip service but involves positively promoting risk management across the organisation.

- The strategy should define the risk appetite and risk register requirements of the organisation.

- It is necessary to ensure that individuals within the risk management framework have defined areas of accountability, and ownership of specified risks or areas of risk. They must also be subject to scrutiny and challenge.

- Risk judgements must be based on sound information. In consequence, risk management requires an internal and external management information system (MIS) that can deliver appropriate detail. An MIS forms an integral part of the operations of many organisations and are particularly effective in monitoring the external environment. The risk management approach needs the MIS to be reconfigured in a way that provides information in a manner compatible with this mode of thinking.

- The risk management mindset must be reinforced across the organisation by education and awareness training with the objective of embedding the importance of risk.

- There needs to be a greater awareness of cross-functional teamworking and the associated risks with joint-working to manage these risks.

3 *Internal risk management systems*

Internal control

3.1 The aim of internal risk management is to ensure that the controls in place are effective in identifying, monitoring and controlling the risks facing the organisation.

3.2 The system of internal control is designed to manage risk to a reasonable level rather than to eliminate all risk of failure to achieve policies, aims and objectives. It can only provide reasonable – not absolute – assurance of effectiveness.

3.3 The system of internal control is based on ongoing processes designed to identify and prioritise risks, to evaluate the likelihood of those risks being realised and their impact should they be realised, and to manage them efficiently, effectively and economically.

3.4 An integral constituent of a system of internal control is an established corporate approach to risk management. The Board of an organisation will ensure that a policy manual is produced and issued to all staff, either directly or indirectly via an intranet. The manual will be subject to regular review.

3.5 The organisation's **governance handbook** describes all the activities and processes associated with the provision of corporate governance within the organisation; audit, risk management and business continuity. The Audit Committee would be responsible for reviewing risk management strategies, in particular strategies for internal control, and for reviewing the arrangement for internal audit.

3.6 A risk advisory group will be put in place to ensure the following outcomes.

- Emerging significant strategic and operational risks are communicated to the Board.

- Corporate risks requiring departmental mitigation are communicated to the departments.

- The risk register is regularly reviewed and updated.

- Key risks are prioritised in terms of probability and impact.

- The risk management process is reviewed and revised as necessary.

- Risk is championed effectively across the organisation.
- Best practice is shared across the organisation.

3.7 A nominated risk coordinator maintains a register of risks and an overview of total risk to the organisation.

3.8 Each department should have risk focal points issued to them. Risk awareness training and effective risk register use is essential at managerial level.

3.9 The strategy for business continuity will be set out in the governance handbook. It will set out overall policies, processes and responsibility for business continuity at corporate and management level. The business continuity plan includes an evaluation of key business priorities that will be subject to ongoing review to ensure that the focus on appropriate and current business critical areas is maintained.

The risk and control framework

3.10 One approach is to base procedures for the management of risk on the strategic risk cycle, principles and terminology as set out in *The Management of Risk* issued by HM Treasury in 2001. The procedure sets out a framework to ensure consistency in the way in which an organisation identifies and assesses risk, reports profitability and impact, and develops mitigation and contingency plans in compliance with the Turnbull Report.

3.11 Organisational policy should actively identify and manage the risk to which it is exposed. Reporting of risks should be encouraged through staff awareness. Risk training and activities are undertaken to manage risks that might endanger strategic and operational objectives.

3.12 In consequence there is a process of continual identification, assessment and reporting of risks throughout the organisation, culminating in the organisational risk register. Risk avoidance, mitigation or contingency plans are developed and monitored as necessary.

3.13 Change management approaches implement all changes and improvements in a systematic manner throughout the organisation.

Review of effectiveness

3.14 An appointed officer will have responsibility for the effectiveness of the system of internal control. The officer will review the system's effectiveness and will receive feedback from the work of internal auditors and the internal managers who have responsibility for the development and maintenance of the internal control framework, together with feedback from external auditors. A plan to address weaknesses and ensure continuous improvement of the system should be put in place.

3.15 The Audit Committee reviews both the internal and external auditing requirement, the adequacy of the financial systems, risk management, control and governance.

3.16 The Board reviews the system of internal controls through its programme boards. Where there are control deficiencies, projects are initiated to remedy them.

3.17 The risk advisory group has a key role in communicating emerging significant risks to the Board and in ensuring that corporate risks requiring operational mitigation are communicated to departments

Roles and responsibilities

3.18 At operational level roles and responsibilities are in place to ensure that day-to-day activities and risks are monitored and managed effectively.

Managers

3.19 All managers have an overall responsibility to ensure that they and their staff have familiarity with the latest risk management guidance. Any staff with particular risk management responsibilities should have these reflected in their work objectives.

Risk managers

3.20 The risk manager is the individual with the day-to-day responsibility for implementing risk countermeasures, monitoring their impact on the risk and reporting on their effectiveness to the risk owner and others. They have a responsibility for providing early warning of current measures becoming ineffective.

Risk owners

3.21 Each risk that is identified in the risk register will have a corresponding risk owner. Ownership must be appropriate to the organisational level with the person able to take effective action (such as switching of resources). If the owner finds they do not have the authority to accomplish this, risk must be escalated to the next level.

3.22 The risk owner is responsible for the quality of information recorded in the risk register. They should oversee any countermeasures and review the contingencies in place.

4 Stages in the risk management process

Identifying risk

4.1 The identification of potential issues, hazards, threats, and vulnerabilities that could negatively affect work efforts or plans is the basis for sound and successful risk management. Risks must be identified and described in an understandable way before they can be analysed and managed properly.

4.2 Risks are documented in a concise statement that includes the context, conditions, and consequences of risk occurrence.

4.3 Risk identification should be an organised, thorough approach to seek out probable or realistic risks in achieving objectives. To be effective, risk identification should not be an attempt to address every possible event regardless of how improbable it may be.

4.4 The use of the categories and parameters developed in the risk management strategy, along with the identified sources of risk, can provide the discipline and streamlining appropriate to risk identification. The identified risks form a baseline to initiate risk management activities.

4.5 The list of risks should be reviewed periodically to re-examine possible sources of risk and changing conditions to uncover sources and risks previously overlooked or non-existent when the risk management strategy was last updated.

4.6 There are many methods for identifying risks. Here are some examples.

- Examine each element of a project's work breakdown structure to uncover risks.
- Conduct a risk assessment using a risk framework.
- Review risk management efforts from similar products. Examine lessons-learned documents or databases.
- Examine design specifications and agreement requirements.

4.7 Identification of risk sources provides a basis for systematically examining changing situations over time to uncover circumstances that impact the ability of a project to meet its objectives.

4.8 Risk sources are both internal and external to the project. As the project progresses, additional sources of risk may be identified. Establishing categories for risks provides a mechanism for collecting and organising risks as well as ensuring appropriate scrutiny and management attention for those risks that can have more serious consequences on meeting project objectives.

4.9 In Chapter 2 we introduced the five categories of risk used by the Canadian Human Rights Commission.

- Strategic perspective
- Business perspective
- Corporate perspective
- Compliance perspective
- Government perspective

4.10 Another commonly used category, particularly in the private sector, is 'environmental risk'.

4.11 Often it is useful to aggregate risks based on their interrelationships, and develop options at an aggregate level. When aggregate risk is formed by cumulatively adding lower level risks, care must be taken to ensure that important lower level risks are not ignored.

Assessing risk

4.12 Risk assessment requires all risks to be managed and monitored at the appropriate organisational level. The risk assessment statement will stress the need to have robust systems in place to ensure that a thorough view can be taken on risk identification and management, ensuring that nothing has been missed or duplicated.

4.13 Risk assessments change as an organisation grows or contracts. This means that the processes in place should be flexible and capable of regular review. These reviews will identify improvements to the processes and equally will indicate when a process is no longer working effectively.

4.14 Parameters for evaluating, categorising, and prioritising risks typically include risk likelihood (the probability of risk occurrence), risk consequence (the impact and severity of risk occurrence), and thresholds to trigger management activities.

Quantifying risk

4.15 For the purposes of assessment, impact refers to consequences or implications if the risk does occur.

- A minor impact indicates that the risk would not have important implications for the organisation.

- A moderate impact indicates that the risk could have implications for the organisation's ability to succeed

- A significant impact indicates that the risk would have important implications for the organisation.

4.16 For assessment purposes, likelihood refers to the probability that the risk may occur, given its nature and the current risk management practices in place. The question to ask is: 'How likely is the risk to occur in the future, given what we currently do about it?'

- A low likelihood indicates that the risk is unlikely to occur, given its nature and current risk management practices in place.

- A medium likelihood of occurrence indicates that the risk has a moderate probability of occurrence.

- A high likelihood of occurrence indicates that the risk is likely to occur, despite the risk management practices in place.

4.17 The following grid (Table 7.1) places the parameters in a visual form (referred to by the examiner as **risk mapping**). These methods help managers to understand the implications of the risk and also to appreciate the actions that should be taken.

Table 7.1 *An impact/likelihood grid*

Impact		Low	Medium	High
	Significant	Considerable management required	Must manage and monitor risks	Extensive management essential
	Moderate	Risk may be worth accepting with monitoring	Management effort worthwhile	Management effort required
	Minor	Accept risk	Accept, but monitor risk	Manage and monitor risks

Low   *Medium*   *High*

Likelihood

4.18 Risk parameters are used to provide common and consistent criteria for comparing the various risks to be managed. Without these parameters, it would be very difficult to gauge the severity of the unwanted change caused by the risk and to prioritise the necessary actions required for risk mitigation planning.

Classifying risk

4.19 There have been many different attempts to classify risks, from the simple to the extremely complex. At the simple end of the spectrum is basic breakdown of risk into strategic risk, operational risk and project risk. More complex classification systems are intended for use as the basis of enterprise risk management or other comprehensive risk management exercises.

4.20 The rationale for attempting to classify risks is that in order to manage your risks effectively you have to know what they are, and a risk classification system is necessary in order to do this. It can provide a basis for both identification and control, two essential parts of the risk management process.

4.21 Within the three areas of strategic, operational and project risk, as discussed in Chapter 2, are a range of risk classifications that can be developed to meet an individual organisation's requirements. Risk can be classified into areas such as compliance, purchasing, disability discrimination etc, across the spectrum of the company's business.

4.22 A comprehensive risk classification system can provide an overall framework for risk identification: simply go through each risk, one by one, and work out where and how it can arise in your organisation. Sometimes there are problems of definition, in that it is not clear exactly how to classify a particular risk that you identify, but having a comprehensive system helps to ensure that you do not double count any risks.

4.23 This process can also assist in the control and mitigation of risks, because risks that are classified in the same way are often susceptible to similar control and mitigation techniques

Monitoring, reporting and reviewing risk

4.24 The monitoring and reporting of risks is an integral part of the risk management programme. There are two main reasons why this is so.

- To monitor whether or not the risk profile is changing
- To gain assurance that risk management is effective and to identify if further action is necessary

4.25 The risk management structure should include a process of review to check whether the envisaged risks still exist, whether new risks have arisen and whether the likelihood and impact of risks has changed. The process should report on any significant changes that adjust risk priorities and should provide assurance on the effectiveness of control mechanisms.

4.26 It is not only the risks that should be monitored and reviewed. The overall risk management process should be the subject of regular review in order to ensure it remains appropriate and effective.

4.27 The HM Treasury Orange Book states that the review processes should:

- Ensure that all aspects of the risk management process are reviewed at least once a year
- Ensure that the risks themselves are subjected to review with appropriate frequency (with appropriate provision for management's own review of risks and for independent review/audit)
- Make provision for alerting the appropriate level of management to new risks or to changes in already identified risks so that the change can be appropriately addressed.

4.28 The review can make use of a number of tools and techniques.

- The role of individuals, work groups and teams should be developed in order to self-assess on an ongoing basis and by regular reviews and meetings.
- **Risk self-assessment** (RSA) is an internal control, sometimes referred to as **control and risk self-assessment** (CRSA), where each area of the organisation reviews its own activities in conjunction with a documented framework or workshop approach. The RSA approach allows risk owners to demonstrate their involvement in the risk process and their understanding of risk management issues.
- Departmental reporting or stewardship reporting requires that managers report upwards on the current status of risk in their areas and on the work they have done in keeping risk and control procedures up to date in their respective areas.
- HM Treasury produces the 'risk management assessment framework', a tool for evaluating the maturity of an organisation's risk management.

4.29 The internal audit function provides an important, independent and objective report about the adequacy of the process of risk management. Internal audit provides a formalised process of reporting but is neither a substitute for ownership of risk nor a substitute for risk management becoming embedded in the organisation.

Chapter summary

- The purpose of risk management is to identify potential problems before they occur. A key aim is to avoid unpleasant surprises.

- Risk management strategy forms part of an organisation's strategic plan.

- The risk strategy provides a framework for the management of risk across the organisation.

- The risk strategy will usually define what risk is to the organisation.

- Governance involves defining policies and setting objectives, allocating resources, appointing senior staff sufficient to meet the objectives, and monitoring progress toward meeting those objectives.

- The aim of internal risk management is to ensure that the controls in place are effective in identifying, monitoring and controlling the risks facing the organisation.

- The system of internal control is designed to manage risk to a reasonable level rather than to eliminate all risk of failure.

- At operational level roles and responsibilities are in place to ensure that day-to-day activities and risks are monitored and managed effectively.

- The identification of potential issues, hazards, threats, and vulnerabilities that could negatively affect work efforts or plans is the basis for sound and successful risk management.

- Risks must be identified and described in an understandable way before they can be analysed and managed properly.

Self-test questions

Numbers in brackets refer to the paragraphs where you can check your answers.

1   Risk management is a process for defining, analysing, controlling and mitigating risk, with a view to providing what assurance? (1.4)

2   How does risk management make a major contribution in helping an organisation to achieve its objectives? (1.5)

3   What is corporate governance? (2.7)

4   What are the responsibilities of the Accounting Officer? (2.10)

5   Suggest six sections that might be included in a risk management strategy. (2.18)

6   What does an organisation's governance handbook describe? (3.5)

7   What is the role of the Audit Committee? (3.15)

8   What is the key role of the risk advisory group? (3.17)

9   List methods for identifying risk. (4.6)

10   Sketch an impact/likelihood grid. (4.17)

11   The HM Treasury Orange Book states that the review processes should achieve what? (4.27)

Further reading

- The Orange Book, www.hmtreasury.gov.uk.
- Kit Sadgrove, *The Complete Guide to Business Risk Management*, Chapter 3.

CHAPTER 8

Building a Risk-Aware Culture

Learning objectives and indicative content

2.3   Evaluate the probability of a risk occurring in particular circumstances, the possible consequences and the potential range of mitigating actions required.

- Definition of probability in relation to the occurrence of a risk event
- How the likelihood of a risk occurrence will affect the approach to risk management
- Application of historical statistical data in predicting the likelihood of future risk occurrences
- Identification of a range of operational risks and assignment of a probability to each one
- Prioritisation of key risks with explanation as to how resources might be allocated appropriately to mitigate such risks

2.4   Analyse the resources required for effective risk management and for building a risk-aware culture within organisations.

- Responsibility of everyone in an organisation
- Definition of risk awareness and the benefits of awareness
- Description of an appropriate communication programme to promote risk awareness
- How different functions can work together to reduce risk
- Promotion of a risk awareness culture among key elements of the supplier base
- How suppliers can assist in the promotion of risk awareness

2.6   Develop an appropriate risk register for the purchasing and supply function.

- Definition of a risk register and the benefits of having one
- Outline of key components of a risk register
- The process of maintaining and reviewing a risk register
- Design of a basic risk register for the purchasing and supply function
- Procedures for monitoring and managing the key risks identified

3.2   Quality systems, total quality management (TQM), quality inspection and quality control.

3.4   Appraise specific key risks and exposures in purchasing and supply and identify appropriate mitigating actions.

- Quality failure, non-conformity and corrective action
- Product liability, reputational damage, consumer confidence

Chapter headings

1   Using a risk register

2   Promoting risk awareness

3   Allocating resources to risk management

4   Quality and its relation to risk

1   *Using a risk register*

Key components of a risk register

1.1   The risk register records all risks identified and the result of their analysis and evaluation, their grading in terms of likelihood of occurrence and seriousness of impact, and initial plans for mitigating each high-level risk and subsequent results.

1.2   The risk register can be a lengthy document but is broken down into the various areas of the business to become more manageable. For example it may begin with corporate and strategic planning objectives, broken down into a number of subheadings (indicative risks, for example an absence of defined strategic planning processes).

1.3   These will then be rated for the likelihood and seriousness of each risk. An organisation might use a rating system such as the following.

*   Level 5 = extreme risk
*   Level 4 = high risk
*   Level 3 = medium risk
*   Level 2 = low risk
*   Level 1 = minimal risk

1.4   The ratings will be referenced against key strategic considerations such as:

*   Financial stability
*   Reputation
*   Competition
*   Planning

1.5   If a number of risks appear against any of these headings we simply accumulate their scores. For example, if three risks to financial stability are identified, one at Level 4, and two at Level 3, the total score against this heading would be 10. A particular organisation might identify a high level of danger in a score of 12 or above, a medium level of danger in a score of 9–11, and a low level of danger for anything below 9.

1.6   Other components of a risk register might include the following.

*   A column indicating the likelihood of each risk occurring
*   A column indicating who bears the lead responsibility
*   A column listing control actions to minimise risk
*   A section addressing additional controls required, targets or comments

The benefits of a risk register

I.7   A risk register is developed so as to achieve the following benefits.

- Provide a useful tool for managing and reducing the risks identified before and during the year

- Provide the project sponsor, Board or senior management with a documented framework from which risk status can be reported

- Ensure the communication of risk management issues to key stakeholders

- Provide a mechanism for seeking and acting on feedback to encourage the involvement of the key stakeholders

- Identify the mitigation actions required for implementation of the risk management plan and associated costings.

I.8   The completed risk register should be brief and to the point, so that it quickly conveys the essential information. It should be updated on a regular basis, at least monthly. The description of the risk should include the associated consequences where these are not obvious. These consequences can be useful in identifying appropriate mitigation actions.

Maintaining and reviewing a risk register

I.9   Risks must be captured and the management of each risk recorded. The recommended method for recording risks is within the risk register and this should contain the following information.

- **Reference number** – this should be a unique reference code for the risk. This will be essential to ensure that no risks are missed and will act as a key where risks are escalated.

- **Description** – this should describe the nature of the risk and how the risk will impact on the organisation.

- **Probability** – this is the likelihood of the risk happening, measured in high, medium and low ratings depending on the organisation's preference. A high rating (H) would suggest that the risk is highly likely to be realised, whilst a low rating (L) would suggest that the risk is unlikely to be realised. It may sometimes be helpful to show intermediate assessments, eg H+. It can also be helpful to show a range for the risk, eg M–H (medium to high), particularly when the risk is first identified and further analysis is required to fully assess the risk.

- **Impact** – this is a rating defining the effect that the risk will have on the ability to achieve objectives, measured in high, medium and low ratings. A high rating would suggest that an incidence would severely impact on the ability of the organisation to deliver its objectives, or where the side effects of achieving the objective are considered undesirable. A low rating would suggest that there would be little impact on the ability to achieve objectives or that any side effects are minor.

- **Mitigation** – this is a description of the action to be taken to reduce the probability of the risk occurring, or to reduce its impact. For each counter-measure indicate whether it reduces probability, impact or both. It is also helpful, especially where there are a number of counter-measures, to indicate the overall level of probability. Where both probability and impact are low, it may be appropriate to accept the risk and not take any mitigating action. In such cases it is still necessary to monitor the risk to ensure that the characteristics have not changed.

- **Contingency** – where a risk is considered to be severe, for example those marked as high probability and high impact, consideration should be given to a contingency plan. The cost of a proposed contingency, and the level of certainty that the counter-measures will prevent the risk occurring, should be considered when deciding whether to spend effort on developing a contingency plan. Contingency plans can be drafted and recorded separately from the risk register but the register should show the document name or other link to the relevant document.

- **Owner** – this is the person that carries the responsibility for ensuring that the risk is monitored and, where appropriate, effectively managed. They might not be the person who has to actually do the necessary tasks but they must be continuously aware of the risk status.

- **Status** – this is a description of the current position for the risk. Include whether the counter-measures are in place and whether they are effective. The status should be reviewed regularly.

1.10 Mitigation actions should include, as appropriate:

- Preventive actions – planned actions to reduce the likelihood that a risk will occur and/or reduce the seriousness should it occur. (What should you do now?)

- Contingency actions – planned actions to reduce the immediate seriousness of the risk when it does occur. (What should you do when it happens?)

- Recovery actions – planned actions taken once a risk has occurred to allow you to move on. (What should you do after it has happened?)

1.11 Each department will make a contribution to the risk register to cover their functional and cross-functional areas. For example, there will be a finance risk register and a purchasing risk register, both of which will be drawn on to contribute to the organisational risk register.

2 *Promoting risk awareness*

Gaining recognition

2.1 Possibly the first step in promoting risk awareness is to gain recognition. Organisations have seen a multitude of 'initiatives' over the years. Some are successful and some are not. There is no doubt that 'system fatigue' affects many companies and individuals.

2.2 Just as quality and quality processes have become embedded in organisations over the years the objective is to build on this thinking and methodology with risk management. There is clearly a lot to do. Many organisations are only just starting to introduce risk management; others remain unaware of it.

2.3 The need for all employees to become risk-aware is increasingly pressing. Risk management is being applied by legal bodies, regulators and shareholders to encourage and ensure compliance. With this emphasis, application of risk management and 'risk awareness' should become embedded within the work routine.

2.4 **Standards Australia 4360** defines risk management as 'the culture, processes and structures that are directed towards realising potential opportunities whilst managing adverse consequences'. The definition highlights the importance of giving as much consideration to loss of opportunity in risk management as to the downside risk.

2.5   Loss of opportunity is sometimes referred to as 'upside risk' and threats and vulnerabilities as 'downside risk'.

2.6   The safest strategy, ie to take no risk at all, would not make for a very successful business, so the broader issue is to balance the downside risk against the core need to engage in business activity.

Organisational culture

2.7   Culture in an organisation clarifies the difference between what behaviour is acceptable and what is not. Some of the most spectacular corporate collapses of modern times occurred when boards were responsible for significant lapses of corporate governance that led, ultimately, to the demise of their companies.

2.8   The Boards may not have been aware of the breaches until too late. Even so, corporate governance, including setting the organisation's corporate culture, is the individual and collective responsibility of Board members.

2.9   This responsibility must continue to drive risk management approaches, despite the mass of regulation that directors must comply with. Mere compliance – with Sarbanes Oxley, the Turnbull Report and other regulations – is not sufficient. Boards and senior management teams need to understand the benefits of a sound framework of corporate governance and a robust risk management ethos to ensure that the right culture becomes embedded in the organisation.

2.10 Although it is not the Board's job to involve itself in the management function of implementing the culture throughout the business it is their responsibility to ensure that the right culture is present at all levels of the organisation.

2.11 A key point is that the Chairman, Chief Executive Officer etc must embrace the organisation's cultural values and communicate these values effectively. Stating and championing a risk management policy will send a clear message to the business that the board sees risk management as a key issue. Good risk management practices should also be reflected in board-approved policies and standards.

2.12 Boards must also ensure that the right reporting mechanisms are in place for disclosing issues and that there is a culture of disclosure. The importance of this was highlighted during investigations into an incident surrounding large foreign exchange losses at a major Australian bank. It transpired that these losses had grown over a two-year period to a colossal $360 million when they were announced in January 2004. According to the audit report, one of the reasons why these losses continued undetected for so long was that the issue was not escalated to the board and its committees; the bad news was suppressed. Boards need to send a clear message to staff that the sooner bad news is identified and reported the sooner action can be taken to rectify the situation.

2.13 In addition to embedding risk management into the corporate culture, companies also need to ensure that risk management is an essential part of business operations. Risk management cannot be something that sits off to the side, happening outside normal business processes. It must be a core function, which the staff considers every day in the course of doing business.

2.14 Responsibility for risk management is then shared between a company's risk and internal audit teams on the one hand, and its business unit managers on the other. The key is getting the entire team to think about risk management every day in every business decision they make.

2.15 An organisation's risk management team can help develop the framework and the policies. They can educate team members about risk management and ensure that robust monitoring and reporting systems are in place. Awareness and operational risk training demonstrates that the organisation is committed to this course of action and is prepared to spend money in ensuring that staff appreciate the new discipline.

2.16 There are two areas that lie outside the remit of risk managers. Firstly they cannot set the corporate culture – that must come from the top of the organisation. Secondly they cannot be the sole manager of risk – that responsibility lies with those in the organisation who create the risks in the first place.

2.17 The role of the risk manager is to ensure that the right people are managing the appropriate risks, that risk management is at the forefront of people's minds, and that bad news is reported quickly. The need is to embed risk management thinking in much the same way that quality thinking has become ingrained into organisations.

3 Allocating resources to risk management

The resources needed for risk management

3.1 Risk management can be viewed as a practice of systematically selecting cost effective approaches for minimising the threats facing an organisation. When looking at the allocation of resources, directors and managers should understand this financial aspect of risk management.

3.2 Risks can never be fully avoided or mitigated as financial and practical implications make that approach unworkable. All organisations have to accept risk to some degree.

3.3 Risk management can be very cost-effective if departments assess their risks properly and determine the most economical way to avoid them entirely, or reduce them to a minimum and limit potential expenditures arising from accidents or emergencies.

3.4 The resources allocated for risk management will reflect the business sector the organisation operates in. Areas such as hospitals, warehouses and logistics will have a high proportion of resources allocated in this area because of the need to comply with health and safety regulations. Other organisations will need to make a judgement based on a range of cost/benefit factors, including:

- Management time
- Costs of comparable systems (such as quality)
- Potential benefits to the organisation
- Costs of not implementing a risk management system
- Systems development and maintenance costs

3.5   The Combined Code and the Turnbull Report impose responsibility for risk management and control at Board level. It is the Board who take responsibility for cascading risk management throughout the organisation, establishing systems and ensuring effective delivery. Resources must be sufficient to meet those obligations.

3.6   Management are required to implement and maintain risk systems in their departments. The introduction of a new and rigorous system will mean an increase in workload for both managers and staff. In certain circumstances it may be appropriate to increase staff levels. This will be a decision reached in conjunction with the human resources department.

3.7   Quality systems will already exist in most organisations. The discipline and systems underpinning quality are not unlike those required for risk management. This gives a good starting point as there may already be a workable understanding of the enhanced and complementary systems required with risk management.

3.8   Infrastructure development (information technology, setting up of committees, scheduling meetings etc) all require allocation of resources, and these must be costed. Risk management does not come free and all establishment and maintenance costs must be considered and evaluated.

3.9   Allocating resources to risk management involves putting up and understanding the business case. As a new discipline there will be an increase in costs but this must be balanced against the confidence and reassurance gained by the organisation and its stakeholders.

Project management resource allocation

3.10   Projects often overrun their cost estimates, sometimes by staggering amounts. This occurs even with carefully constructed bottom-up cost estimates completed to a very detailed level by experienced project teams.

3.11   The problem with the usual method of constructing a project **estimate at completion (EAC)** is that adding the estimates for all work breakdown structure (WBS) components does not necessarily produce the most likely cost for the entire project. A cost-risk analysis can provide a more accurate, realistic and honest estimate of project costs.

3.12   A formal risk analysis involves discussing, within a risk management framework, those problems and fears which have been recognised but are often hidden. In addition, this can help in calculating the contingency needed to provide the project explicitly with different measures of protection against cost overruns. It can also provide the project manager with a list of the most risky WBS elements leading to better risk management strategies.

3.13   A cost-risk analysis starts with the WBS. The next step is to collect data on the extreme optimistic and pessimistic ranges of cost for each of the risky elements. The data collection is the most important phase of a cost-risk analysis, and the most difficult. It involves interviewing the team leaders about the risks they see in their own areas of expertise and responsibility and placing these in the risk register.

3.14   Risk awareness helps in allocating the appropriate resources early in the project lifecycle and recognition at an early stage leads to better risk management throughout the entire life of the project.

4 *Quality and its relation to risk*

Total quality management

4.1 For an organisation to be effective each part of it must integrate and work together. With the modern views of supply chain management and closer supplier relationships this role of integration and working effectively together will often extend outside an operation and cascade through the supply chain. Total quality management (TQM) is conventionally a commitment to quality adopted by an organisation, but with the increasing drive toward supply chain management the TQM philosophy is one that impacts along the supply chain as suppliers strive to meet customer needs in relation to quality.

4.2 TQM is an extension of quality thinking. Quality has long been achieved by inspection of products to check that they meet the required specifications. Increasingly, however, emphasis is placed on building quality in to new products, processes or services from the beginning. The customer is at the heart of this thinking. Terms such as 'satisfying customer needs' or 'delighting the customer' are not only marketing terms – they are the drivers for delivering quality.

4.3 Business culture has put quality at the heart of competitiveness over recent years and new ways of considering quality issues have been developed.

- Quality control has developed a more refined and systematic approach. This has led to recognisable gains and improvements for many organisations.

- Quality assurance has widened the concept of and responsibility for quality management by introducing a formalised approach that extends beyond production and encompasses the service element of organisational operations.

4.4 TQM has been developed as a way of management that seeks to improve the effectiveness, flexibility, reputation and competitiveness of a business overall. TQM can be defined as 'a continuous improvement in quality, efficiency and effectiveness' and has the following features.

- It aims towards an environment of zero defects at a minimum cost.

- It involves measuring and examining all costs that are quality related.

- It requires awareness by all personnel of the quality requirements involved in supplying the customer with products that meet the agreed specification.

- It is a philosophy that involves all parts of the organisation and everyone working in it.

- It aims at the elimination of waste, where waste is defined as anything other than the minimum essential amount of equipment, materials, space and workers' time.

- It must embrace all aspects of operations from pre-production to post-production.

- It involves an emphasis on supply chain thinking (working with suppliers to improve quality along the supply chain).

- It works toward a continuous process of improvement.

4.5 TQM will seek changes in methods and processes that will help in achieving these objectives and lead to measurable quality improvement.

4.6   TQM comprises three major components.

- A documented and auditable quality management system such as ISO 9000 and its derivatives
- The application of relevant online and offline controls
- The development of cross-functional teams

4.7   The three components are complementary and support each other. They share the same requirement – a commitment to quality.

4.8   TQM is designed to include everyone in the organisation. It is designed with the 'internal customer' very much as a focus. The concept of 'total quality' is just that. No one, no part of the organisation, is excluded. All have a role to play in attaining total quality.

4.9   Other approaches that are adopted include quality councils, quality improvement teams and corrective action teams. The approach will depend on the organisation and its needs. The 'six sigma' approach, discussed later in this chapter, utilises quality improvement teams in a way that updates the TQM approach in a format particularly relevant to meet today's modern business needs.

ISO 9000

4.10   ISO 9000 was launched in 1987 and comprises a group of quality management standards laid down by the International Organisation for Standardisation (ISO). It was a development of the BS (British Standards) 5750 system. Although not an essential ingredient of TQM, the integration of ISO 9000 standards provides a quality assurance structure that ensures good practice is applied and is seen to be applied. The ISO 9000 standards are built around business processes, with an emphasis on improvement and on meeting the needs of customers.

4.11   The ISO 9000 model contains eight quality management principles on which to base an efficient, effective and adaptable quality management system. The principles reflect best practice and are designed so as to enable continuous improvement in the business.

- **Customer focus**. Customer needs and expectations must be determined and converted into product and/or service requirements.
- **Leadership**. Good leaders establish a direction and a unity of purpose for an organisation. They formulate an acceptable and appropriate quality policy and ensure that measurable objectives are set for the organisation.
- **Involvement of people**. The role of people in the organisation and their full involvement in the quality ethos enables their abilities to be used for the organisation's benefit while also enhancing their own personal role. Management must act as the enablers of this process.
- **Process approach**. A desired result is achieved more efficiently when related resources and activities are managed as a process. In consequence a quality management system must have, at its core, a process approach, with each process transforming one or more inputs to create an output of value to the customer.
- **Systems approach to management**. Identifying, understanding and managing a system of inter-related processes for a given objective contributes to both the efficiency and the effectiveness of the organisation. These processes must be fully appreciated and understood in order that the most efficient use is made of them.

- **Continuous improvement**. This is a permanent and ongoing objective. Customer satisfaction is a moving target and the quality management system must take this into account. Monitoring of customer feedback and proactive research supported by the measuring and monitoring of performance delivery must be an integral part of the system.

- **Factual approach to decision-making**. Effective decision-making is based on the logical, intuitive analysis of data and information. This requires that a system is in place that provides current and relevant information to managers to assist in the decision-making process.

- **Mutually beneficial supplier relationships**. These types of relationships between an organisation and its suppliers (commonly known as 'win-win' relationships) enhance the ability of both organisations to create value. Each organisation is just one of the links in a much larger supply chain. In order to serve the long-term needs of the community and the organisation itself, mutually beneficial relationships must exist at all points in the supply chain.

4.12 The importance of quality assurance is to maintain the gains made and embed them within the organisation. A similar approach, developing this method of working, underpins risk management thinking.

The costs of quality

4.13 We have seen that the main objective of quality is to meet customer requirements. If these requirements are not met for any reason there are possible repercussions, most notably a decrease in sales and a loss of future business.

4.14 The cost of quality is defined (BS 6143) as 'the cost of ensuring and assuring quality, as well as the loss incurred when quality is not achieved'. It is the latter part of this definition that prompts quality control measures; losses incurred as a result of poor quality are generally perceived to be higher than the costs of securing quality in the first place.

4.15 Quality related costs are the expenditure incurred in defect prevention and appraisal activities and the losses due to internal and external failure of a product or service through failure to meet agreed specifications. Quality related costs can be classified as failure costs (internal and external), appraisal costs and prevention costs.

Figure 8.1 *The costs related to quality*

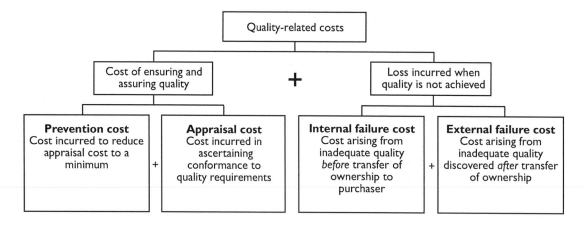

Failure costs

4.16 Failure costs can be categorised under two headings: internal and external.

4.17 **Internal failure costs** are those that arise from inadequate quality before transfer of ownership to the purchaser.

- Loss or reworking of faulty items discovered during the production or inspection process
- Scrapping of defective products that cannot be repaired, used or sold
- The re-inspection cost of output that has been modified or corrected
- Downgrading of products with the subsequent loss of income
- The waste incurred in holding contingency stocks, providing additional storage and duplicating work
- Failure analysis and the cost of those activities required to establish the causes of internal product failure

4.18 **External failure costs** arise when products or services fail to meet the standards expected of them, perhaps because of poor design, inadequate materials, or production errors.

- Repair of products (either returned products or the costs of servicing in an outside location)
- Guarantee and warranty claims
- The administration of complaints and refunds
- Potential liabilities arising from claims
- Possible loss of customers and contracts
- Loss of goodwill, which may have a long-term effect on the organisation's business
- The physical handling of returns and the costs involved in the returns process
- The cost of either returning repaired goods to stock or writing stock off

4.19 Both internal and external failures are the cost of getting things wrong.

Appraisal and prevention costs

4.20 Appraisal costs are the costs incurred as part of the inspection process in order to ensure that products meet specification. This can be extended to include the inspection of parts and components being delivered from suppliers for incorporation into a more refined product.

- The costs involved in physical or machine inspection; the staff required and the investment in measuring or weighing machinery etc
- Verification of incoming material, process set-up, process running, vendor rating and performance appraisal against specification
- Quality audits to ensure the quality system is performing as intended

4.21 Prevention costs are those incurred in order to reduce appraisal costs to a minimum. Costs include investment in machinery, technology and training programs designed to reduce the number of defective products during production. The resources invested in prevention are aimed at getting it right first time.

- The determination of quality requirements and the establishment of specifications for suppliers
- Investment in improved production equipment and processes
- Customer research and surveys
- Supplier appraisal and reviews
- Quality circles
- Quality engineering
- ISO 9000 approval

Six sigma

4.22 Six sigma is a new form of quality program with its origins in Motorola (1980s). It is a quality management tool that targets three main areas: improving customer satisfaction, reducing cycle time and reducing defects.

4.23 Six sigma has a focus that differentiates it from other quality programs.

- The needs of the customer are the priority. The focus is on the customer's critical-to-quality needs (CTQs).
- It maximises the cross-functional approach that many organisations are taking towards business.
- It concentrates on measuring product quality and improving related processes.

4.24 It has a strategic aspect in that top management commitment is required and implementation introduces new tools, methods and approaches, at all levels, in order to achieve results.

How it works

4.25 The purpose of six sigma is to reduce process variation in order that nearly all the products and services provided by an organisation meet or exceed customer expectations. The name derives from the use in statistics of the Greek character sigma (σ) as a measure of 'standard deviation'.

4.26 An organisation reaching the six sigma stage has its processes in such tight control that only a tiny minority of defects will emerge from its business processes (approximately two defects per billion transactions). At the one sigma stage a high level of defects can be expected. By the time the organisation has improved its processes to the four sigma level only tiny error levels are experienced, but an organisation fully committed to quality will still wish to improve to the five sigma or six sigma level.

4.27 There are three key elements to six sigma: process improvement, process design (or redesign), process management.

4.28   With regard to process improvement, a five-stage approach known as DMAIC is applied.

- **Define**: a serious problem is identified and a project team is formed and given the responsibility and resources to attain the defined project goals.
- **Measure**: the process to determine the existing level of performance. The data gathered is analysed in order to produce initial ideas about what might be causing the problem.
- **Analyse**: based on preliminary ideas, theories are generated and investigated to determine the root cause(s) of the defects.
- **Improve**: the identified root causes are removed by designing and implementing changes to the process.
- **Control**: new controls are designed and implemented to control future process performance and sustain the gains made.

4.29   Each of these stages has a variable number of substages, known as tollgates. These are identified steps that the project team must complete as they progress through each stage.

4.30   With regard to **process design** (or **redesign**) there is again a five-stage model (DMADV) used to achieve design for six sigma (DfSS).

- **Define**: identify and set the goals for the new process taking into account internal and external requirements.
- **Match/measure**: determine customer needs. Benchmark where appropriate and develop performance measures that meet these goals.
- **Analyse**: undertake an analysis of these performance measurements and develop an outline design for the new process that will meet customer needs.
- **Design (and implement)**: detail the process to meet the performance and customer criteria and implement.
- **Verify**: the design performance by introducing controls to ensure the stated goals are being met.

4.31   With regard to **process management**, six sigma fundamentally changes an organisation in the way it is structured and managed. Process management involves the following steps.

- Understanding and defining processes, understanding customer requirements and identifying the process owners, both internal and external.
- Ongoing measurement of performance against customer requirements and key performance indicators.
- Analysing data to monitor and refine measures.
- Controlling process performance by monitoring inputs, transformation and outputs and responding to variations outside those anticipated.

Selecting a team

4.32   Having identified a project to be carried out a 'problem statement' is prepared describing specific detail on the problem area. Expressed in measurable terms, the statement forms the basis for the size of the task and the resources and manpower needed. Will it be one project or involve a number of smaller, cross-functional teams reporting back to a central leader?

4.33 Six sigma uses a core of experts who provide the base for the organisational infrastructure to support the program. A typical six sigma team will consist of the following personnel.

- **Champions**: executives who understand six sigma and serve as mentors to black belts and interface with senior management.

- **Mentors** who drive the project forward and give support and direction.

- **Master black belts** are experienced, full-time leaders with a developed knowledge of six sigma. They provide advice, feedback, coaching, project planning advice and training where appropriate.

- **Black belts** who will lead quality projects, usually on a full-time basis until they are complete. It is envisaged that most six sigma projects will be between three and six months in duration.

- **Green belts** who work on projects on a part-time basis but will often lead teams in their own area or function.

4.34 There are six widely accepted themes of six sigma.

- A genuine focus on the customer with improvements measured in terms of customer satisfaction and value.

- It is based on data and fact so that problems can be effectively defined, analysed and resolved.

- Process improvement or design is at the heart of six sigma. Analysing and remedying the process itself leads to measurable improvements in quality.

- Six sigma demands proactive management. Instead of reacting to situations management focus on defining ambitious goals and setting clear priorities, questioning why things are done as they are.

- Boundaryless collaboration: six sigma involves both internal and external providers and contributors to the six sigma program.

- Strive for perfection, tolerate failure. New ideas come with risk. Learn from mistakes but encourage original thinking.

4.35 Quality is important as it demonstrates how risk management can come become embedded within organisations. Many of the themes of quality and quality management are reflected in the risk management approach (eg the need for systems, cross-functional teamwork, support from the top of the organisation and a customer focussed approach).

Product liability and consumer confidence

4.36 Apart from aiming to satisfy their customers, manufacturers have strong legal reasons for trying to ensure product quality. The Consumer Protection Act 1987 imposes **strict liability** on manufacturers whose defective products cause damage. Strict liabiilty means that the law is not concerned with whether or not the manufacturer was negligent; if his products were defective, he is liable even if he was not negligent.

4.37 This of course makes things very difficult for manufacturers, but the need for **consumer confidence** is paramount. With a régime of strict product liability consumers can be confident that their claims in respect of defective products will be upheld. Without it, consumers would have to prove what a manufacturer did or did not do during the manufacturing process, and for most ordinary citizens that is not a realistic possibility.

4.38 Manufacturers must naturally consider the possibility of product liability claims and will have to cover this cost, along with all others, in the pricing of their products. In effect, an amount will be included in the selling price as a kind of insurance premium. We come back to the question of quality-related costs: it is preferable to ensure quality first time round than to bear the costs of product failure, which could include product liability claims.

4.39 From the buyer's perspective, this applies not just within the boundaries of his own firm. Product defects in a bought-in component can lead to defects in the buyer's own products. For this reason, it is vital to ensure quality right along the supply chain. Refer back to Chapter 6 – the massive product recall forced upon Dell, the computer manufacturer – for an example of the damage that can be caused by quality failures.

Chapter summary

- The risk register records all risks identified and the result of their analysis and evaluation, their grading in terms of likelihood of occurrence and seriousness of impact on the organisation, and initial plans for mitigating each high-level risk and subsequent results.

- The completed risk register should be brief and to the point, so it quickly conveys the essential information.

- Loss of opportunity is sometimes referred to as 'upside risk' and threats and vulnerabilities as 'downside risk'.

- The sooner bad news is identified and reported the sooner action can be taken to rectify the situation.

- Risk management can be viewed as a practice of systematically selecting cost effective approaches for minimising the threats facing an organisation.

- The resources allocated for risk management will reflect the business sector the organisation operates in.

- The discipline and systems underpinning quality are not unlike those required for risk management.

- A formal project risk analysis involves discussing, within a risk management framework, those problems and fears which have been recognised but are often hidden.

- Total quality management (TQM) is an extension of quality thinking.

- The purpose of six sigma is to reduce process variation in order that nearly all the products and services provided by an organisation meet or exceed customer expectations.

Self-test questions

Numbers in brackets refer to the paragraphs where you can check your answers.

1   What ratings might be given in the risk register for the likelihood and seriousness of each risk? (1.3)

2   Why is a risk register developed? (1.7)

3   Explain 'probability' and 'impact'. (1.9)

4   What three actions should mitigation include? (1.10)

5   How does Standards Australia 4360 define risk management? (2.4)

6   What two areas lie outside the remit of risk managers? (2.16)

7   What cost/benefit factors could the Board use to consider resource allocation? (3.4)

8   What does a cost-risk analysis provide to project management? (3.13)

9   Define total quality management. (4.4)

10   The ISO 9000 model contains what eight quality management principles? (4.11)

CHAPTER 9

Using Third Party Resources

Learning objectives and indicative content

2.5 Propose ways in which third party supplier resources are used to reduce risk and mitigate losses during a risk event.

- Range of supply solutions for mitigating losses in the aftermath of a risk event: insurance, loss adjusting, alternative accommodation, disaster recovery plus restoration and recovery services
- Appropriate methods of purchasing and paying for disaster recovery services both during a risk event and in the normal run of business
- Incentives to retain specialist services at times of national disaster, including flood and hurricane damage

2.7 Evaluate insurance as a financial means of risk protection.

- The insurance service, including the role of the broker and the insurer
- How insurers use the re-insurance market to spread their risk
- The key stages to resolve a claims event
- Definition of captive insurance or self insurance with description of its practical application
- The relative merits of captive self insurance

Chapter headings

1 Insurance

2 Disaster recovery services

3 Sharing risk up and down the supply chain

1 Insurance

Why insure?

1.1 Even the most risk-averse of organisations will not be able to avoid losses completely. For this reason it is important to consider ways in which losses may be mitigated; in other words, we seek to minimise the adverse effects of the loss.

1.2 One obvious way of doing this is by means of appropriate insurance. Most readers will already be thoroughly familiar with this procedure. The person seeking insurance agrees to pay a premium (or regular premiums, perhaps monthly, quarterly or annually) to an insurance company. In return, the insurer agrees to pay financial compensation if a loss arises from certain events agreed in advance.

1.3   Most of the risks faced by an organisation can be insured against. For some categories of risk, organisations are legally required to take out insurance; for example, UK companies are obliged to take out a policy of employer's liability insurance for the benefit of their employees. Even where insurance is not a legal requirement it may well be a sensible precaution.

1.4   There are numerous risks that can be, and usually are, covered by insurance. Here are just a few of them.

*   Theft

*   Fraud

*   Damage to property

*   Fire and flood

*   Public liability (eg to cover the case where a member of the public suffers injury on the company's premises)

*   Product liability

The insurance contract

1.5   A firm taking out insurance is entering into a contract of **utmost good faith** (a contract *uberrimae fidei*, to use the Latin term). Utmost good faith, or *uberrima fides*, means that the firm must disclose all relevant factors to the insurer, even if the insurer does not specifically ask about it. Otherwise, the contract will be invalid. (This is different from a normal contract, in which the silence of one party cannot normally be regarded as a misrepresentation.)

1.6   This means that the firm must disclose all relevant circumstances at the time of taking out the insurance policy, and must also keep the insurer informed of any changes in circumstances that may affect the level of risk.

1.7   The insurer will usually be a large company. This is necessary so that the persons seeking cover can rely on sufficient financial resources in the event that they have to make a claim on their policy. But the firm seeking cover will not normally deal direct with the insurer. Instead, it is normal to deal with an **insurance broker**. This is a 'middleman' who acts as the agent of the firm seeking insurance and negotiates the insurance contract on the firm's behalf.

1.8   A broker will usually be paid commission by the insurer with whom he eventually places the contract. From the perspective of the firm seeking cover, the value added by the broker is his knowledge of the insurance market. This should enable him to source the most suitable policy at the most favourable rate of premium.

1.9   In some cases, the insurer may enter a contract of **reinsurance**. This means that he shares the risk (and the premium income) with another insurer or insurers in order to reduce his own exposure. The contract of reinsurance is between the two insurance companies, and does not affect the firm seeking cover. That firm's contract is entirely with the original insurer, who is solely liable to the firm in the event of a claim.

Making a claim

1.10 Insurance companies make their money by underwriting risks. This means that they collect premiums from numerous clients, which provide funds from which to compensate the relatively small number of clients who will suffer loss and make a claim. (Insurance companies also make significant profits from careful investment of their premium income, but this does not concern us here.)

1.11 If the insured party suffers loss arising from one of the events covered by the insurance policy, he makes a claim to the insurer for financial compensation. The insurance company will naturally investigate the claim in some detail. They will wish to ensure that the claim is valid (ie that the loss really has occurred, and that it arose from a risk covered by the insurance contract).

1.12 Moreover, there is usually an 'excess' on an insurance policy. This means that the insured party agrees, on taking out the policy, to bear the first part of any loss suffered. You may well be familiar with this from everyday insurance policies, such as a car insurance policy. Typically, premiums will be very high if you insist that the insurance company underwrites every minor instance of damage. The premium will be much less expensive if you accept, say, a £250 excess – meaning that the first £250 of any claim is borne by the insured party rather than by the insurer.

Loss adjusting

1.13 Assuming that the insurance company can agree the claim, they will pay out an appropriate sum of compensation to the insured party. Determining the appropriate amount to pay out may not be straightforward; often the insurer will employ a loss adjuster to negotiate with the insured party as to the correct sum.

1.14 In some cases this can be a lengthy process. The loss adjuster is paid by the insurance company, and his role is to ensure that the insurer is not paying out more on the claim than is really justified. The insured party will naturally be seeking the highest possible compensation payment to cover the loss he has suffered. The loss adjuster will typically challenge the amounts claimed and will seek to show that the true amount of the loss is less than stated.

1.15 The role of the loss adjuster does not imply that there is any intention on the part of the insured party to defraud the insurer (though naturally insurance companies are alert to the possibility of fraudulent claims too). It is simply that evaluation of the amount of the loss may be quite subjective. An insured party may argue that an item of equipment has been ruined by water damage and may seek the full cost of replacement. The loss adjuster may claim in response that the item is not ruined, but merely needs an inexpensive repair.

1.16 This simple example illustrates the possibility of dispute on the appropriate amount of compensation. Eventually, though, a process of negotiation will lead to agreement on the amount claimed and at that point the insurer will pay up.

Self-insurance

1.17 From your earlier studies, you will be familiar with the 'make or buy' decision. Firms must decide which activities they should conduct in-house ('make') and which they should buy in from external suppliers ('buy'). In this respect, insurance services are no different from any other input that a firm needs in order to conduct its business. In other words, in some cases a firm may elect not to purchase insurance from an external provider; instead, the firm maintains sufficient emergency funds to cover any risks that may befall it. This is called **self-insurance**.

1.18 The motivation for this is often to avoid paying expensive insurance premiums to an outside party. After all, most firms will pay more in premiums than they ever claim on their insurance policies – that's how insurance companies make their underwriting profits. So it may seem commercially sensible to adopt such a policy.

1.19 However, a firm in this situation must be very careful in its risk management. The danger is of suffering a loss greater than can easily be covered from funds on hand. Usually, such firms will set aside money in a dedicated fund, and will ensure that the level of the fund is calculated so as to cover all eventualities.

Captive insurance

1.20 A variation of self-insurance is captive insurance. This is the practice of forming (or acquiring) a specialised insurance company dedicated to covering the risks of its parent company (and other group companies). In some ways, the captive company is just like an external insurer: group companies pay premiums and, if appropriate, make claims. The only difference is that the insurer is a part of the parent group, and its profits are not lost to the organisation.

1.21 As before, a primary objective is to avoid large premium payments leaving the entity and ending up in the hands of a third party. There may also be important tax advantages, but this is beyond the scope of the syllabus. Captive insurance is a more formal system than self-insurance, in that the captive company will observe all the financial disciplines expected of a specialist insurer.

Liability and indemnity insurance

1.22 As we mentioned at the end of the previous chapter, 'liability' is a financial obligation arising from a legal relationship. An organisation may be liable to pay damages (or the costs of other remedies) where the courts uphold a claim of breach of contract; negligence resulting in damage, injury or economic loss to another party; breach of a statutory duty (eg to provide safe and healthy premises and employment practices under the Health and Safety at Work Act 1974); or provision of defective goods (eg under the Consumer Protection Act 1987).

1.23 The risk of liability for the costs of meeting such a claim (if not for the reputational and other associated risks) can be transferred to an insurer, by taking out relevant liability insurances. An organisation may take out insurances to cover:

- Product liability
- Contract liability
- Employer's liability
- Professional liability

- Public liability
- Other specific project risks (eg damage to works, contractors risks)

1.24 Indemnity insurance, on the other hand, is the technical name for insurance that compensates for damage to assets, eg from fire or flood, from fraud or theft etc.

Specialist forms of losses

1.25 Near the beginning of this chapter we listed the types of risk that an organisation might seek to insure against. The examples we gave are very common, and most organisations of any size will have insurance policies to cover such risks. Some risks, though, are more specialised, and specialised forms of insurance may be required to cover them.

1.26 As an example, consider a UK company with extensive importing activities. Suppose that on Day 1 the company contracts with a US supplier to purchase goods valued at US$1m. The exchange rate is such that £1 sterling buys exactly US$2. The credit terms agreed between the two companies are that payment is due on Day 60.

1.27 From the importer's point of view, the danger is that the exchange rate will move unfavourably between Day 1 and Day 60. For example, suppose that on Day 60 the prevailing exchange rate is £1 = US$1.8. A purchase that was expected to cost £500,000 ($1m/2) will now cost £555,555 ($1m/1.8). The adverse currency movement has cost the importer no less than £55,555.

1.28 The financial markets have developed specialised products to cover such risks (enabling the importer to 'hedge' the risk). For example, the importer might enter a forward exchange contract on Day 1, agreeing to purchase $1m on Day 60 in order to pay his US supplier. The cost of the US dollars will be fixed by the bank on Day 1, the rate being determined by market conditions and expectations of future exchange rate movements.

1.29 To the importer, the value of such a contract is that he knows on Day 1 exactly how much his purchase will cost him.

1.30 This is not the place for a detailed description of financial instruments. Suffice to say that for companies with specialised types of financial risk, the market offers a bewildering array of specialised products designed to hedge the risks.

2 *Disaster recovery services*

Introduction

2.1 In recent years, organisations have paid increasing attention to the need for disaster recovery planning. Partly this has been because organisations are increasingly dependent on information systems, which are susceptible to many risks of damage or destruction. Partly it has arisen from a sense of increasing danger in the external environment, especially a perceived increase in risks from terrorism.

2.2 There is duplication in your syllabus here. While it is true that disaster recovery planning and business continuity planning are by no means the same thing, they share many common features. This makes it surprising that disaster recovery is listed under syllabus area 2.5, while business continuity appears under syllabus area 3.3. We follow the syllabus by discussing disaster recovery here, but there will inevitably be some duplication when we come to discuss business continuity in Chapter 15.

2.3   A natural first step is to consider what disasters an organisation may be prone to. These could include any or all of the following.

- Fire and/or explosion, whether accidental or arising through arson
- Flooding
- Natural disasters, such as hurricanes, tsunami, earthquakes etc
- Terrorist action
- Sabotage (by employees or by competitors)
- Computer failures, eg those caused by viruses

2.4   Organisations nowadays seek to promote awareness of these hazards in all of their employees. They also attempt to devise plans to overcome the worst consequences of potential disasters. Often, the worst threat is the loss of computerised systems, and disaster recovery has for many years focused on just this area. However, it is important to consider wider consequences as well, such as the loss of buildings in a flood or earthquake, or the loss of key employees arising from a terrorist attack.

2.5   Staying for the moment with the threat to computerised systems, an organisation may put in place any of the following measures.

- Uninterruptible power supply (UPS) to guard against power failure. This is now a standard part of almost all computerised systems.
- Anti-virus software and firewalls
- Automatic data back-up routines, combined with remote storage of back-up devices
- Surge protectors, which minimise the effect of power surges on electronic equipment

2.6   If a computer failure occurs, here are some of the steps that may form part of the recovery plan.

- Set in motion a **telephone cascade** – informing all relevant employees of the need for pre-defined action
- Ensure equipment is restored to working order (eg by removing viruses, or if necessary by purchasing new equipment)
- Retrieve back-up devices from their off-site storage areas
- Re-install software and data
- Re-enter data from the period since the last back-up
- Notify business contacts as appropriate – it may help to minimise ill-informed panic reactions if key customers, suppliers etc are made aware of possible temporary problems

Alternative accommodation

2.7   One particular aspect of disaster recovery is highlighted in the syllabus: alternative accommodation. This refers to a measure adopted by many large organisations who need to resume business as quickly as possible after a disaster. To help with this, they maintain 'reserve' or back-up accommodation as a precaution against their normal premises being impossible to work in.

2.8 The need for this could arise from the various disasters identified above. For example, a building might be subject to an explosion, a fire or a terrorist attack. Until the building can be restored to its normal state – which might take months – the organisation requires alternative accommodation from which to carry on its activities.

2.9 In some cases it may be possible to make use of spare space in another building occupied by the same organisation. For example, if fire breaks out in the Swindon branch of a paper company, it may be possible for the Swindon staff to temporarily move in with their colleagues in the Slough branch. This obviously depends on there being sufficient spare space in the Slough branch.

2.10 More formally, top management of the paper company may have adopted a disaster recovery plan under which sufficient spare space must be kept available in each branch. As a variant of this, a company might have an agreement with another company in a nearby location whereby each one keeps spare space to house the other in the event of a disaster. And a final variant of the same general idea is for a company to use space managed by specialist providers of disaster recovery services.

2.11 So far we have referred only to the physical space required to house staff. There is also the very important consideration that staff must have the desks, computer equipment, and up to date data required for effective completion of their daily work. In this connection it is common to classify the back-up accommodation as being a cold site, a warm site or a hot site.

- A cold site simply contains the space required to house the staff. It does not contain back-up equipment, software and data files.
- A warm site additionally contains computer equipment similar to that abandoned in the original location, but does not contain software and back-up data files.
- A hot site is effectively a duplicate of the original location. It contains both computer equipment and all the software and back-up data files required for the business to resume operations immediately.

2.12 Needless to say, these possibilities are arranged in ascending order of costliness. Maintaining a hot site involves purchasing computer equipment that in the natural course of things may never be used. It also involves a regular process of ensuring that up to date data files are always on hand.

Natural disasters

2.13 Your syllabus refers to 'national disasters', but this is presumably an error for natural disasters, ie floods, hurricanes etc. Similar risks include fire (whether 'natural' or caused by human negligence), tsunami, earthquakes etc.

2.14 In all of these cases a prime risk mitigation strategy is to prevent damage by ensuring that buildings are well designed and strongly built. This is particularly important in geographical areas where such events are known to occur regularly. Appropriate insurance is also essential.

2.15 Other precautions can include alarm systems (eg fire alarms) and properly designed escape routes (eg fire escapes). These are normally a legal requirement in workplaces. Finally, the disaster recovery procedures already discussed of course are relevant to the aftermath of natural disasters.

3 Sharing risk up and down the supply chain

Outsourcing

3.1 In this final section of the chapter we look at ways in which we can mitigate risk by sharing it with other members of the supply chain. Use of insurance (Section 1 of this chapter) and use of disaster recovery services (Section 2 above) are two specialist methods of doing this. However, it is possible more generally to mitigate our risks by using the fact that we are just one link in an extended supply chain. The trick then is to ensure that other links in the chain bear as much of the strain as possible.

3.2 The modern focus on core competencies has led many companies to buy in products, components or assemblies previously produced in-house, and to outsource a range of support functions (such as maintenance, catering, warehousing and transport, and staff recruitment and training) and even core functions such as sales and customer service (eg in call centres).

3.3 The advantages and disadvantages of strategic outsourcing are summarised in Table 9.1.

Table 9.1 *Advantages and disadvantages of strategic outsourcing*

Advantages	*Disadvantages*
• Support for downsizing: reduction in staffing/space/facilities costs	• Costs of services and relationship/ contract management
• Allows focused investment of managerial, staff and other resources on core/distinctive competencies	• Loss of control and difficulties ensuring service standards
• Leverages the specialist expertise, technologies, resources and economies of scale of suppliers, with potential to add more value at less cost than the organisation could achieve itself (for non-core activities)	• Potential reputational damage if service or ethical issues arise
	• Loss of in-house knowledge and competencies (for future needs)
	• Loss of control over confidential information and intellectual property
• Enables synergy through collaborative supply relationships	• Ethical and employee relations issues of downsizing

3.4 Recent high-profile examples (such as British Airways' problems arising from poor employee relations at Gate Gourmet, to whom it had outsourced all its catering) show that careful management is required to control the relationship, output/service quality, ethical/employment standards – and their consequences for the outsourcing organisation and its brand.

3.5 Strategic outsourcing should only be applied to:

(a) Non-core competencies which, if outsourced:

- Will benefit from expertise/cost efficiency/synergy of specialist supplier

- Will enable firm to leverage its core competencies

- Will not disadvantage the organisation with loss of in-house capability or vulnerability to market risks

- Will enable firm to exploit technology or other operational capabilities which it lacks (and would find too costly to develop) in-house

(b) Activities for which external contractors have required competence/capability. Various options can be summarised in a simple matrix: Figure 9.1.

Figure 9.1 *Competencies and contractor competence*

Competence of contractors

	High	Low
Low (Core importance)	Outsource/buy in	Develop contracting
High (Core importance)	Collaboration	In-house

(c) Activities for which value for money is offered by outsourcing (due to the supplier's cost/profit structure, economies of scale, or potential for the buyer to divest itself of assets), in relation to the service levels that can be obtained.

3.6 Outsourcing is a way of getting suppliers to do things that we would otherwise do ourselves. This seems like a simple way of transferring risk from our own organisation to the supplier. However, in doing so we take on new risks.

- We risk the loss of expertise and competence no longer needed in-house.
- We risk cutting ourselves off from market knowledge.
- We risk the difficulties of insourcing (ie having to take the outsourced activity back in-house because of changed circumstances or supplier failure).

3.7 Apart from this, it is also important that we cannot outsource our duty to our own customers. If our customers are disappointed with our products or services, we cannot blame the outsource providers. The fault lies with our own organisation, and can only be remedied by more effective management of the outsource relationship.

Joint ventures

3.8 Another form of inter-organisational relationship is a joint venture. This is a formal arrangement whereby two independent companies establish a new company which they jointly own and manage. Their other businesses remain separate from this new, shared venture. (Where more than two companies enter this arrangement it is called a **consortium**.)

3.9 Joint ventures are often used to overcome barriers to entry in international markets: Western companies operating in Eastern Europe and China, for example, have formed joint ventures with local partners. One provides technical and managerial expertise and investment, while the other supplies access to labour and local markets.

3.10 From our present perspective, the particular interest of joint ventures is that they may enable two organisations to take on a potentially valuable opportunity that would be too risky for either one of them alone. For example, the level of financial investment might be prohibitive for either company, but acceptable when shared. Or each company might lack crucial areas of expertise that will be needed for the project; between them, all areas may be covered well.

Protecting stock

3.11   Stock is an asset that is to some extent provided by suppliers. It is therefore an obvious target for risk reduction in that we can quite easily make the suppliers responsible for it. One method for achieving this is **vendor managed inventory** (VMI).

3.12   VMI is an alternative to traditional buyer/supplier relationships, which gives the vendor access to information (production plans, ordering, sales forecasts) and delegates responsibility to the vendor for managing and replenishing the buyer's inventory, within policy guidelines. Such stocks as need to be carried are mostly held on the vendor's premises. The buyer benefits from freedom to focus on more strategic decision-making, while also transferring most of the stockholding risk to the vendor.

Using supply contracts to provide protection

3.13   Most commercial relationships are formalised with a written contract, setting out the undertakings and the rights of both parties, the buyer and the supplier.

3.14   Where there is a written contract, and there is a dispute about performance, the contract will be used as a point of reference to establish what the rights and obligations of the buyer and the supplier are. And, written contracts have other benefits, particularly where:

- the purchase is a one-off transaction
- the buyer is using a supplier for the first time, or
- the supplier is relatively new, and the relationship has not yet had time to develop.

3.15   In these circumstances, written contracts can have a number of other advantages, as well as helping with the resolution of disputes.

- Either party can refer to the contract, in case it is in doubt about what it has undertaken to do.
- The product specifications might be included in the contract, in which case the contract will be an essential point of reference.
- A written contract can be a short document, and need not be long, complex, legalistic and adversarial.

3.16   For a transactional supply contract, or a supply arrangement with a new supplier, a written contract can be used to identify potential risks that might arise, and to determine in advance how these risks should be dealt with. This considerably reduces the supply risk that arises in all purchase transactions. Table 9.2 lists just a few such problems and how a contract can provide for dealing with them.

Table 9.2 *Contract provisions*

Potential risk	Contract provision
The supplier delivers the wrong quantity.	The quantity to be supplied, how the quantity delivered should be established, and who in the supplier's organisation should deal with any query.
The product is not made to the correct specification.	The contract provides the product specification, and sets out how rectification should be made in the event of the product not being supplied to specification.
The buyer fails to pay a supplier invoice.	The contract specifies when payments should be due, and perhaps provides for an 'interest payment' if the buyer pays after the due date.
The supplier is late with delivery.	How potentially late deliveries should be dealt with, and by whom.
There is disagreement about who should pay for transportation charges.	The contract will specify how the goods should be delivered and who is responsible for the cost.
The service might be performed or installation carried out by individuals who are insufficiently qualified.	The contract will specify the qualifications or experience of anyone carrying out a service or making an installation, and will state how the qualifications or experience of the individuals will be established.
Employees of the buyer organisation will be unfamiliar with how to use the item delivered.	The contract could provide for training of a number of the buyer's employees by staff of the supplier.
The product might be dangerous to handle.	The contract will specify how the product should be delivered and packaged, or what type of containers it should be delivered in, so as to avoid health and safety risk.
Changes may be required to the contract, relating to the specification, the provision of new services, design or performance measurement.	A variation clause, detailing the procedures that should be followed if changes are needed which still ensure value for money.
The parties may wish to vary the prices charged.	A price variation or contract price adjustment (CPA) clause, possibly based on a mutually agreed cost index.
A dispute arises	A dispute resolution clause, detailing the procedures that should be followed, such as mediation or arbitration.

Contractual failure

3.17   Of course, even with a written contract things can go wrong. This risk must be managed as much as any of the other risks we have considered in this text. The possible damage to the buyer includes financial loss, disruption to production, loss of customer goodwill, and investment of management time to resolve the dispute.

3.18 This is not a law text and it would not be appropriate to go into too much detail. However, you should be aware that a buyer has certain remedies against a seller who fails to perform his side of the contractual bargain.

- The normal remedy is **damages**: the seller must provide monetary compensation to cover any loss suffered by the buyer.

- In some cases, the buyer may be able to claim **specific performance**. This means that the seller is compelled by the courts to carry out his side of the bargain.

- The buyer may obtain an **injunction**, forbidding the supplier from doing something that would breach the contract.

3.19 Neither specific performance or an injunction is at all a common remedy. By far the most common remedy is damages. Damages are assessed in such a way as to restore the injured party to the financial situation he would have been in if the breach of contract had not occurred. In other words, they are meant as a remedy for the injured party, not as a punishment for the party at fault.

3.20 From the buyer's point of view, damages are often an unsatisfactory remedy. If a supplier fails to deliver a key material, and the buyer has to source it from elsewhere at a higher price, the damages will only compensate him for the difference in price. He is unlikely to be compensated for the consequential disruption to production.

3.21 One final point to bear in mind about all of these remedies is that they are only available if the seller remains in business. If the breach of contract arose through the buyer's insolvency, the buyer is unlikely to have any recourse at all. His main hope in such a case would be an insurance claim, assuming he has a policy that covers the circumstances.

3.22 Looking beyond the legal position, a buyer who suffers from a contractual breach must also take practical action to remedy any disruption to operations. For example, he may have to identify an alternative source of supply, and promptly. If sound risk management disciplines are in place, the buyer will have prepared for this eventuality in advance. Sharing risk with customers

3.23 We have already looked at moving risk upstream to our suppliers. It also makes sense to consider the ways in which our customers – both internal and external – can share risk.

3.24 Internal customers of the purchasing function are all those departments within the organisation who use the services of purchasing staff. Purchasing will naturally aim to provide the best possible service to their colleagues in other departments, but in return buyers should expect a level of cooperation from customer functions.

3.25 In many organisations, purchasing aim to formalise this kind of relationship by drawing up a statement of service levels that customer functions can expect. For example, they may undertake to process requisitions and convert them into purchase orders within 24 hours of receipt, provided the requisitions are correctly and completely filled out. It is this two-way obligation that protects purchasing from the risk of customer dissatisfaction.

3.26 As far as external customers are concerned, a particular problem is over-optimistic estimates of sales volumes. The customer is naturally keen to earn the best possible undertakings on service levels and price. To achieve this, he may make an over-optimistic estimate of his likely requirements. This puts the selling organisation at risk: if actual volumes are considerably less, the price quoted may be lower than is justified. Moreover, the seller may have produced excessive stock in anticipation of sales that never materialise.

3.27   With good planning, these risks can be minimised. For example, rather than agreeing a low price in anticipation of future sales, the seller may consider basing prices on actual orders received. If all goes well, and actual sales volumes are high, the buyer can always be rewarded by a *retrospective* discount.

3.28   Another risk arises when customers require modifications to standard products. This may involve the seller in expensive re-tooling or investment in new machinery. To protect against the obvious risks here, the customer must be contractually bound to purchase a volume of product that justifies the seller's additional investment.

Chapter summary

- Numerous risks can be covered by taking out appropriate insurance. In the event of the risk materialising, the insured party will at least be able to rely on financial compensation.

- Some companies bypass external insurance companies, either by relying on internal funds to insure against risk (self-insurance), or by forming or acquiring an intra-group insurance company (captive insurance).

- Some specialist forms of losses (eg exchange rate losses) require specialised forms of financial instrument to protect against them.

- Disaster recovery planning is an increasing preoccupation of managers, partly because of a perceived increase in external risks (eg from terrorist activity).

- One precaution against disaster is the use of alternative accommodation. This may involve sharing space with another group company, or with another company on a reciprocal basis, or may mean hiring space from a specialist disaster recovery firm.

- An organisation is part of a supply chain. It can mitigate its own risks by sharing them with other members of the chain.

- Means of transferring risk onto suppliers include outsourcing, joint ventures, vendor managed inventory, and appropriately drafted supply contracts. Risks can also be shared with customers, both internal and external.

Self-test questions

Numbers in brackets refer to the paragraphs where you can check your answers.

1   List typical risks that can be insured against. (1.4)

2   What is meant by a contract *uberrimae fidei*? (1.5)

3   Explain the process of making an insurance claim. (1.10–1.12)

4   Explain what is meant by self-insurance. (1.17)

5   What is a forward exchange contract? (1.28)

6   What kinds of disasters are organisations prone to? (2.3)

7   If a computer failure occurs, what steps should be undertaken as part of the recovery plan? (2.6)

8   Distinguish between cold sites, warm sites and hot sites in the context of disaster recovery. (2.11)

9   List advantages and disadvantages of outsourcing. (3.3)

10   What are the risks involved in outsourcing? (3.6)

11   How can a joint venture enable an organisation to mitigate risk? (3.10)

12   List risks that may arise in dealing with suppliers and explain how these can be mitigated by appropriate terms in the supply contract. (3.16)

CHAPTER 10

Qualitative and Quantitative Techniques

Learning objectives and indicative content

1.3   Basic quantification methods for measuring [risk]

2.8   Identify and apply a range of qualitative and quantitative risk identification and analysis techniques to ensure better decision quality in reviewing alternatives for a superior project outcome.

- Scenario analysis and planning
- Auditing
- Decision tree analysis
- Fault tree analysis
- Dependency modelling
- External environment analysis
- Assumption
- Identification frameworks

Chapter headings

1   Qualitative techniques

2   Quantifying hazards and risks

3   Quantitative techniques

1   Qualitative techniques

Risk identification frameworks

1.1   In previous chapters we have said a good deal about identifying risks. We elaborate on these comments in the paragraphs that follow. Then in the remainder of the chapter we move on to consider methods – both qualitative and quantitative – for evaluating the seriousness of risks.

1.2   There are many techniques that are useful in identifying risks. For example, guidance published by CIPS for this unit (drawing on the work of the Institute of Risk Management) cites the following possibilities.

- Brainstorming
- Questionnaires
- Business studies, examining business processes and the factors that influence them
- Industry benchmarking
- Scenario analysis
- Risk assessment workshops
- Incident investigation

- Auditing and investigation
- Hazard and operability studies

1.3 Another possibility, widely used in strategic forecasting, is the so-called **Delphi method** (named after the site of the famous oracle in ancient Greece). This involves submitting a questionnaire to different people who are able to form a sound judgement of likely future risks. Each of these experts submits answers and also studies the answers produced by others. They are all then invited to reconsider their original answers, until an informed consensus is reached.

1.4 Finally in this area we mention the use of **Ishikawa diagrams** (sometimes called **fishbone diagrams**). This is a recognised tool of quality management, but its use can be extended to assist in the identification of risks. See Figure 10.1

Figure 10.1 *The 5M fishbone diagram*

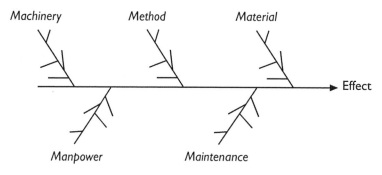

1.5 Each of the five headings in the diagram is a possible source of risk. The branches are subsidiary areas of each main heading. By labelling the diagram appropriately we can identify all the main possibilities of risk in a structured way.

1.6 Once a risk has been identified, it should be logged in the risk register, as explained in an earlier chapter.

Auditors

1.7 In an earlier chapter we referred briefly to the role of internal and external auditors. In the context of risk identification this topic is relevant again here.

1.8 Many organisations are subject to an independent financial investigation by specialist **external auditors**. In the private sector, such an external audit is a legal requirement for large companies and must be carried out annually. In the public sector a similar role is carried out by the Audit Commission and the National Audit Office.

1.9 The external auditor will normally investigate the systems of internal controls operating within the organisation. The outcome of this review will often include identification of areas of potential weakness and risk. By including such matters in his report, the external auditor performs a function that is valuable in identifying risks.

1.10 The external audit is carried out only at intervals (usually once a year) and with only limited objectives (usually to report on the financial performance of the organisation). Though valuable, this is not regarded as sufficient in most organisations of any significant size. Such organisations will invariably maintain a team of **internal auditors**.

1.11   The internal auditors are of course employed by the organisation and in that sense are not independent. Nevertheless, independence is of crucial importance in carrying out their work, and for that reason it is normal for internal audit to report to the highest level of the organisation.

1.12   The work of the internal audit department covers all aspects of the organisation's activities, not just the financial aspects. Moreover, it is an ongoing function, carrying out its work throughout the year. Much of the work done will be recurring checks and investigations on defined areas of operation, but there will also be project work designed to focus on specific activities in greater detail.

1.13   The Institute of Internal Auditors (IIA) publishes standards that lay down principles according to which internal auditors should carry out their work. Typically, senior members of an internal audit team (and sometimes all members of the team) will be full members of the IIA or at least working towards achieving the qualification.

1.14   Internal audit have responsibility for examining and testing all the internal controls in the organisation. Where weaknesses are discovered, internal audit will make recommendations for improvement. Because the department normally reports to the highest level of management their recommendations will be treated very seriously.

1.15   In addition to this, internal audit increasingly play a role in corporate governance. Internal auditors are ideally placed, by virtue of their quasi-independent position, to examine the accountability of senior managers in the organisation. In organisations that appoint an **audit committee** (an important tool of corporate governance), there will invariably be a close reporting relationship between the committee and the internal audit team.

1.16   In the context of risk identification, internal audit will also work closely with other departments (such as purchasing) to identify and assess potential risks specific to those departments.

External environment analysis

1.17   The syllabus topic duplicates syllabus area 1.3. This has already been covered in Chapter 2 as 'The PESTLE framework'.

2   Quantifying hazards and risks

Estimating the probability of a risk

2.1   Once risks have been identified, the next step is to analyse them. As explained in an earlier chapter, two crucial aspects are the likelihood of a risk and its potential impact if it materialises.

2.2   How can we estimate the likelihood of a risk? To answer this question it is worthwhile to distinguish between upside risk and downside risk (mentioned briefly in an earlier chapter).

- **Upside risk** – a slightly non-intuitive expression – means the possibility of a favourable outcome, for example the possibility that a new project will prove profitable. We can estimate the likelihood of this using techniques such as market research or test marketing.

- **Downside risk** is what we usually mean when we talk about risk, namely the possibility of things going badly. Later in this chapter we will discuss some quantitative techniques for assessing downside risk (decision tree analysis, fault tree analysis, dependency modelling and 'value at risk').

2.3 To some extent the estimation of likelihood can be based on qualitative approaches, as we saw earlier in this chapter. It is also possible to apply more quantitative tools, but don't be fooled by the apparent sophistication of such calculations. In the end, anything in the future is based on guesswork, and even if numerical calculations are used, they should be tested in the light of sound business judgement.

2.4 Two techniques in particular are worth describing at this stage: statistical sampling, and time series analysis.

2.5 **Statistical sampling** is an easily understood concept. In many cases, the total 'population' we are interested in may be vast. It would be impractical to examine every member of the population individually. Instead, we may select a carefully structured sample for testing. Provided our sample is representative, statistical techniques then enable us to draw conclusions about the wider population.

2.6 As an example, we may be interested in the likelihood of a new product being regarded favourably in the consumer market. Clearly we cannot approach every individual in the world, or even in the UK, to ask them their reaction to our new product. But we can carry out market research among a sample of consumers and from the results we can estimate the future popularity of the product nationwide or even worldwide.

2.7 We used the term 'carefully structured sample' earlier on. This reflects the fact that selecting a sample is itself a statistical technique. The sample must be of sufficient size; otherwise, it is not valid to draw statistical conclusions from the results. And similarly the sample must be representative of the wider population. For example, it might not be valid to select a sample of consumers from a particular geographical region, because that region might not be typical of the entire country in its reaction to our proposed new product.

2.8 **Time series analysis** is another technique that can help in forecasting outcomes. In its simplest form, this is simply a matter of logging the value of a variable at regular intervals. For example, a buyer's office wall might carry a chart on which the buyer each month logs the total value of his spend. By referring back to his total spend in, say, March 2007 he perhaps has a starting point for estimating his spend in March 2008.

2.9 It is possible to apply detailed statistical analysis to this technique, for example to isolate the underlying trend in the buyer's spending level, the amount of seasonal variation and so on. However, for many purposes the simple application described above provides valuable input.

2.10 Of course, in the modern office we are more likely to see this kind of analysis carried out on computer than on a manual wallchart. Computer software can streamline all kinds of statistical analysis. In terms of time series analysis, it may simply involve inputting historical data onto a spreadsheet and graphing the outcome. This can easily be extrapolated to the future so as to provide a very rough estimate of what lies ahead.

Probability theory

2.11   The general concept of probability is an everyday one: we all speak in general terms of whether it is likely to rain today and how unlikely we are to win the lottery! Probability as a quantitative tool aims to add a numerical scale of measurement to ideas such as 'very unlikely' or 'quite likely'.

2.12   By convention, the measurement scale ranges from 0 (impossible) to 1 (certainty): 0.5 therefore represents an even or 50:50 chance.

2.13   If there are **m** equally likely outcomes to a trial, **n** of which result in a given outcome **x**, the probability of that outcome – symbolised as P(x) – is n/m.

For example, if an unbiased die is thrown in an unbiased way, each of the scores 1 to 6 is equally likely. The probability of an even number being thrown can be calculated as follows: P(even) = 3/6 = ½. (Three of the six outcomes are even numbers: 2, 4 and 6.)

2.14   Where events are **mutually exclusive** (that is, one event precludes the other): then P (A and B) = 0. However, the probability that either A or B will occur is the sum of the separate probabilities of each occurring: P (A or B) = P (A) + P (B). So your probability of throwing a 6 or a 1 on your die is: 1/6 + 1/6 = 2/6 = 1/3.

2.15   Where events are **independent** (that is, one happening or not happening does not affect whether the other happens or doesn't happen), then the probability of both A and B occurring is the product of the separate probabilities: P (A and B) = P(A) x P (B). As an example, say a delivery contains 12 components of which 4 are defective and the rest are OK. P (defective) = 4/12, while P (OK) = 8/12. The probability of drawing two OK components (if you replace the first before the second is selected) is calculated as follows.

P (component 1 OK) = 8/12; P (component 2 OK) = 8/12.
P (component 1 and 2 OK) = 8/12 x 8/12 = 2/3 x 2/3 = 4/9 (or 0.44).

Probability distributions

2.16   There are three main statistical distributions: Table 10.1.

Table 10.1: *Probability distributions*

Type	Focus	Example applications
Binomial distribution	The probability of discrete events with only two outcomes (p or q: eg success or failure, has or doesn't have a particular attribute, answer is yes or no, event will or won't happen). P (p + q) = 1. So if p = ½ , q = 1 – ½ = ½ .	• Probability of a batch containing defects or non-defects; x or more/less-than-x defects • Customers buying or not buying a brand. • Success or failure of a project; delivery on time or late.
Poisson distribution	The probability of a discrete event (p) within a continuous stream of events or tests (n). Should be applied when there is a small probability of the event occurring in a single test, and a very large number of tests.	• Quality control: defects (or non-defects) within eg a length of cable or time period. • Risk assessment: problems occurring, or success/failure within a given time period
Normal distribution	Ranges of possibilities, and how likely they are to occur, based on: continuous historical data, formed into a frequency distribution, diagrammed as a histogram.	'If defects are normally distributed, calculate the probability that defects are between 3 and 7 (tolerance level) per delivery.'

Estimating the impact of a risk

2.17 Clearly risks will differ in their potential impact on the business. We should devote more management attention to serious risks than to trivial risks. This implies that we must attempt to estimate the potential effect of each risk event.

2.18 What kinds of impact might we be examining? Here are some of the adverse effects we may suffer if a risk event materialises.

- Loss of revenue
- Increase in costs
- Fall in share price or owners' equity
- Failure in quality
- Failure in health and safety
- Environmental damage
- Damage to reputation
- Hostile legal action

2.19 With some of these (in particular, the first three) it is conceivable, though perhaps not easy, to place a financial figure on the potential impact. The other examples are far more difficult to quantify. A failure in quality could lead to many consequences: not just the costs of rework and scrap, but possibly loss of customer confidence. Environmental damage may lead to fines in some cases, but again the full impact goes beyond this if we are serious about environmental responsibilities.

2.20 Some authorities have suggested classifying the potential impact of a risk as simply high, medium or low. However, this is somewhat simplistic, and even then may be difficult to get right in view of the intangible factors mentioned above. And in any case, how can we achieve agreement on what is meant by a high impact or a low impact?

2.21 Others have suggested a different three-level classification: risks may either be so great as to be totally unacceptable, or so small that no action is necessary, or somewhere in between. Again, this is somewhat simplistic, and has the disadvantage of not discriminating very well between risks – almost all risks will be placed in the middle category.

2.22 Kit Sadgrove (in *The Complete Guide to Business Risk Management*) suggests a classification of impact into four categories: catastrophic (financial loss of over £10m); serious (£1m–£10m); minor (£100,000–£1m); and insignificant (less than £100,000). The problem with this is that the figures are arbitrary: a loss of £1m may be minor to some organisations, while fatal to others.

2.23 This should be sufficient to illustrate the real difficulties of classifying impact in a meaningful way. Nevertheless, some such attempt must be made in order that we can focus management effort where it is most needed.

Combining probability and impact

2.24 It is the combination of probability and impact that determines our reaction to a potential risk.

- A very unlikely risk with a very small potential impact can be ignored.
- A very likely risk with a very high potential impact may require drastic action.
- Most risks will fall somewhere in between these extremes.

2.25 As we have already seen, a problem with this kind of analysis is that it is both simplistic and vague (vague in the sense that different people may have a different conception of what is meant by 'high impact', for example). Writing in *Accountancy* magazine (January 2007), Mike Brooks expresses his frustration at this: 'I might physically assault the next person to present me with a three-by-three matrix, showing low–medium–high on each axis'.

2.26 Brooks suggests a different classification, using terms that are more likely to elicit agreement among different people. His classification is indicated in Table 10.2.

Table 10.2 *A classification of likelihood and impact*

Classifying likelihood	**Classifying impact**
1 Has never happened in this industry	1 Would have no discernible effect
2 Has happened in this industry but never in this group of companies	2 Would cost 10% of this business unit's net assets if it happened
3 Has happened in this group but never in this business unit	3 Would wipe out this business unit if it happened
4 Happens occasionally in this business unit	4 Would cost 10% of group net assets if it happened
5 Happens frequently in this business unit	5 Would wipe out the group if it happened

2.27 Using this classification, we would pay little attention to a risk classified as 'has never happened in this industry' and 'would have no discernible effect even if it happened'. But alarm bells would ring if a risk is classified as 'happens frequently in this business unit' and 'would wipe out the group if this happened' (admittedly a rather extreme combination).

2.28 For greater precision, we could use the numbers indicated in Table 10.1. For example, the first risk just referred to would have a score of 1 × 1 = 1, whereas the second risk would have a score of 5 × 5 = 25. The higher the combined score, the more we need to focus management attention on the risk.

3 Quantitative techniques

Failure mode and effect analysis (FMEA)

3.1 In this final section of the chapter we look at a number of quantitative techniques that may be used in risk analysis. Although these may be used relatively infrequently in practice, they all have relevance to your exam, either because they are specified in the syllabus, or because they are discussed in the guidance published by CIPS for this unit despite not being specified in the syllabus (FMEA is in this latter category).

3.2 FMEA has its origins in manufacturing. It is a technique for determining the different ways (modes) in which a product can fail, and assessing the seriousness of the effects in each case. By using appropriate numerical values the different modes can be ranked in order of how critical they are. This should remind you strongly of the five-by-five risk classification discussed just above. Indeed, that is the relevance of FMEA in this area: when adapted from its manufacturing context it can be re-fashioned as a slightly more sophisticated version of this earlier risk classification.

3.3 Staying with the manufacturing context for now, the analysis is conducted as follows.

- Identify the components forming part of the product.

- For each component, list the different ways in which failure may occur and the causes of each.

- For each failure mode identified, list the effects on the overall product. (These first steps correspond to identifying potential risks and evaluating the potential impact of each.)

- Assess the probability (P) of each failure mode on a scale of 1 (not very probable) to 10 (extremely probable). This step corresponds to estimating the likelihood of a risk.

- Assess the seriousness (S) of each failure mode by considering its effects; again, a scale of 1 (not very serious) to 10 (extremely serious) may be used. This step corresponds to placing a numerical value on the impact of each risk.

- Assess the difficulty (D) of detecting the failure before the customer uses the product; the scale may run from 1 (easy to detect) to 10 (very difficult to detect). This does not correspond to anything in the model discussed earlier, but could easily be adapted so that our considerations extend to three different dimensions instead of just two. For example, a third dimension that we did not consider in the earlier model was the cost of measures to avoid the risk.

- Calculate a criticality index (C) for each failure mode by use of the formula C = P × S × D. This corresponds exactly to the calculation we used in the previous model, except that we are here considering three relevant factors instead of just two. As before, a low value for C indicates lower importance; a high value for C indicates a need for management attention.

Decision tree analysis

3.4   Decision tree analysis is a technique for coping with a series of decisions, each one having a variety of possible outcomes. The decision tree enables us to map the various combinations of decisions and outcomes in a structured way. If we can estimate the probabilities of the various possible outcomes, and assign monetary values to them, the tree enables us to evaluate the decision options and select the one leading to the most favourable monetary outcome.

3.5   As an example, suppose a company is considering the production of a new consumer item with a five-year product life. To manufacture the item requires the building of a new plant. Management has identified three options.

- Option A is to build a large plant now at a cost of £1m. If market conditions are good (probability 70%), the company can expect an annual profit from the new product of £350,000 for five years. If market conditions are poor (probability 30%) there would be a loss of £75,000 in each of the five years.

- Option B is to build a small plant now at a cost of £550,000. If market conditions are good, we profit by £200,000 per year; if market conditions are bad, we make a loss of £25,000 per year.

- Option C is to wait for a year while more information is collected. If the resulting information is unfavourable (probability 20%), management would abandon the idea. If it is favourable (probability 80%) management would build either the small or the large plant, and again would face either good or poor market conditions thereafter.

3.6   The position is shown in Figure 10.2. The squares represent decision points: points at which managers must make up their minds on how to proceed. The circles indicate the possible outcomes that may ensue: market conditions may be good or poor; information received under Option C may be favourable or unfavourable. The financial outcomes depend both on the decisions taken and on the circumstances that prevail afterwards.

3.7   Using the estimated probabilities and the estimated cashflows arising from each outcome it is possible to evaluate the expected value of each Option. In general, management will choose the option with the most profitable expected value (though of course there are many non-financial considerations that should not be overlooked in such a decision).

3.8   In the above example, we have not performed the mathematics, because it would take us well beyond your syllabus. In practice, decision trees are nowadays invariably produced using appropriate computer software so that manual calculations are never necessary.

Figure 10.2 *A simple decision tree*

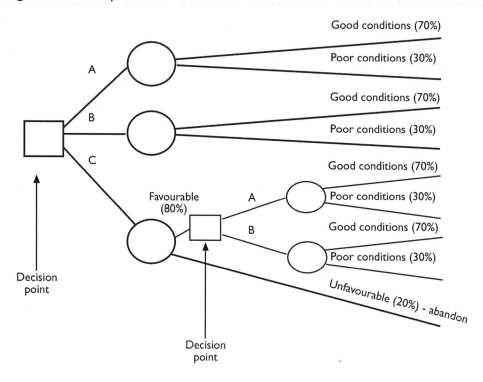

Fault tree analysis

3.9 Fault tree analysis is similar to decision tree analysis, except that it is concerned solely with the possibility of failure. This technique has been defined as 'a graphical technique that provides a systematic description of the combinations of possible occurrences in a system, which can result in an undesirable outcome. The method can combine hardware failures and computer failures'. (Institute of Engineering and Technology)

3.10 The IET website illustrates a fault tree showing the probability that a crash will occur at a particular road junction. It does this by tracking back to analyse what possible failures might have occurred to cause the crash: there must have been a car at the main junction; there must have been another car emerging from a side road and unable to stop; this in turn must have been caused by poor driving, or by poor road conditions. By tracking back to ultimate causes it is possible to estimate how many crashes might be expected to occur at the junction over a period.

3.11 This technique has obvious relevance to the analysis of risk, but once again it would take us too far afield to pursue the mathematics any further. At this stage we merely point out some of the limitations of the technique.

- A fault tree can only deal with a single failure (or a single risk). Each risk requires a separate tree, which is cumbersome and time consuming.

- There is inevitably a great degree of subjectivity in determining the possible factors that could contribute to the eventual failure, and the likelihood of each.

- The mathematics is forbidding; in practice, this is overcome by using specialised software.

Dependency modelling

3.12   Risks do not necessarily arise from a single failure. On the contrary, it is very often a combination of factors (people, systems, processes, technology) that gives rise to risk. Dependency modelling is a software tool that helps organisations to analyse the links between different factors that between them can give rise to risk.

3.13   The outputs from the software include:

- Analysis of risks faced by the organisation
- Potential impact of the risks in financial and operating terms
- Possible countermeasures to counter the risks

Value at risk

3.14   Value at risk (VaR) is a measurement tool used to assess the size of an organisation's risk exposure. It was developed in the banking and financial sector and at first applied primarily to organisations (such as banks and securities houses) with many different investments. However, the principles of VaR can equally be applied to non-financial organisations. For example, a large construction company may have many projects in progress at a given time, each of which can be regarded as a financial investment.

3.15   VaR measures the volatility of a firm's investment portfolio in the light of market conditions. It is defined as the maximum amount of loss that we can expect (with a predetermined level of probability) to suffer on a given investment over a given time frame.

3.16   This is a somewhat subtle concept. The first thing to grasp is that VaR, like any other tool of estimation, cannot give a definite answer: we cannot say with 100% certainty that our losses will be less than £X. But we can say – using complex statistical techniques beyond the scope of your syllabus – that we have, say, a 95% chance, or a 99% chance, that our loss will be less than a certain amount.

3.17   What that amount may be will depend partly on our assessment of market conditions, and partly on the degree of confidence that we want to obtain in our estimate. For example, on a particular investment we may be able to calculate with 99% confidence that our loss will not exceed £250,000. But if we are concerned about losing, say, £150,000, our calculations may give us only 95% confidence of being within that amount.

3.18   To simplify matters, we have referred above to a single investment. However, in real life the statistical analysis applies to a portfolio of investments rather than to a single investment. This is because part of the analysis is concerned with correlations between one investment and another. This reflects the fact that in a particular market, a development that impacts badly on Investment A may have a favourable impact on Investment B. A company holding both investments is to some extent hedging its bets and increasing its confidence of keeping losses within bounds.

3.19   This kind of correlation has a material effect on the VaR calculations. Bear in mind that correlation can also work the other way: in a particular market, a certain change in circumstances may have a damaging effect on Investments X, Y and Z. A firm holding all three of these investments could lose out badly.

3.20 There are four steps in a VaR calculation.

- Determine the time horizon over which the firm wishes to estimate a potential loss. For example, we may be concerned about our exposure in the period of one month ahead.

- Select the degree of certainty required: is it sufficient to estimate our possible losses with 95% certainty, or is a higher level of certainty (say 99%) necessary for us?

- Create a probability distribution of likely returns for the investment(s). This is where the statistics become complicated. As inputs to this step we would need historical market data combined with our assessment of market conditions in the period ahead.

- Calculate the VaR estimate. The mathematics of this need not concern us.

3.21 As can be seen, the output of the process is our VaR estimate. This measures the largest likely loss arising from market risk that the investment(s) will suffer over a particular time horizon and with a degree of certainty selected by the user.

Chapter summary

- Many techniques may be used for identifying risks: brainstorming, questionnaires etc.

- Both external and internal auditors have important roles to play in the identification of risk and in suggesting means to reduce risk.

- Statistical sampling is one method of estimating the probability of a risk. By selecting and investigating a carefully structured sample we can draw conclusions about the whole 'population' of items that we are interested in.

- Another technique for estimating probability is time series analysis. What happened in previous periods can be a starting point for estimating what will happen in the future.

- Various frameworks have been proposed for estimating the impact of a risk: for example, high, medium, low; catastrophic, serious, minor and insignificant.

- By combining the likelihood of a risk with its potential impact we arrive at a measure of how much management attention the risk deserves.

- Failure mode and effect analysis is a technique with its origins in manufacturing. It can be adapted to form a means of evaluating risks by taking account of their likelihood and their potential impacts.

- Decision tree analysis is another quantitative technique, designed to cope with situations where a series of decisions may be needed.

- Fault tree analysis is a method of analysing how a risk can materialise by tracking back to identify what must first have gone wrong.

- Value at risk (VaR) is a measurement tool used to assess the size of an organisation's risk exposure. Though it originated in the banking and financial sector its use can be extended to other types of organisation.

Self-test questions

Numbers in brackets refer to the paragraphs where you can check your answers.

1   List techniques that can be used to identify risks. (1.2)

2   Explain how Ishikawa diagrams can be used in identifying risk. (1.5)

3   Explain the role of internal auditors in corporate governance. (1.15)

4   Distinguish between upside risk and downside risk. (2.2)

5   Why must a statistical sample be carefully structured? (2.7)

6   List possible ways in which a risk may impact on an organisation. (2.18)

7   List the five classifications of risk likelihood suggested by Mike Brooks, and his five classifications of risk impact. (Table 10.2)

8   List the steps in a failure mode and effect analysis. (3.3)

9   Describe what is meant by decision tree analysis. (3.4)

10 What is 'value at risk'? (3.14)

CHAPTER 11

Finding Solutions for Risks (I)

Learning objectives and indicative content

3.1   Develop appropriate solutions to mitigate the inherent risk in the following supply chain issues:

- Supplier appraisal, selection and management
- International sourcing
- Corporate social responsibility (CSR) including ethical, environmental and health and safety issues

3.4   Appraise specific key risks and exposures in purchasing and supply and identify appropriate mitigating actions.

- Contractual failure, consequential loss and provision for remedies
- Supplier insolvency, monitoring and guarantees
- Security of supply, contingency planning, stock holding and alternative sources of supply
- Fraud, accounting and payment exposures, conflicts of interest, purchasing ethics and codes of conduct

Chapter headings

1   Supplier risks

2   International sourcing

3   Ethics and corporate social responsibility

4   Environmental risk

1   Supplier risks

Supplier appraisal and selection

1.1   Supplier failure (discussed in Chapter 3) can have severe repercussions for all supply chain members. To reduce the risk caused by supplier failure it is important to assess the supplier's integrity, financial stability and delivery capability. Supplier appraisal has always been part of the purchasing discipline but the role is enhanced when considered in the context of supply chains. The impact of supplier failure will cascade along the chain.

1.2   The need for supplier appraisal may arise in several circumstances. For example, a supplier may apply to be placed on a list of approved suppliers, or a buyer may need to source a part or component that has not been purchased before, or is not available from existing suppliers. Alternatively there may be a major one-off project that does not fall within the scope of existing suppliers.

1.3   In any of these cases, the buyer's aim is to ensure that the potential supplier can perform the contract to the required standard. Supplier appraisal forms an element of both quality assurance and risk management.

Identifying potential suppliers

1.4   A wide variety of information is available to assist the buyer in identifying potential suppliers. In many instances there is too much information. In consequence the purchaser needs to be focused in his research.

1.5   Past experience is a good starting point. Most of the tasks in a purchasing department are to a greater or lesser extent repetitive. A well organised purchasing function will ensure that a good supplier database is maintained, enabling buyers to locate suitable suppliers quickly from those known to the organisation.

1.6   Salespeople from suppliers are another common source of information. Many buying organisations tap this source systematically by displaying both their finished products and major components in public, in effect inviting visiting salespeople to deploy their knowledge to the advantage of both organisations.

1.7   Contacts with other buyers, both inside and outside the organisation, can help in keeping up to date with new developments.

1.8   All purchasing departments receive published catalogues and direct mail from potential suppliers. They contain a mass of information, particularly for standard parts, but access to this information requires good recording and filing.

1.9   Trade directories are available in hard copy and electronic form. Certain industries have specialist publications more focused to the needs of organisations. The search facility and hyperlinking facilities make research faster.

1.10   Trade journals are another common source of topical information in the form of editorials, news items and advertisements. Trade shows and exhibitions enable suppliers to display and demonstrate their products, provide information and pass on news of developments.

The supplier appraisal questionnaire

1.11   A key part of the supplier appraisal process is the supplier appraisal questionnaire. This will ask questions of a potential supplier in such areas as the following.

- Financial standing
- Production capacity and facilities
- Human resource profile including disputes that may have affected production
- Quality, supported by relevant accreditations as appropriate
- Performance (such as benchmarking key performance indicators, major failures to deliver against contracts and other relevant factors relating to the specific business area)
- Information technology
- Corporate social responsibility
- Risk management

1.12 The questionnaire itself will usually follow a standard template. This allows for direct comparison of responses with those received from other suppliers and for evaluation against predetermined criteria.

1.13 The responses gained help to provide a profile of the supply organisation. This reduces the supply risk but is not enough in itself. To gain confirmation of the information provided by the supplier in the questionnaire it is good practice to follow this up with a supplier visit. This enables the buyer not only to vet the suppliers and their facilities but also to discuss the products and services and the ways in which the supplier can contribute to the buyer's requirements.

1.14 The site visit forms an important part of the supplier evaluation process but it is important not to underestimate the amount of resources it consumes. It will not be necessary in cases of small purchases where recurring business is not expected.

1.15 Supplier visits are an important source of information on such matters as the following.

- Production equipment and operations
- Operation of key materials management activities
- Existence of adequate production capacity
- Expertise and motivation of personnel
- Technological expertise of supervisory personnel
- Management capabilities

1.16 The visit offers a chance to resolve uncertainties and discuss potential problems or uncertainty areas. It also provides the opportunity to establish personal relationships between key personnel of the purchasing and selling organisations.

1.17 The appraisal and visit forms only the first part of the assessment of suppliers. The need to monitor the supplier is an ongoing commitment. The appraisal and visit help in reducing risk but risk management demands more rigour in the continued monitoring of not only the supplier but also the internal and external factors influencing the supply chain.

Supplier financial stability

1.18 The assessment of a supplier's financial position will take place early in the appraisal process. Suppliers will be required to complete the supplier appraisal questionnaire. Among the question areas are sections requiring details about their company, their financial situation and references.

1.19 The most accessible source of information on a supplier is their published financial accounts. Financial analysis carried out by the buyer's Finance Department will examine aspects such as financial gearing, ratio analysis and other financial tools that allow an understanding to be gained of the financial status of the supplier. It is common to ask the supplier to provide this information on an ongoing annual basis, as the financial situation of an organisation will change over time.

1.20   The supplier's financial accounts present historical data, but when supplemented by financial forecasting techniques (where appropriate) and comparison with accounts of similar companies they can provide a useful source of information to the buyer. Research organisations such as Dun and Bradstreet can be used to provide more tailored information should be situation demand.

1.21   Financial stability is important. Dobler and Burt cite three scenarios that can arise if dealing with a financially weak supplier.

   •   You need to insist on maintaining quality but the supplier is forced to cut costs.

   •   You have a financial claim against the supplier, but he does not have sufficient working capital to meet it.

   •   You need to insist on speedy delivery to meet a promised delivery date, but the supplier cannot afford to pay overtime.

1.22   Financial benchmarks could be included as part of the risk management process with a responsibility placed on the supplier to inform other supply chain members when acceptable ratios or gearing criteria are not being met.

1.23   As discussed earlier in the text, the risk management process can involve requiring suppliers to have a risk management policy and process and to insist on the same in their own suppliers.

1.24   It can be part of the risk management process that when certain criteria are not being met then formal notification must be given to nominated supply chain members. This could be one tier above or whatever is agreed and included in the contract.

1.25   Risk management can place obligations on suppliers and tier members to provide information on identified issues that may impact on the supply chain.

The impact of the supply chain concept

1.26   Adoption of a supply chain perspective requires supplier appraisal to be viewed in a wider context. That is not to say that traditional approaches to supplier appraisal are invalid; only that they should be extended as appropriate to meet the more integrated needs of the supply chain.

1.27   The nature of the supply chain (lean, flexible, agile or a combination of these approaches) will make different demands on suppliers. An understanding of the approach to the supply chain is fundamental in appraising a supplier's ability to contribute effectively as a chain member.

1.28   The appraisal process should assess the benefits of closer collaboration and the willingness and ability of supply chain partners to embrace this approach. We are not only looking at factors such as the capacity to meet requirements. We are looking at a long-term commitment where organisations will work together for the mutual benefit of each other, developing and refining the relationship over the longer term.

1.29   Where a long-term relationship is contemplated, the supplier should be viewed strategically. Strategic sourcing is a core activity in purchasing and is defined by CIPS as 'satisfying business needs from markets via the proactive and planned analysis of supply markets and the selection of suppliers with the objective of delivering solutions to meet predetermined and agreed business goals'.

1.30 Strategic sourcing requires a logical and long-term approach, supported at Board level in organisations. To develop a strategic sourcing approach requires a clear understanding of our own organisation and of what we require from suppliers or partners.

Supply risk

1.31 The workbook *Understanding Supply Chain Risk* (Cranfield School of Management/Department of Transport; see www.cranfield.ac.uk/som/scr) identifies a series of generic questions that should be considered when looking at supply risk.

- Is the chain dependent on dominant or specialist suppliers where failure to supply could disrupt output?

- Are any suppliers, particularly critical suppliers, in potential financial difficulties that could interrupt output?

- Do any suppliers offer extended lead times that impact on inventory or customer service?

- Is there a record of poor quality from any suppliers and are there risks that could arise as a result?

- Are there any suppliers who have poor schedule compliance, and if so, are they among the suppliers on whom there is a dependency?

- What is the state of the supply market? Is our company taking a large slice of the supply? And are there any tight spots in the supply market that might disrupt output?

- Are there measures of performance in place with suppliers that provide a platform for an improvement programme?

- Make an assessment of supplier capabilities to plan and fulfil demand. Are they using good methods or working hand to mouth?

1.32 The workbook suggests ranking the outcomes of these questions (0 = none, 1 = some, 2 = significant), not as a ranking of the likelihood of the risk occurring but as an assessment of the risk should it occur. The identification of key supply risk factors again serves to focus supply chain management in these areas.

1.33 Here are some possible methods of mitigating supply risk.

- Materials: perhaps increase stock levels to cover an identified potential supply risk

- Supplier performance measurement: putting processes in place if they do not exist already or enabling effective computer linked measurement on key areas such as price, delivery and quality giving real-time measurement

- Lead time reduction: working with supply chain partners on process improvements that will lead to overall supply chain gains

- Transport contingency: the development of fallback positions should transport links become disrupted

Strategic supply chain relationships

1.34 As we suggested in Chapter 3, procurement positioning models suggest that critical or strategic items (which are subject to high supply risk) should be procured via long-term, selective 'partnership' or 'alliance' relationships with key suppliers, in order to minimise supply chain vulnerability.

1.35 The benefits and risks of long-term partnership relations can be summarised as follows.

Table 11.1: *Benefits and risks of long-term supply relationships*

Benefits for the buyer	Risks for the buyer
Established contacts/track record create trust	Complacent performance by the supplier
Supplier knowledge of requirements allows better service, collaborative improvement	Dependence on supplier may erode price or performance gains: lowering bargaining power
Sharing of data/plans allows forward planning, joint product/service development	Dependence increases vulnerability to supplier failure or supply disruption (eg strike, disaster)
Quality problems ironed out over time: pooled expertise enhances quality, added value	Vulnerability to reputational damage by association (eg re supplier ethical failure)
Reduced supplier evaluation/selection, contracting, transaction and dispute costs	Investment in integration raises cost of switching where this may be necessary or advantageous
Supplier may give preferential treatment in event of materials shortages, crisis demand etc	Collaboration increases risk of loss of control over confidential data, intellectual property etc.
Suppliers are motivated to invest in R&D, low-cost solutions, quality improvements	Investment in collaboration may not be warranted by priority/frequency of purchases
Suppliers are motivated to dependable performance	Investment may be wasted if supplier turns out to be unsuitable/incompatible
Systems can be progressively integrated for greater efficiency, reduced transaction costs	
Enhanced supply chain competitiveness	

Benefits for the supplier	Risks for the supplier
Established contacts/track record create trust	Complacent conduct by buyer (eg re payment)
Buyer knowledge of capabilities allows managed expectations	Dependence may enhance buyer power, forcing price/margins down
Knowledge of buyer requirements reduces risk of disputes, misunderstandings, rejects etc.	Dependence increases vulnerability to buyer failure or unforeseen drop in demand
Sharing of data/plans allows forward planning, joint product/service development	Vulnerability to reputational damage by association (eg re buyer ethical failure)
Supplier development enhances value-adding capabilities for wider development, competition	Collaboration increases risk of loss of control over confidential data, intellectual property etc.
Less costs of selling + reduced production costs over time due to learning effect	Investment in collaboration may not be warranted by priority/frequency of purchases
Managerial time is freed for focus on added value, business development	Investment may be wasted if supplier turns out to be unsuitable/incompatible
Trust in long-term business enables better revenue/cashflow and capacity planning	
Systems can be progressively integrated for greater efficiency, reduced transaction costs	

1.36   In order to mitigate the risks, it may be necessary for either or both organisations to:

- Analyse the most appropriate relationship type for the situation (eg using procurement positioning and supplier preferencing tools)
- Engage in careful partner evaluation, selection, contracting and relationship management processes
- Put in place multiple or back-up sourcing arrangements (buyer) or diversified customer base (supplier)
- Establish joint (or mutual) performance measures and continuous improvement targets and incentives
- Use legal means to protect intellectual property rights and confidentiality
- Share information for accurate demand forecasting
- Engage in joint contingency and continuity planning
- Prepare exit strategies for managing relationship termination.

1.37   One of the key elements of partner evaluation and selection will be to appraise the operational and strategic compatibility of any prospective partner: in other words, to ensure that both organisations' processes, objectives and cultures are compatible. This is sometimes referred to as 'cross-organisational goal and process alignment'.

KPI alignment

1.38   One approach to ensuring strategic compatibility and expectation management in a supply relationship, highlighted in recent CIPS exams, is 'KPI alignment'. Key performance indicators (KPIs) are agreed, quantifiable measures of the performance of an organisation in relation to its critical success factors (areas of key competitive advantage, or factors necessary for success in its market).

1.39   KPI alignment uses facilitated interviews with key representatives and stakeholders of both the buyer/client and the supplier/contractor, to capture data on what is important to each party in terms of its desired outcomes from a contract or supply relationship. This ensures that both parties have to clarify their expectations and understand each others' expectations: identification and comparison of potential differences (misalignments) can support pre-contract clarification and negotiation – to avoid conflict (and resulting risk) as the contract or relationship progresses.

1.40   Misalignments may come in the form of conflicting or diverging KPIs (desired outcomes) and/or 'gaps' between the level of importance given to a particular KPI: for example, if one party considers CSR or innovation crucial, while the other considers it unimportant. The responses can be scored (eg on a scale from 0 to 5 or 0 to 10), so that the extent of the misalignment or 'gap' can be quantified: a larger gap may be both more urgent to discuss – and harder to overcome.

Negotiation risks

1.41   Negotiations with suppliers are often carried out by means of a win-lose approach: the buyer regards the supplier as an opponent, guards relevant information jealously, and insists on a deal that meets his own objectives, regardless of the supplier's. The risk here is that, even if the buyer is successful, the supplier could be resentful, which could lead to damaging consequences at a later date.

1.42   Other risks which might be identified as inherent in the negotiation process can be summarised as follows.

- The risk of 'losing out' from the negotiation, if a zero-sum or 'win-lose' approach is used

- The risk that unacceptable or unfeasible concessions will be made, which will cause economic loss, conflict and other negative impacts if followed through

- The risk of reaching an impasse: not being able to reach a solution or agreement that is acceptable to both parties – and therefore wasting negotiation time and cost without ratifying or implementing an agreement

- Adversarial relations with the other party, if the negotiations have been win-lose in style: this may have critical secondary risks (eg if key suppliers or employees are alienated or resentful, and co-operation is damaged).

- Conflict or divergent tactics within a negotiating team undermining the bargaining position (and/or the acceptability of the result to internal stakeholders)

- Ethical/reputational risk: eg if negotiating power is used for personal gain, or there is breach of confidentiality during or following negotiations

- Compliance risk: eg if statutory procedures (eg competitive tendering under Public Sector Procurement Directives) are not complied with.

1.43 Here are some measures to control and mitigate these risks.

- Detailed pre-negotiation research (eg supplier appraisal, price research)
- Careful position planning: establishing the 'range of negotiation' between best possible and worst acceptable outcomes, and having a prepared BATNA and walk-away position (resistance point)
- Making provision for third-party mediation or arbitration, where negotiation is insufficient to resolve a deadlock
- The segmentation of supply relationships, in order to select appropriate negotiating approaches and styles: for example, a more integrative, problem-solving approach for suppliers of strategic/critical items
- Rehearsals of negotiation tactics (especially by negotiating teams)
- Ethical policies and awareness programmes, supporting ethical negotiation
- Pre- and post-negotiation stakeholder communication, in order to minimise the risk of failure to accept and ratify the resulting agreement
- Evaluation, reporting and learning from negotiations, to improve performance next time.

1.44 The November 2007 exam also highlighted the question of risk in particular negotiating contexts: for example, the negotiation of exclusive supply (or distribution) contracts. In addition to the 'negotiation risks' discussed above, this scenario raises the risks associated with exclusive relationships: similar to those of long-term partnership relationships (discussed above) – but with increased vulnerability due to the unavailability of multiple/back-up relationships in the event of problems; the lost potential to access wider options and capabilities (which may reduce flexibility and increase exposure in complex and dynamic markets); and the risk of negative impacts on other relationships within the supply chain/market.

1.45 We will discuss negotiation risks in more detail in Chapter 13.

2 International sourcing

Introduction

2.1 The international aspect of supply chain management means that participants require at least a basic understanding of the nature of international trading. The more involved organisations become, the greater the necessity for a detailed understanding of the risks and benefits of international trade.

2.2 In this section of the chapter we look at some specific aspects of international trading: culture and communications, legal aspects (including incoterms), and payment methods.

Culture and communications

2.3 One of the more obvious problems in dealing with overseas suppliers is that they are not British! This remark is not intended in any racist or xenophobic sense. It is merely intended to make the obvious point that the residents of a particular country, such as the United Kingdom, share a common culture and a common language, both of which influence their business dealings with each other. When dealing with overseas suppliers it is necessary to adjust to a different culture and language.

2.4   The difficulties here are both technical and behavioural. Technical difficulties concern the simple issue of understanding what is being offered and accepted, and what has eventually been agreed. Behavioural difficulties are related to how people interact with each other and form pleasant and rewarding business relations.

2.5   To deal first with the technical difficulty of communication, it is clearly vital that agreements once concluded are expressed in language that both parties understand. But before that stage is reached oral discussions will take place during which offers and commitments will be expressed that have a great influence on the course of negotiations. Buyers must make every effort to ensure that such discussions are unambiguous.

2.6   It is an essential element in a binding contract that the parties reach agreement. That element is absent if there is misunderstanding: one party believes he understands what the other has said, but in fact has not done so. Even leaving aside the legal niceties, it is clear that successful business relations are endangered if the two parties have different ideas as to what has been agreed.

2.7   Native speakers of English are in a fortunate position in that their first language is widely recognised as the standard language of international trade. However, that should not lead buyers to think that they can ignore communication difficulties. Even if negotiations are conducted in English, it is important to ensure that the supplier understands technical terms and idioms in the same way as the buyer.

2.8   An effort to acquire some understanding of the relevant foreign language can be a great help in this respect. It is also a major step in improving business relations. It is a positive sign that the buyer has made efforts to adapt to the supplier's position and will usually be welcomed even if the level of proficiency is not great.

2.9   This leads on naturally to the less technical and more behavioural problems of dealing with overseas suppliers. As in all negotiations, it is important to make a positive impression on one's business partners. This is more difficult in the case of overseas partners because of cultural differences.

2.10   Many of these differences have been described in the purchasing literature. For example, it is common to refer to Japanese patterns of business behaviour which can cause confusion to British and American buyers.

2.11   One instance of this is the much greater link between social and business relations in Japan; social communication forms a larger part of the negotiation process than is common in Britain or America. Buyers doing business in Japan should not assume that extensive entertaining by their hosts is an unimportant prelude to the main talks.

2.12   Another instance sometimes cited is the Japanese practice of avoiding a direct 'no', so as not to cause embarrassment to their guests. This can sometimes leave a British or American buyer believing that something is still up for debate, when the truth is that the supplier regards it as unacceptable.

2.13   Instances such as this could be multiplied by reference to other countries where business practices differ from those of Britain and America. However, the best practical measure is to benefit from the experience of others. Buyers doing business with overseas suppliers should brief themselves by discussing such points with colleagues who have previous experience.

Table 11.2 *Suggestions for negotiating with overseas suppliers*

1.	Speak slowly and ask questions to check understanding.
2.	Print business cards in both English and the foreign language.
3.	Study the culture in advance.
4.	Be prepared for negotiations to be drawn out over a longer period than usual.
5.	Become familiar with local regulations, tax laws etc.
6.	Prepare in advance on technical issues, financing arrangements, cost and price analyses etc.
7.	If possible, ensure that the person recording the discussions is drawn from your team
8.	Arrange discussions so that the other team can 'win' their share of the issues.

Legal aspects

2.14 One issue that is important when contracting on an international scale is to determine the proper law of the contract. In other words, which nation's legal rules apply in determining any legal dispute?

2.15 The Contracts (Applicable Law) Act 1990 gave statutory effect to the Rome Convention on the Law Applicable to Contractual Obligations 1980. The Rome Convention allows the contracting parties to choose the law that will govern the contract between them. The choice must be made expressly within the contract documentation. Where the parties, for whatever reason, do not make a choice on the law of the contract, then article 4(1) of the Rome Convention states that the law of the country with which it is most closely connected will govern the contract.

2.16 Litigation (taking legal action through the courts) can be complex and involved particularly when international considerations are involved. To reduce the risks involved, parties involved in dispute may seek to avoid legislation and seek to use an alternative means of dispute settlement, such as **arbitration**.

2.17 The parties to the contract have to agree to arbitration before it can be applied. The parties can agree to this either before or after the dispute has arisen but good risk management process would ensure this is considered prior to entering into an international purchase contract.

2.18 Arbitration is a formal procedure and the award given by the arbitrator is in most cases enforceable. However, it does not always provide a quick solution to a dispute: in fact it is not uncommon for arbitration proceedings to last as long as court hearings.

2.19 Arbitration does have some positive advantages over litigation.

- The contracting parties have the freedom to choose who they desire to arbitrate. These can be people who, for example, possess expertise in a particular trade and might be best suited to resolving the dispute. This often makes for smoother resolution of the dispute.

- The parties can choose rules of procedure, such as rules published by the International Chamber of Commerce (ICC).

- The parties can often choose the time and place to hold arbitration proceedings.

- The parties can keep the dispute between themselves as arbitration proceedings are undertaken behind closed doors, as opposed to litigation which is in the public domain.

- Arbitration awards are generally final, meaning there is little likelihood of protracted dealings through appeals.

2.20 There are other alternatives to litigation.

- Mediation: the mediator is prevented from suggesting solutions but has the role of looking for common ground and encouraging the parties to keep talking.

- Conciliation: the conciliator is allowed to act as a catalyst bringing the two sides together and proposing compromises.

- Assisted dispute resolution (ADR): this brings the opposing parties together and acts out their cases. The procedure does follow legal principles but allows parties to reach their own solution to the dispute.

Incoterms 2000

2.21 Sending goods from one country to another as part of a commercial transaction can be a risky business. If they are lost or damaged, or if delivery does not take place, then the climate of confidence between the parties involved may degenerate to a point where legal action is considered or brought.

2.22 However, the sellers and buyers in international contracts inevitably want their contracts to be successfully completed. The use of *Incoterms 2000* can assist in achieving this objective.

2.23 Incoterms are a set of contractual conditions or terms that can be adopted into international contracts and which are designed to be understood and interpreted correctly on a worldwide basis. Terms of trade define the risks and responsibilities of buyers and sellers in the sale and delivery of goods to overseas markets.

2.24 Defined in *Incoterms 2000* (published by the International Chamber of Commerce) they represent a set of internationally agreed and widely accepted trade terms that are used by the vast majority of trading nations.

2.25 There is no legal requirement to use incoterms when drawing up an international commercial contract. However, if the parties adopt incoterms into their contract they are agreeing to be bound by the detailed specifications laid out in *Incoterms 2000*.

2.26 Although the adoption of incoterms into a contract will mean that courts will imply the standards of incoterms in law, the ICC will arbitrate on disputes. This will often prove a cheaper option than going to law. If this course of action is considered worthwhile the ICC recommends inclusion of the following term in the contract:

'All disputes arising in connection with the present contract shall be finally settled under the Rules of Conciliation and Arbitration of the International Chamber of Commerce by one or more arbitrators appointed in accordance with the said Rules.'

2.27 Incoterms are best viewed and understood from the exporter's perspective. They are arranged in order of increasing responsibility for the exporter. As we move through the list, the amount of responsibility borne by the supplier increases. This is seen in the four main groups of incoterms below: Table 11.3.

Table 11.3 *The four groups of incoterms*

Group	Duties of buyer/seller
'E' terms	The seller's only duty is to make the goods available at own premises. May assist with transit, but not a requirement.
'F' terms	Seller will undertake all pre-carriage duties, but main carriage arrangements are the responsibility of the buyer.
'C' terms	Seller arranges for carriage of goods, but once they are despatched he has fulfilled his obligations.
'D' terms	Seller's obligations extend to delivery of goods at the specified destination; eg seller is liable for damage in transit.

Figure 11.1 *The basic concept of Incoterms*

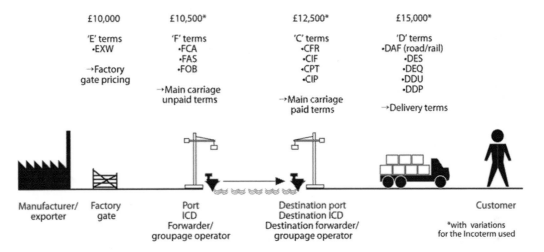

2.28 The use of incoterms in a contract can save pages of detailed negotiation because the detailed specifications relating to the relevant incoterm will apply, defining areas of risk and responsibility. Areas detailed within incoterms specify the obligations of buyer and seller in regard to, among other things:

- where delivery should be made;
- who insures;
- what level of insurance is required;
- who raises particular documents.

Payment methods

2.29 Payment for goods purchased from abroad may in some cases be no different from payment in a domestic transaction. For example, companies who have a long history of trading together will have developed a mutual trust enabling ordinary trade credit terms to be operated. The seller simply invoices the buyer and the buyer pays on the due date.

2.30 This situation however is far from being the norm in international trading. The distances involved, the risks of international transportation, the limited direct contact between the parties, and the different legal systems involved, all reduce the seller's confidence of being paid. To protect the seller's position, alternatives to open account trading have been developed.

2.31 The simplest alternative, though highly undesirable from the buyer's point of view, is payment in advance. The dangers of this are so obvious as to require no comment, and in practice this procedure would be highly unusual. More probably, buyer and seller would resort to one of the various methods that have been developed to provide reasonable security on both sides. These methods involve the use of banks as intermediaries. By far the most common method is the use of a **letter of credit**, and this is described below.

2.32 Using letters of credit is essential in international trade, and importers need a reasonable understanding of how they work. However, the procedure is somewhat complex and to help your understanding it is worthwhile to bear in mind what the system attempts to achieve.

- For the seller, the aim is to ensure payment without recourse to litigation, especially since such litigation might involve a foreign jurisdiction. Preferably, the seller would like the source of funds to be located in his own country.

- For the buyer, the aim is mainly to ensure that payment is not made until he has received assurance that the goods have been transferred to himself.

2.33 These aims are achieved by the use of two banks as intermediaries: one in the seller's country (the advising bank), and one in the buyer's country (the issuing bank). In brief, the buyer instructs the issuing bank to open a credit with the advising bank in favour of the seller. The seller will be able to draw on this credit – ie obtain funds from the advising bank in his own country – once he has delivered to the advising bank any documents specified by the buyer, such as a clean bill of lading.

2.34 Having paid the seller, the advising bank passes on the documents to the issuing bank and is reimbursed for the sum advanced. The issuing bank in turn presents the documents to the buyer in return for payment. The end result is that the buyer has paid, and the seller has received, the contract price, while the intermediary banks have received fees for handling the transaction.

2.35 The seller will invariably insist that a **confirmed irrevocable letter of credit** is used.

- 'Confirmed' means that the advising bank has confirmed the arrangement with the seller in its own country, and the seller therefore has confidence in receiving funds from a local source once he has delivered the required documents.

- 'Irrevocable' means that the issuing bank receives an irrevocable authority from the buyer, and also undertakes irrevocably to act on that authority. This means that the issuing bank must honour the credit, even if the buyer attempts to revoke the agreement (as might happen, for example, if some dispute arose between buyer and seller).

2.36 The banks involved in this transaction act as agents of the buyer, and they run the risk that he, as principal, will refuse to ratify their actions. This he might do, for example, if the documents tendered to him do not comply with the requirements that he laid down. To protect themselves against this possibility, banks will normally refuse to accept documents from the seller unless they comply in every respect with the buyer's stipulations.

2.37 Use of letters of credit is by no means a fail-safe system. In particular, the number of parties involved can mean that delays arise. It can happen, for example, that goods arrive at the port of destination before the buyer has received the bill of lading from the issuing bank. The carrier will be reluctant in that case to hand over the goods. In practice, the buyer may persuade him to do so by indemnifying him against any loss he may suffer as a result.

2.38 One final point to mention in connection with payment is the risk of volatility in foreign currency exchange rates. This was described in Chapter 9.

3 Ethics and corporate social responsibility

Ethical behaviour in purchasing

3.1 'Ethics is concerned with the moral principles and values that govern our beliefs, actions and desires' (Lysons). Ethical behaviour is high on the agenda within purchasing, encouraging buyers to operate to a principled standard. Ethics are also shaped more deliberately by public and professional bodies, in the form of agreed principles and guidelines that are designed to protect society's best interests.

3.2 Ethical issues may affect businesses and public sector organisations at three levels.

- At the wider macro level, there are issues concerning the role of business and capitalism in society: the debate about globalisation, the exploitation of labour, the impact of industrialisation and so on.

- At the corporate level, there are issues that face an individual organisation as it formulates strategies and policies about how it interacts with its various stakeholders. The sphere generally referred to as corporate social responsibility covers policies that the organisation adopts for the good and wellbeing of stakeholders: this is further discussed later in this chapter.

- At the individual level, there are issues that face individuals as they act and interact within the organisation and supply chain: whether to accept gifts or hospitality which might be perceived as an attempt to influence supplier selection, as an example. This is the sphere that is often covered in Professional Codes of Ethics.

3.3 Buyers are, arguably, more exposed to ethical temptations than most professionals. They control large sums of organisational funds. Their decisions typically benefit some suppliers over others – creating an incentive to try and influence those decisions.

3.4 Within purchasing there is a high priority placed on ethical behaviour, outlined by CIPS advice on ethical procurement.

- Members must declare any personal interest that may impinge on their work activities.

- Members must respect confidentiality of information.

- Members should avoid any arrangement that might prevent fair competition.

- Except for small-value items, business gifts should not be accepted.

- Any doubts on the last two points should be discussed with the individual's superior.

3.5 Ethics in purchasing and supply has two aspects: ethical behaviour and ethical sourcing. Ethical behaviour is outlined in the above advice that those in purchasing should follow. Ethical sourcing is a wide business area that has grown more complex as global sourcing and supply chain management in particular have continued to develop. Purchasing has the responsibility for certain types and levels of organisational spend and should consistently consider both ethical behaviour and ethical sourcing.

3.6 Closer relationships increase risk, as companies within the supply chain are more integrated and reliant on each other. Hard measures on delivery, quality etc, can be put in place but it is the softer measures, the effective interface between suppliers/partners, that underpin the relationship.

Ethical sourcing

3.7 Ethical sourcing establishes an organisation's responsibility for labour and human rights in the supply chain. In today's wider marketplace it is not enough to look only at basic purchasing criteria such as price, quality and delivery. Buyers must take responsibility for sourcing decisions in the wider context.

3.8 We have discussed reputational risk throughout this text. The decisions that purchasing make can have serious reputational risk ramifications and need to be viewed with the entire supply chain in mind.

3.9 With the development of the supply chain approach there is an increasing distance, both geographical and cultural, between tiers in the supply chain. There is a clear need both to reduce the impact of reputational risk to the organisation and to act in an ethical manner towards workers and others within the supply chain.

The Ethical Trading Initiative (ETI)

3.10 The Ethical Trading Initiative is an alliance of companies, non-governmental organisations and trade union organisations committed to working together to identify and promote good practice in the implementation of codes of labour practice.

3.11 The ETI Base Code covers the following areas.

- Employment is freely chosen.

- Freedom of association and the right to collective bargaining is respected.

- Working conditions are safe and hygienic.

- Child labour shall not be used.

- Living wages are paid.

- Working hours are not excessive.

- No discrimination is practised.

- Regular employment is provided.

- No harsh or inhumane treatment is allowed.

3.12 The awareness of ethical issues is particularly important in purchasing, as purchasing is the interface between the organisation and the outside world. An ethical sourcing policy places a clear obligation on both an organisation and the purchasing department to ensure compliance.

3.13 This obligation will often be accomplished by the issuing of 'Codes of Conduct' which will be placed on the next tier suppliers. These suppliers, in turn, place similar obligations on their suppliers.

3.14 The question arises 'Is this enough?' The answer is often no. To protect both the workforce and the reputational risk it is often necessary to put in place procedures covering both documentary and physical audits. These will form part of the risk management process. In doing this, a degree of rigour is brought to the process with a direct line of accountability at Board level.

3.15 There may be considerable costs and challenges involved in ethical monitoring of suppliers in an extensive, highly tiered, shifting and/or geographically dispersed supply chain. Supply chain managers should focus on developing supply chain policies that express ethical standards.

Corporate social responsibility (CSR)

3.16 Corporate social responsibility has become the broadly accepted concept used to describe a collection of related disciplines that combine to represent an organisation's overall ethos, its personality, philosophy and character with regard to the world in its widest sense.

3.17 CSR is defined by CIPS as 'an approach by which a company recognises that its activities have a wider impact on the society in which it operates; and that developments in society in turn impact on its ability to pursue business successfully'.

3.18 CSR offers opportunities to organisations. The increased emphasis on environmental responsibility, sustainability etc, enables organisations to adapt their business model to take advantage of new attitudes and potential and as a result to enhance their perception in the mind of stakeholders. It is not enough merely to put a CSR policy in place – it must be seen to be delivered effectively

3.19 There are a number of key drivers to develop and improve CSR within a purchasing and supply environment.

- Board level directives
- Meeting stakeholder expectations
- Public opinion and media concerns
- Expectations of trade unions and employees

3.20 Not all aspects of CSR fall within the remit of purchasing and supply chain management, or if they do the involvement may be minor. Where the involvement is apparent the relationship will often involve risk issues. In consequence, there is a clear requirement to consider purchasing and supply chain issues with reference to CSR expectations: see Table 11.4.

Table 11.4 *CSR issues for buyers*

Issue	Considerations for buyers
Environmental responsibility	Environmental issues will evidence themselves in the manner in which goods are made, the energy used and the pollution caused. It may be necessary to visit manufacturing facilities and/or obtain documentary evidence that environmental standards are being met.
Community involvement	Limited purchasing involvement
Equal opportunities	Purchasing can ensure that equal opportunities is an issue included in and monitored in the Code of Conduct that suppliers/partners need to comply with.
Sustainability	This is already highly developed in certain supply chains (eg sustainable forests used to make paper and paper products). Where influence is possible it is often necessary to go to the start of the supply chain and influence at this tier is increasingly being achieved.
Diversity and supplier diversity	Diversity issues are high on the agenda of many UK companies who are seeking to establish a workforce that mirrors the society it serves. Supplier diversity is an issue currently highlighted in public sector procurement where smaller, ethnically representative suppliers are being encouraged to provide goods and services.
Corporate governance	Limited purchasing involvement
Human rights	The Code of Conduct should have robust statements relating to human rights issues (forced labour, freedom of association, child labour etc) and should be enforced rigorously.
Impact on society	The extraction or harvesting of certain commodities has historically displaced, contaminated or aided in dispersing communities. Purchasing and supply chain management needs to adopt the wider view when considering impact on society.
Ethics and ethical trading	Considered previously
Bio-diversity	Usually limited purchasing and supply chain involvement. However, protecting wildlife, endangered species and plants is increasingly important in maintaining an organisation's profile and offers positive opportunities to enhance the organisation's reputation.

3.21 CIPS give a number of hints on minimising the negative impact and maximising the positive impact that purchasing and supply chain management can bring to CSR.

- Link with the organisation's overall CSR policy and exert influence on its approach from the supply-side perspective.

- Ensure the CSR sourcing strategy delivers what the organisation as a whole is aiming for and that its commitments are entirely practicable within overall existing policies in more general terms, such as value for money or cost reduction.

- Identify which aspects of CSR are likely to be important to the organisation overall, and particularly within the supply chain.

- Get high-level corporate buy-in for the supply-side and communicate this to suppliers.

- Review products, services and suppliers for potential benefits or risks from CSR impact, and identify the likelihood and potential impact of risk/reward from each.

- Prioritise analysis and action on higher risk/reward areas and check the likely impact throughout the supply chain.

- Involve suppliers in the analysis. If there is a potentially excellent supplier who is poor on a particular aspect of CSR then assess whether it is worth working with them to improve this aspect of their business.

- Balance the CSR impact within the organisation's overall sourcing strategy.

- No two organisations have the same requirements and therefore a unique risk rank model will need to be developed that encompasses social, environmental and economic risks.

3.22 CSR in the supply chain can be formalised by codes of conduct passed through the tiering system. Owing to the fluid nature of supply chains these Codes of Conduct should be regularly reviewed in the light of ever changing situations. CSR is a feature of modern business and has a high impact on supply chain management. Purchasing professionals must embrace this facet of SCM and act proactively to develop their organisation's approach.

4 Environmental risk

Damage to the environment

4.1 The environment is defined in the Environmental Protection Act 1990 as 'consisting of all, or any, of the following media, namely the air, water and land'.

4.2 There is an increasing awareness in society of the damage our activities can do to the environment. The interaction between the activities of society and the environment is often difficult to quantify. However, a balance must be struck between environmental responsibility and the need to attain organisational success.

4.3 Kit Sadgrove in *The Complete Guide to Business Risk Management* gives eight ways to pollute.

1   Emissions to air

2   Discharges to water

3   Solid waste

4   Owning (or acquiring) environmentally damaged assets such as land

5   Producing or using toxic or hazardous materials

6   Consuming fossil fuels or energy derived from them (non-renewable energy)

7   Consuming scarce or non-renewable resources

8   Damage to nature such as building projects or deforestation

4.4 Sadgrove also highlights the 'seven penalties of environmental damage', which focus on the social and financial penalties of polluting behaviour: see Table 11.5.

Table 11.5 *Seven penalties of environmental damage*

Penalty	Comment
Costs of compliance	There are increasing regulatory strictures that have to be met across a wide range of environment issues ranging from establishing low-polluting factories to the recycling of used products. This is a global approach affecting developing and developed countries to different degrees but is highly influential in making companies take a wider view of their activities.
The costs of breaking the law	Compliance with environmental law is essential. The risks of reputational damage, as well as the cost of fines, help ensure that organisations view environmental risk seriously.
The polluting company is more vulnerable to changes in environmental legislation	Environmental laws and regulations will become more stringent. This presents a risk to purchasing in particular, as it is more difficult to estimate whole life costing. The cost of disposal can be calculated at the time of purchase, but regulations and costs will often be more rigorous at the time of disposal.
Polluters will increasingly find it difficult to get finance and insurance	Organisations with a poor environmental record, or those liable for environmental fines, will find it difficult to get finance and insurance, particularly at competitive rates. Stakeholders and pressure groups may cause unrest and share prices may fall as a result.
The polluting organisation will find it harder to attract and retain good staff	Sadgrove gives the results of a National Union of Students survey which found that three-quarters of students would not work for a company with a poor ethical and environmental reputation.
A company that damages the environment can be attacked for being anti-social and uncaring	Many companies have gained a bad image through the impact of the media, press reports and journalistic exposés. Environmental and related CSR issues must be viewed in a global perspective.
The polluting company can find itself left behind competitors, who adopt greener products and processes	An environmentally friendly approach can bring both reputational and competitive advantages. Organisations that adopt a proactive environmental approach can find themselves in advance of competitors and in a position to gain opportunities from this progressive position.

The precautionary principle

4.5 Recent years have seen a shift in thinking from a reactive or remedial approach to environmental issues to a more proactive approach directed at preventing or minimising negative environmental impact. The change in emphasis is reflected in the application of risk assessment that now focuses on assessment at the outset rather than after the event.

4.6 The *Rio Declaration* adopted by governments at the United Nations Conference on Environment and Development in 1992 defined the precautionary principle as follows.

'Where there are threats of serious or irreversible damage, lack of full scientific certainty shall not be used as a reason for postponing cost-effective measures to prevent environmental degradation.'

4.7   When forming risk assessment strategies the precautionary principle should be fully considered. Concern, rather than scientific evidence, should be applied.

4.8   The evaluation of risk requires a judgement about how significant the risk is to the receiving environment. In consequence it involves questions regarding risk acceptability. Assessment relating to environmental quality involves both scientific judgements and social judgements and it is important to consider both aspects when developing risk management approaches.

The social aspects of risk

4.9   Society as a whole is aware of the harm that its activities can do to the environment. Risk management has been highlighted in this area as environmental crises have shown that procedures and processes in place at the time were found wanting.

4.10   The *Guidelines for Environmental Risk Assessment and Management* published by the UK government department DEFRA (www.defra.gov.uk/environment/risk) states that decisions regarding social risks should take account of social issues for the following reasons.

•   General awareness of environmental risks has increased and this is often associated with heightened levels of concern.

•   Recent experience has shown how essential it is to have in place a framework that ensures transparency in decision-making and which forms a justifiable basis for policies on environmental protection.

•   Calls have been made for a greater degree of public involvement in decision-making processes for environmental protection.

•   There is increasing pressure on those who create and regulate risk to inform the public about the risks to which they and their environment are exposed.

The environmental audit

4.11   An environmental audit is an approach where an organisation collates all the information on its environmental impact. By carrying out an environmental audit an organisation can assess the risks caused by environmental impacts and also assess the risks against the wider criteria outlined above.

4.12   In practical terms many organisations have difficulty in gathering effective environmental data for analysis. This is simply because no business discipline of this type has existed before. This also creates an opportunity in that gathering information for the environmental audit requires a fresh and innovative approach that can often be in line with the thinking required to develop this business area.

4.13   An organisation should consider its approach to environmental issues at corporate level. Three categories of approach are identified.

•   Environmentally friendly, defined as conforming with best practice

•   Environmentally neutral, defined as doing what is adequate

•   Environmentally unfriendly, defined as doing nothing or the bare minimum to conform, or continuing with existing poor practice

ISO 14000

4.14   ISO 14000 and its associated standards provide a framework for the management of environmental matters. ISO environmental management standards help organisations by focusing on how to minimise the negative environmental effects of their processes and operations, how to comply with applicable laws, regulations, and other environmentally oriented requirements, and how to continually improve in these areas.

4.15   ISO 14000 is a series of standards and guideline reference documents, covering the following issues.

- Environmental Management Systems
- Environmental Auditing
- Eco Labelling
- Life Cycle Assessment
- Environmental Aspects in Product Standards
- Environmental Performance Evaluation

4.16   The material included in this family of specifications is very broad. The major parts of ISO 14000 are as follows.

- ISO 14001 is the requirements standard against which organisations are assessed. ISO 14001 is generic and flexible enough to apply to any organisation producing any product or service anywhere in the world.
- ISO 14004 is a guidance document that explains the 14001 requirements in more detail. These present a structured approach to setting environmental objectives and targets, and to establishing and monitoring operational controls.

4.17   ISO 14001 is an internationally accepted specification for an environmental management system. It specifies requirements for establishing an environmental policy, determining environmental aspects and impacts of products, activities and services, planning environmental objectives and measurable targets, implementation and operation of programs to meet objectives and targets, checking and corrective action, and management review.

4.18   At present many countries and regional groupings generate their own requirements for environmental issues, and these vary between the groupings. A single standard ensures that there are no conflicts between regional interpretations of good environmental practice.

4.19   The fact that companies may need environmental management certification to compete in the global marketplace could easily overshadow all ethical reasons for environmental management. ISO14001 requires an environmental policy to be in existence within the organisation, fully supported by senior management, and outlining the policies of the company, not only to the staff but also to the public.

4.20   The policy should clarify compliance with environmental legislation and stress a commitment to continuous improvement. Emphasis has been placed on policy as this provides the direction for the remainder of the management system.

4.21 Environmental risk management can be carried out using similar methodology to the risk management structures already discussed. ISO 14000 develops an 'aspects register' (similar to a risk register) in which identified risks and actions are recorded. Environmental auditing is carried out both internally and externally, when required.

Sustainable development

4.22 The aim of sustainable development is to achieve a better quality of life for everyone now and for generations to come. Sustainable development is concerned with achieving economic development in the form of higher living standards while protecting and enhancing the environment.

4.23 *Supply Management* (18 January 2007) discusses the sustainable issues facing the purchasing profession. 'In May 2005 Prime Minister Tony Blair set up a business-led group called the Sustainable Procurement Task Force (SPTF) to examine how the public sector's £150 billion budget for goods and services can be spent in a sustainable manner. The aim of the group was to show how to get value for money from the public purse throughout the lifetime of a product or service, from creation or purchase to disposal. At the same time, sustainable purchases should benefit the organisation that buys them, help society, boost the economy and support the natural environment'.

4.24 The challenge for the wider purchasing community is to take this perspective on board and integrate it into its procurement processes.

Chapter summary

- Buyers have numerous sources from which to identify potential suppliers: past experience, salespeople from suppliers, catalogues etc.

- Use of a supplier appraisal questionnaire is common in getting to know new suppliers. A key issue is the supplier's financial stability.

- To identify supply risk, a Cranfield workbook recommends a number of generic questions that can be asked.

- In international trading, additional barriers to communication arise from cultural and language differences.

- Litigation is not the only possible way to resolve a dispute in international trade. Buyers should consider alternatives, such as arbitration.

- Incoterms are standard business terms widely used in international trade to reduce the likelihood of misunderstanding.

- Payment is a particular issue in international trade, often resolved by the use of letters of credit.

- Ethical issues are becoming increasingly important to modern purchasers. This includes ethical personal behaviour, but also extends to ethical sourcing.

- The Ethical Trading Initiative lays down guidelines to help in formulating an ethical sourcing policy.

- The concept of CSR is that an organisation has responsibilities that extend more widely than its immediate stakeholders and embrace society as a whole.

- Organisations can cause damage to the environment. Modern thinking suggests that organisations have an obligation to avoid this.

- International standards (particularly the ISO 14000 series) lay down guidelines by which organisations can formulate an environmental policy.

Self-test questions

The numbers in brackets refer to the paragraphs where you can check your answers.

1   List sources of information from which buyers can identify potential new suppliers. (1.4ff)

2   List questions that might appear on a supplier appraisal questionnaire. (1.11)

3   What sources of information assist a buyer in assessing a supplier's financial stability? (1.18ff)

4   List questions that might be asked when assessing supply risk. (1.31)

5   List suggestions for overcoming the cultural barriers when dealing with overseas suppliers. (Table 11.2)

6   What are the advantages of arbitration over litigation? (2.19)

7   List and briefly describe the four main groups of incoterms. (2.27)

8   What is the system of payment by letter of credit trying to achieve for buyer and seller? (2.32)

9   List five requirements that CIPS place on their members in relation to ethical behaviour. (3.4)

10   What main areas are covered by the ETI base code? (3.11)

11   Define CSR. (3.17)

12   What eight ways of causing pollution are identified by Sadgrove? (4.3)

13   What are the seven penalties of environmental damage identified by Sadgrove? (4.4)

14   What is an environmental audit? (4.11)

CHAPTER 12

Finding Solutions for Risks (II)

Learning objectives and indicative content

3.1   Develop appropriate solutions to mitigate the inherent risk in the following supply chain issues.

- •   Project failure (eg capital procurement – investment appraisal)
- •   Implementation of new technologies
- •   Public sector procurement

3.4   Appraise specific key risks and exposures in purchasing and supply and identify appropriate mitigating actions.

- •   Project failure, project planning principles and corrective action
- •   Technology failure, impact on supply, use of back-up systems and disaster recovery
- •   Security, theft and damage
- •   Fraud, accounting and payment exposures, conflicts of interest, purchasing ethics and codes of conduct

Chapter headings

1   Investment appraisal

2   Project failure

3   Implementation of new technologies

4   Public sector procurement

5   Fraud and conflicts of interest

1   *Investment appraisal*

Principles of investment appraisal

1.1   When a business spends money to acquire assets it does so in order to generate revenue which will more than cover the money expended. In other words, businesses invest cash in productive assets in order to make profits. When the sums invested are large, detailed techniques of investment appraisal are worthwhile.

1.2   As an example, a company might be quoting for a large project to be carried out for a customer, possibly involving the acquisition of major assets, hiring of employees and other significant expenditure. The size of the sums involved makes it vitally important for the business to evaluate such investment projects rigorously, and a number of techniques have been evolved to help with this.

1.3 The nub of the question in investment decisions is the (usually) extended time period involved. In the case where a large capital asset is acquired heavy expenditure takes place up front, but benefits of quality and productivity are expected over years to come.

1.4 The starting point is to estimate the types and magnitude of the cash inflows and outflows that will arise if the investment goes ahead. The **timing** of cashflows is also important; in general, the negative cashflows in early years are reasonably certain, while positive cashflows expected later are inevitably more speculative. The longer the period before cashflows become positive, the less attractive the project will seem.

1.5 To evaluate these various factors businesses use a variety of investment appraisal techniques. We will look at three: the payback method; the accounting rate of return (ARR) method; and the use of discounted cashflow techniques to determine the net present value of a project.

The payback method

1.6 The great virtue of this method is its simplicity. The idea is to assess how long a project will take to 'pay back' the initial investment. An example will make this clear. Suppose that a company proposes to purchase a replacement machine for £200,000, payment to be made immediately. The new machine is much more productive than existing plant, and this will lead to financial benefits of £50,000 per annum for each of the five years that the machine is in use.

1.7 The pattern here is clear. In year 1, the initial negative cashflow of £200,000 is only partly compensated by operating savings of £50,000. This negative is gradually wiped out by operating savings in later years. By the end of year 4 the net cumulative cashflow is zero. We say that the project has paid back by the end of year 4. By the time the machine's useful life is finished the cumulative net cashflow has reached a positive figure of £50,000.

1.8 Managers favour the use of this method partly because of its simplicity, but partly also because of its relative safety compared with other methods. In the above example, we expect to recoup our investment after four years, which is not a long time in investment terms. Projects which appear very profitable, but which will not pay back until well into the future, are regarded with suspicion: after all, there must be considerable uncertainty whether the distant benefits will ever be realised.

1.9 The payback method has a valid place in preliminary screening of potential projects. For example, managers might adopt a rule of thumb that any project not expected to pay back within ten years should be rejected without further investigation. But it is an unsophisticated guide to investment decisions, mainly because it takes no account of cashflows that may arise after the payback period.

The accounting rate of return (ARR) method

1.10 This is another relatively simple method, easily understood by managers faced with investment decisions. The idea is simply to calculate the average rate of return earned by the money invested. This procedure is familiar to anyone who has ever compared rates of interest offered by building societies and banks on their savings accounts.

1.11 As the name suggests, the relevant rate of return is based on the accounting profits generated by the investment. Accounting profits are not identical with cashflows, but for simplicity we will ignore this distinction and illustrate the procedure using the cashflow figures already given above in relation to the purchase of a replacement machine.

1.12 The overall return over five years is £50,000, being savings of £250,000 compared with expenditure of £200,000. This means that average annual returns of £10,000 are expected on an investment of £200,000, a 5 per cent rate of return.

1.13 Strictly speaking, it is incorrect to use £200,000 as the investment figure in the ARR calculation. This is because the business is not investing this entire sum for the duration of the project. Indeed, the whole of the initial investment is recouped before the project ends. This means that the average amount invested over the lifetime of the project is far less than £200,000. These complications do not affect the general principles involved.

1.14 A number of criticisms can be made of the ARR approach.

- It takes no account of the project's life. A 20 per cent return may seem more attractive than a 15 per cent return, but a project offering 15 per cent for five years may be more attractive than one that offers 20 per cent for only two years.
- It takes no account of the timing of cashflows. Later cashflows are more speculative than earlier ones, but all are given equal weight in the ARR calculation.
- The measurement of accounting profits is subjective. (We avoided this problem above by using cashflows instead of accounting profits.)

Discounted cashflow (DCF)

1.15 The methods of investment appraisal described so far are relatively crude. Although they are in widespread use (particularly the payback method) they should really be regarded as providing only preliminary criteria for evaluation. If a large-scale capital project warrants detailed appraisal, the use of discounted cashflow (DCF) techniques is essential.

1.16 The reason for this is the crucial importance of timing in the generation of cashflows. To understand this you need to be familiar with the concept of the **time value of money**. This can be illustrated by considering the difference between a sum of £1,000 receivable today and the same sum receivable in one year's time. Which would you prefer?

1.17 Clearly there are several reasons why £1,000 right now is preferable. One reason is the element of risk. Perhaps circumstances will change over the next year, and the promised £1,000 will not materialise at the end of that period. Another reason is inflation. In most developed economies inflation erodes the value of money over time. The amount you can purchase with £1,000 today is greater than you will be able to purchase in one year's time. Finally, if the money is received today it can be put to work immediately. If it is invested it will amount to more than £1,000 by the end of the year.

1.18 This final point is easy to illustrate. Suppose your local bank is offering interest of 5 per cent per annum on savings accounts. If you receive £1,000 today and invest it, your account will be worth £1,050 after a year. In this sense it is fair to say that £1,000 today is worth £1,050 in one year's time. If you leave the cash on deposit for a further twelve months you will receive a further interest payment of £52.50 (£1,050 x 5% = £52.50). This boosts the value of the account to £1,102.50, so we can say that £1,102.50 receivable in two years is equivalent to £1,000 receivable today.

1.19 To put this the other way around, what is the value in today's terms of £1,000 receivable twelve months hence? This can be calculated by working out the amount you would need to deposit in the savings account in order for your balance to reach £1,000 in one year's time. The answer is £952.38, because this sum plus 5 per cent interest will amount to £1,000 in twelve months. We say that the present value of £1,000 receivable after a year at a discount rate of 5 per cent is £952.38.

1.20 These calculations illustrate the main principle of discounted cashflow. Cashflows arising in the future must be discounted to arrive at their present value, ie their value in today's terms. The exact rate of discount reflects the time value of money. This value may be different at different times, or even for different firms at the same time. It reflects the fact that a particular firm at a particular time may have a stronger or weaker preference for receiving money now rather than in the future. But whatever the circumstances, there is always some preference for receiving cash now.

1.21 So far we have illustrated the time value of money by reference to cash receivable. However, similar principles apply in reverse to cash payable. In this case firms prefer to pay money in one year's time rather than now. For example, a firm which is due to pay a bill of £1,000 in one year's time can pay £952.38 today into a building society account at 5 per cent interest. After a year there will be £1,000 in the account to pay the bill. From the firm's point of view the liability of £1,000 is equivalent to a liability of only £952.38 in today's terms.

1.22 These calculations are simplified in practice by the use of published tables. The present value of a future sum of money depends on two things: the discount rate, and how far in the future the money will be paid or received. Published tables are arranged in the form of a grid in which any combination of these two factors can be identified and a 'discount factor' read off. Table 12.1 is an illustrative extract from such a table.

Table 12.1 *Discount factors for DCF calculations*

			Rate of discount			
Year	5%	6%	7%	8%	9%	10%
0	1.000	1.000	1.000	1.000	1.000	1.000
1	0.952	0.943	0.935	0.926	0.917	0.909
2	0.907	0.890	0.873	0.857	0.842	0.826
3	0.864	0.840	0.816	0.794	0.772	0.751
4	0.823	0.792	0.763	0.735	0.708	0.683
5	0.784	0.747	0.713	0.681	0.650	0.621
6	0.746	0.705	0.666	0.630	0.596	0.564

1.23 The discount factor in each case shows the present value of £1 receivable or payable after the stated number of years at the stated rate of discount. For example, with a discount rate of 5 per cent, a sum of £1 receivable in two years time has a present value of £0.907 or 90.7p. Using this information it is easy to calculate that £1,000 receivable in two years has a present value of £907.

1.24 Given that careful appraisal is needed, DCF offers significant advantages over other methods.

- Unlike the payback method, DCF takes account of all cashflows over the life of the project, not just those in the early years.

- Unlike the ARR method, DCF concentrates on the most relevant factor: actual cashflows rather than accounting profit or loss.

- DCF is the only method to take account of the crucial factor of the time value of money.

1.25 Despite this it is sensible to recognise the limitations of DCF techniques. The apparent precision of the calculations should not mask the subjective assumptions on which they are based. The flows estimated to arise in the future are necessarily uncertain in amount, and this uncertainty increases as the time horizon becomes more distant. Moreover, we have entirely ignored the very great practical difficulties of determining an appropriate discount rate in respect of a particular firm or a particular investment.

Risk analysis

1.26 In considering investment appraisal techniques we have made the assumption that predictions can be made about future outcomes. For example, we have considered the purchase of a replacement machine which we claim will give rise to certain cashflows over a future period of five years.

1.27 In reality, of course, there is no way we can be certain that such cashflows will materialise. In other words, there is risk attached to our forecasts. A problem that managers must address is how to analyse the amount of risk involved. This obviously has an impact on the attractiveness or otherwise of any project we are considering.

1.28 One way of dealing with risk is simply to adopt very prudent criteria in deciding whether to make an investment. For example, if we think the likely positive cashflow in Year 3 is £120,000, we could scale this estimate down by, say, a factor of one third, to £80,000. If the project continues to look attractive on these pessimistic forecasts we can invest in it with some confidence: we have left ourselves a good margin for error.

1.29 A similar technique would be to impose an overriding criterion for acceptance of a project, eg a maximum payback period. For example, we might adopt a rule of never investing in a project that will take more than three years to pay back. Using this criterion we would reject even very attractive projects unless their positive cashflows were expected to arise in the first three years. Of course, this means we may lose out on high payouts further down the line, but we minimise the risk of expensive disasters.

1.30 Another possible technique would be to calculate not just one net present value, but a range of NPVs based on different discount rates and different estimates of future cashflows. For example, instead of forecasting that the positive cashflow in Year 3 will be £120,000 we might forecast that (with a high degree of likelihood) the amount would lie between £90,000 and £140,000. We could then compute the consequences at these extreme values and estimate how our decision would be affected in each case.

1.31 More sophisticated than all of these approaches would be the use of **sensitivity analysis**. This is defined as 'a modelling and risk assessment procedure in which changes are made to significant variables in order to determine the effect of these changes on the planned outcome'. This is essentially an extension of the technique described in the paragraph above.

1.32 As an example of sensitivity analysis, we could focus on one factor influencing our estimates of future cashflows. For example, we might consider the likely unit production cost of a new product that we intend to produce on a machine we contemplate purchasing. Our initial estimate of the unit production cost might suggest that the new machine is well worth buying, because it enables us to produce a product that can be sold profitably.

1.33 Use of sensitivity analysis would allow us to probe more deeply. By setting up the formulae on a spreadsheet we could estimate the degree of 'tolerance' in our forecasts. For example, in a particular case it might turn out that the production cost is absolutely critical: even a small mistake in our estimate would make a big impact on the decision to invest. In such a case, we would revisit our estimate and look at it very carefully.

1.34 In another case, it might turn out that our decision is barely affected by the production cost. Even if our estimate understates the true production cost by 20 per cent the machine is still worth buying. In this case we would conclude that we are not much at risk from a mistake in forecasting this particular variable, and we should therefore concentrate our attention on other factors involved in the forecast (eg the volume of sales we might achieve).

1.35 In practice, all of these techniques have a strongly mathematical flavour and use of a computer would be routine nowadays. In the exam you are unlikely to be confronted with numerical work, but you should be aware of the principles involved.

2 Project failure

Introduction

2.1 There is duplication in the syllabus at this point, and indeed throughout syllabus area 3.1. Project risks are mentioned in both syllabus area 1.5 (see earlier coverage in Chapter 4 of this text) and again here in syllabus area 3.1. In this section we will concentrate on the risks involved in capital procurement, which leads on from the previous section on investment appraisal.

Capital procurement

2.2 Two main characteristics distinguish capital goods. The first is the **length of their lifecycle**. Many goods are purchased for immediate use in a manufacturing process or for onward sale; these are not capital goods. A capital item is one which the purchasing organisation will be using for a number of accounting periods. The second characteristic is the cost of such goods – items of small value are not regarded as capital goods even if their expected useful life is relatively long.

2.3 Typical examples of capital goods include buildings, manufacturing plant, computer hardware and software systems. All of these have a reasonably long lifecycle (possibly very long in the case of buildings), and are expensive. They may be items which are peculiar to one industry, or even one firm, or alternatively they may be of a type that many firms purchase.

2.4   Distinguishing features of this type of purchase have often been discussed in the purchasing literature. They include the following main points.

- The monetary value of the purchase is high, suggesting a need for specialised techniques of evaluation and control. This also raises questions relating to the financing of the purchase: outright purchase, leasing or some other means?

- The purchase of a capital item tends to be non-recurring. There is unlikely to have been a similar purchase in the recent past and specific experience is therefore lacking.

- The benefits to be obtained from the purchase are often somewhat intangible and difficult to evaluate. For example, a machine may be replaced by a superior model in order to secure quality improvements.

- Buying a capital asset usually means buying a service too – including installation, training of operators and after-sales maintenance. The purchase of services introduces additional difficulties.

- Negotiations are usually more extended and complex than in other acquisitions.

- Specifications are usually more difficult to draft because of the technical complexity of the item to be purchased.

- A team approach is usually needed in which the contributions of other departments must be effectively coordinated and managed.

2.5   All of these features give rise to risk and the project literature is full of examples of projects that have failed completely or have drastically overrun in terms of timescale, budget or both. Familiar examples in the UK are the construction of the Scottish Parliament building and the new Wembley stadium.

The buyer's role in the purchase of capital assets

2.6   There are many departments that deserve a voice in decisions about capital assets: purchasing, user departments, top management, finance staff and possibly others. To coordinate the various inputs so as to arrive at the best possible decisions requires careful management, usually under the leadership of purchasing staff. In many cases, it will be appropriate to adopt a formal team approach to the purchase decision.

2.7   What should be the contribution of purchasing staff in the work of such a team? This is a topic that has been very extensively discussed in the purchasing literature. Table 12.2 summarises the main tasks that are usually identified as the province of the purchasing function.

2.8   A further important aspect, though one which is seldom performed by purchasing staff, is formal investment appraisal. This was discussed in Section 1 of this chapter.

2.9   The concept of teamwork should not be taken to imply that all staff can take a hand in all aspects of the work. In particular, in dealings with potential suppliers it is vitally important that all communications move through purchasing staff. Otherwise there is a danger that non-purchasing staff will effectively give the supplier the authority to proceed before all necessary matters have been considered. This situation has been a frequent source of examination questions in the past.

Table 12.2 *The role of purchasing in the acquisition of capital assets*

1.	Performing research to identify potential vendors and to obtain relevant data about them
2.	Consulting with referees – ie existing users of products manufactured by the potential suppliers
3.	Requesting quotations and evaluating bids, including consideration of price, lead time, operating characteristics, expected useful life, performance criteria, operating costs, recommended spares and maintenance schedules, warranty terms, payment terms and so on
4.	Organising and managing discussions and negotiations with suppliers, finalising agreed terms and conditions
5.	Awarding contract and placing order
6.	Checking supplier's compliance with agreed terms, eg in submission of drawings, meeting deadlines etc
7.	Monitoring installation, and performance post installation

Selecting a supplier

2.10 The eventual choice of a supplier will depend partly on familiar purchasing criteria, but partly too on specific aspects peculiar to capital assets. Some of the main criteria are described below. Notice that a key theme is the need to reduce risk.

2.11 An obvious starting point is the previous experience that the supplier has in producing the type of asset required. Even if the exact asset is a special one-off design specified by the purchaser, the supplier should be able to point to experience with similar assets. It is quite reasonable to ask for details of other satisfied customers to act as referees.

2.12 The organisation and management of the potential supplier is also important. What is his approach to innovation? What is his approach to quality (does he have ISO 9000 accreditation)? What design and manufacturing capacity is available?

2.13 Once invited to submit a quotation, the potential suppliers are entitled to receive a detailed description of what is required. In return, they should propose solutions which match the buyer's requirements, and perhaps go beyond them to suggest alternatives that might be more efficient and/or cost-effective.

Reducing the risks

2.14 We have already mentioned various procedures and disciplines that form part of good purchasing practice and contribute to risk reduction (eg careful supplier selection). Here are some other steps that buyers can take to minimise the risk of capital purchases.

- Use of appropriate project management software, incorporating techniques such as critical path analysis
- Constant monitoring of project progress against predetermined 'milestones'
- Careful advance planning of the project scope and specifications so as to avoid constant changes as the work progresses (a frequent cause of project failure and overruns)
- Involvement of professional purchasing input from the earliest stages
- Careful planning in the procurement of funds

2.15 This final point – the **procurement of funds** – deserves further consideration. In some respects procuring funds involves the same kind of purchasing disciplines as procuring materials and supplies.

- We aim to secure the lowest cost, for example the lowest interest rate if the money is being borrowed.
- We aim for 'just in time' procurement. If the funds are not available on time, the project may be jeopardised. If the funds are received too soon (a kind of 'overstocking') they are costing us interest at a time when we cannot put them to use.
- We observe normal CSR objectives. For example, if the funds originate in overseas tax havens, can we be sure they do not originate in money laundering?

2.16 It is also important to consider CSR when the funds are invested. For example, if the investment is in an overseas project we must be alert to risks of fraud, corruption and diversion of funds.

2.17 Risk management is vital in project work because of the serious implications if things go wrong.

- Large sums of money are at stake – the financial damage could be disastrous if the project fails or overruns.
- Reputation is also at stake – many project failures have been extremely public, and have brought serious embarrassment to the parties concerned. The examples already quoted of the Scottish Parliament building and the new Wembley stadium illustrate this clearly.
- There may be public interest at stake – if the project fails to satisfy public expectations there may be consequences in terms of both reputation and CSR.

3 Implementation of new technologies

Introduction

3.1 Once again there is an issue of duplication in this area. Syllabus area 1.8 is entirely devoted to risks associated with technology, and this area was covered in Chapter 2. In this section we focus on issues associated with new technology implementation, but you should refer back to Chapter 2 for discussion of ongoing technological risks.

Project management

3.2 Modern organisations increasingly rely on technology to achieve gains in efficiency and economy. Technology can also be an important factor in achieving competitive advantage, eg by the implementation of sophisticated marketing information systems. However, the extent to which IT is crucial in operating modern businesses naturally brings risk: what happens if IT fails?

3.3 This has been a particular concern in organisations where new systems have been introduced. A number of high-profile examples illustrate the dangerous level of exposure.

3.4   One case frequently cited in the project management literature is that of the London Ambulance Service, which in the early 1990s attempted to introduce new automated systems. The attempt suffered numerous failures and setbacks, and is now regarded as a textbook example of how not to manage an IT project. Among the many failings cited were the selection of a software development company lacking sufficient resources and expertise for the job, and the absence of professional purchasing involvement.

3.5   Another example in recent years was the botched implementation of the tax credits system operated in the UK by the Inland Revenue (nowadays H M Revenue and Customs). The Inland Revenue was the UK authority responsible for assessing and collecting direct taxes. Under new legislation they were also given responsibility for issuing tax credits (ie making payments to taxpayers). The computerised system introduced for this purpose was unable to cope, and the result was literally billions of pounds in excess payments.

3.6   These examples are enough to suggest that implementation of new technologies should be treated as a project in its own right, with all of the traditional project disciplines already discussed above and in Chapter 4. This applies whether the project is to introduce a new system in one particular area, or to integrate already existing systems (eg when introducing **enterprise resource planning** or ERP).

3.7   Good project management in this area is assisted by published standards such as ISO 17799 (see earlier discussion in Chapter 2).

Planning the implementation

3.8   The guidance published by CIPS for this module suggests that there are four key elements in a successful implementation of new technology.

- Adoption of a lifecycle perspective. This means that the project manager guides the project through a series of predetermined stages.
- Taking a participative approach. This means that individuals affected by the new system are encouraged to participate in the implementation, so that they can feel motivated and take ownership of the changes.
- Accepting that changes will emerge as the project develops. This does not mean that we just ignore the original plans; it does mean that we should accept new behaviours or innovative approaches if they are valuable.
- Taking account of the politics. This means that the project plan must recognise that personal ambition may be as much a driving force in the implementation as a desire for beneficial change.

3.9   The CIPS guidance also suggests a checklist of issues to be considered ahead of implementation.

- Objectives – was there a good set of reasons for change, and a business case?
- Personnel – do we have staff members and an organisational culture that will respond well to change?
- Relationships – can we cope with the changes in relationships that will arise when the new system is implemented?
- Technology – do we have sufficient expertise in-house, or sufficient knowledge to source from outside?
- Finance – has the project been appraised in financial terms?
- Power – will the new system shift power from one department or individual to another?

4   Public sector procurement

Introduction

4.1   We have already discussed the particular factors relating to public sector procurement from the perspective of stakeholders: refer back to Chapter 5 to refresh your memory. In this chapter we look at some more general features of public sector procurement to highlight areas in which risk management practice differs from the private sector.

4.2   The principal differences arise from the fact that funding for public services comes, in the main, from taxpayers' money. All taxpayers have an interest in how such money is spent. In general, this fosters a lower risk appetite in the public sector: whereas private shareholders may accept risk in return for the chance of reward, in general taxpayers are not expecting public authorities to invest money speculatively.

4.3   By the same token, managers in the public sector are less ready to risk taxpayers' money because of the level of accountability they undergo. Spending decisions in the public sector are more tightly constrained by regulations, and are more subject to public scrutiny.

4.4   We now begin to consider how these differences manifest themselves in public sector procurement.

Differences compared with the private sector

4.5   The main influence on strategic decisions in a private sector firm is the achievement of commercial objectives. In most cases, this can be simplified further: private sector firms are profit-maximisers, and managerial decisions are assessed on the extent to which they contribute to organisational profit.

4.6   Related to this is the very strong influence of competition. In nearly all cases, a private sector firm will be one of several, or many, firms offering goods or services of a particular type. Consumers are free to choose between the offerings of different firms, and their choices of course have a dramatic impact on the revenue and profits earned by the firms concerned. Securing competitive advantage is a large step towards realising the objective of profit maximisation.

4.7   The 'constituency' served by a private sector firm is limited in number – shareholders, customers, employees, all referred to collectively as 'stakeholders' in the modern phrase. This helps the firm to be focused in its strategy: it is usually clear which outcomes will benefit the stakeholders. Moreover, all members of the constituency are there by choice. They could have invested their money elsewhere, or in the case of employees they could have offered their labour and talents elsewhere.

4.8   In these respects, and others, public sector organisations differ from their counterparts in the private sector. The differences are well analysed by Gary J Zenz in *Purchasing and the Management of Materials*. His analysis forms a starting point for Table 12.3.

4.9   The implication so far appears to be that purchasing in the private and public sectors are two completely different disciplines. However, this is far from the truth and the differences cited above should not mask many essential similarities between the work of the public sector buyer and his private sector counterpart.

Table 12.3 *Differences between public and private sector purchasing*

Area of difference	Private sector	Public sector
Objectives	Usually, to increase profit	Usually, to achieve defined service levels
Ownership and control	Buyers are responsible to directors, who in turn are responsible to shareholders, the owners of the organisation	Buyers are responsible ultimately to the general public, the 'owners' of the organisation
Legal and regulatory environment	Activities are regulated by company law, employment law, product liability law etc	Most of this applies equally to public sector, but additional regulations are present too (eg compulsory competitive tendering)
Competition	There is usually strong competition between many different firms	There is usually no competition
Publicity	Confidentiality applies in dealings between suppliers and buyers	Confidentiality is limited because of public interest in disclosure
Budgetary limits	Investment is constrained only by availability of attractive opportunities; funding can be found if prospects are good	Investment is constrained by externally imposed spending limits
Sources of finance	Typically this comes from shareholders and lenders	Ultimately the source of public funding is the taxpayer
Information exchange	Private sector buyers do not exchange information with other firms, because of confidentiality and competition	Public sector buyers are willing to exchange notes
Defined procedures	Private sector buyers can cut red tape when speed of action is necessary	Public sector buyers are often constrained to follow established procedures

4.10 One reason for this is that differences in objectives and organisational constraints may not necessarily lead to differences in procedure. For example, public sector buyers may not be seeking to maximise profit, but their concern to achieve value for money is stimulated by other influences, equally strong; in particular, the public sector buyer must achieve a defined level of service within a defined budget. He is just as concerned as his private sector counterpart to minimise the risk of failing in his objectives.

4.11 Similarly, the private sector buyer faced with a profit objective will identify customer satisfaction as a key criterion in meeting the objective. But equally, the public sector buyer will work in an environment where providing a quality service so as to delight 'customers' is an essential part of the organisational ethos.

4.12 Differences between public sector and private sector buying also arise from the question of **accountability**. As we have noted already, the stakeholders in a public service are more diverse than those of a private firm. Buyers in the public sector may be required to account for their actions to a wide constituency, most of whose members are entirely unknown quantities as far as managers in the public service are concerned. One effect of this is an insistence on detailed procedures and record keeping: it may be difficult later to justify a course of action which breaches defined procedures or which is poorly documented. We can say that **compliance risk** – the risk of failing to observe regulations – is higher in the public sector.

4.13 **Budgetary control** is another area where differences surface. The demand for funds in a private sector firm is limited, in that only some projects are commercially attractive. Other projects are not regarded as viable because, for example, they do not meet criteria for return on capital. In the public sector, by contrast, the demand for funds is limitless: no taxpayer ever complains that too much of a service is provided.

Financing the public sector

4.14 To provide public sector services we naturally require finance. Where does this come from?

4.15 All sources of public sector income derive ultimately from the taxpayer. Funds are collected in various different forms: direct taxes (ie taxes on income, such as the corporation tax paid by companies and the income tax paid by individuals); indirect taxes (ie taxes on expenditure, such as value added tax and excise duties); local taxes (such as council tax and business rates).

4.16 In the UK, most of this income is collected by central government (though some of it, such as council tax, is collected by local authorities). It is the task of government, and specifically the Treasury department, to then distribute the income for use on the purposes prioritised by government policy.

4.17 Where funds are collected locally (eg council tax) they are also spent locally on such services as law and order, waste disposal etc.

The impact of regulation on public sector procurement

4.18 Public sector regulators are intended to ensure compliance with defined standards. For example, a buyer in the public sector must ensure that the goods he purchases match up to all public standards and specifications (as well as, obviously, matching up to the specification generated by the buyer himself). This includes compliance with relevant health and safety standards, not just in the products purchased, but in the entire purchase process (eg compliance with manual handling regulations in the delivery and handling of the goods).

4.19 The public sector buyer must also comply with relevant environmental standards.

4.20 The public sector buyer is subject to a high level of accountability. He must ensure that appropriate processes have been followed to acquire best value for the taxpayers' money he is responsible for, and must equally ensure that a full 'audit trail' exists so that his actions and decisions can be vetted.

4.21 The public sector buyer must ensure that appropriate service levels are achieved in the provision of services to members of the public.

The effects of European procurement directives

4.22 EU procurement directives are an important influence on the activities of buyers in the public sector. Their principal objective is to promote free, open and non-discriminatory competition within the EU.

4.23 Once a buyer has specified the product or service he requires, and has decided to use the tendering method, he must ensure that he complies with EU directives. These do not apply to private sector buying, but do cover purchases by public authorities unless their value is below a certain (low) threshold.

4.24 Subject to certain exceptions, the directives require public bodies to use open tendering procedures. They must advertise the invitation to tender according to defined rules designed to secure maximum publicity.

4.25 In general, buyers are obliged to award the contract on the basis of the lowest quoted price, or on the basis of the economically most advantageous tender. If they choose the latter alternative, they must make the fact known to candidates, and must explain by what criteria they mean to assess 'economic advantage'. The purchaser is allowed to exclude firms if they fail to meet defined criteria relating to general suitability, financial and economic standing and technical competence.

4.26 The results of the tendering procedure must be notified to the Office of Official Publications of the European Communities, and will then be made public.

4.27 This regime of compulsory open tendering has certain disadvantages. All vendors are aware that a large number of bids are likely to be made, and this may deter some suitable applicants. Moreover, since very little prequalification of vendors is allowed under the directives, it is likely also that some will take risks in attempting to undercut potential rivals. The result may be a contract awarded at a price that gives no incentive to high quality performance. Finally, there is of course a great administrative burden on the purchaser who is faced with a large number of tenders to evaluate.

Public and private funding initiatives

4.28 Increasingly, UK governments (in common with many others across the world) have tried to involve private investors in works that traditionally would have been carried out by means of public funding. This kind of collaborative arrangement is referred to by the general term **public private partnership** (PPP).

4.29 The usual reason for involving the private sector in public works, apart from risk reduction, is to gain the benefit of increased efficiency, management skills and financial acumen – or so the government typically states! Critics of such schemes, most notably the trade unions, believe that a more important reason is a short-term financing advantage, which in the long term may lead to vital public assets being owned by private sector companies.

4.30 One way in which a PPP may be structured is by means of the **private finance initiative** (PFI). This was a creation of the Conservative government in the early 1990s, but has been carried forward with enthusiasm by the current Labour government. The basic idea of a PFI scheme is that the private partner pays for the construction cost (of a road, a hospital, a prison or whatever), and then rents the finished product back to the public sector. Ownership of the asset remains with the contractor. This kind of scheme is sometimes referred to as a DBFO scheme – the contractor **d**esigns, **b**uilds, **f**inances and **o**perates the project.

4.31 From the government's point of view, this reduces the need for unpopular measures (such as raising taxes). The contractor's payback comes in the form of the rental payments, and also from retaining any cash left over from the design and construction process.

4.32 Critics of PPP/PFI are inclined to exaggerate the extent of the problem: after all, it remains true that the majority of public projects are financed by government. Even so, the number of such projects is significant. Many new prisons and hospitals have been financed in this way, and major road schemes such as the Thames crossing and the Birmingham relief road are being financed through PFI.

4.33 The drawbacks of PPP/PFI are firstly, that in the long term taxpayers will pay more for the projects than if they were wholly financed by the government, and secondly, that some PFI projects appear to have been below acceptable standards. This, it is argued by some, is because the private sector contractors are motivated to maximise profits by cutting corners on quality and safety issues.

5 Fraud and conflicts of interest

The nature of fraud and corruption

5.1 Fraud is defined (*Chambers Concise Dictionary*) as 'an act of deliberate deception, with the intention of gaining some benefit'. In a commercial context, the fraudster may be an employee or someone external to the organisation, such as a supplier. He acts deliberately to deceive and typically will attempt to conceal his actions. Needless to say, organisations can lose significant amounts of money if fraud is unchecked, and in some cases may risk reputational damage as well.

5.2 As examples, an employee may authorise salary payments to fictional members of staff, pocketing the proceeds for himself. Or a supplier may attempt to win business by lying about his client list or his financial resources in order to present a more favourable impression.

5.3 The same dictionary defines corruption as the condition of being corrupt, and defines corrupt as 'morally evil; involving bribery; dishonest'. For a buyer, the middle term ('involving bribery') is perhaps the most immediate threat. Buyers handle large amounts of money on behalf of their organisations and historically have been regarded as a target for bribery. A supplier looking to land a large and profitable contract may regard it as money well spent if he can induce a buyer to favour his tender over anyone else's.

5.4 A problem that faces organisations doing business overseas is cultural differences compared with the UK. For example, in some countries (typically, developing nations) the use of inducements in order to win business is regarded as normal. A UK company trying to win business in such a culture faces a dilemma: risk failing to win the business or risk compromising ethical standards.

The impact on purchasing staff

5.5 For purchasing staff, the issue of bribery is a long-term source of problems. It arises in a small way every Christmas: the traditional business courtesy whereby suppliers offer gifts to their customers is now frowned upon by many buying organisations. Every year the issue surfaces for debate in the pages of *Supply Management* magazine. A wide range of opinions is expressed: some hold that small-scale Christmas presents offer no danger to anyone, while others believe that any kind of gift, however small, may rank as an inducement to award business for the wrong reasons.

5.6 For buyers, the problem is a potential **conflict of interest**. A buyer is employed in order to further his organisation's commercial objectives. To do this he must deal with suppliers on a basis of strict impartiality, and must award contracts only for the best possible commercial reasons.

5.7 However, the buyer is also an individual with his own personal interests. He may be very tempted by the offer of a free holiday or similar inducement. The danger is that his own private interests may take precedence over his employer's interests when it comes to selecting suppliers.

Detecting and preventing fraud and corruption

5.8 There are many signs that can indicate fraud, corruption or conflicts of interest. Here are some of the things managers should look out for.

- Purchasing staff who decline to delegate and don't take holidays – this may indicate that they fear discovery by a subordinate or someone covering during holiday leave.

- Suppliers who insist on payment in cash – they may have good reasons for not wanting any lasting record of the payment.

- Unusual patterns in dealing with tenders – for example, if a particular supplier is consistently successful in winning tenders he may be colluding with a buyer.

- Evidence of close relationships between a buyer and a supplier – for example, if the supplier provides generous presents to the buyer.

5.9 Of course, it is even better if corruption can be prevented before it happens. There are many measures a buying organisation can take to help with this.

5.10 To begin with, ethical values should be a key criterion in recruitment and selection of staff to work in the purchasing function. Previous record will be a useful guide, and it should be standard practice to take out references in relation to new recruits. This should be reinforced during staff training, which should emphasise ethical principles as strongly as technical issues.

5.11 This kind of training will be supported by a strong CSR stance devolved downwards from the most senior levels of the organisation. It is the responsibility of top management to ensure the highest standards of corporate governance throughout the firm.

5.12 Unduly close relationships between buyers and suppliers can be checked by a systematic process of rotating buyer responsibilities. In this way, no buyer has time to become a 'crony' of a particular supplier. This can be reinforced by communicating directly with suppliers, emphasising the buying organisation's stance on issues of fraud and corruption and outlining the sanctions that will operate in case of abuse.

5.13 Another control is to ensure division of responsibilities. The buyer who awards a contract and authorises purchase of goods and services should not also be the person responsible for authorising payment. A separate individual will authorise payment only once he is satisfied that value has been received. This is an important control over collusion between buyer and supplier.

5.14 Where this division of duties is not possible – eg for transactions using purchasing cards, where the buyer makes payment at the same time as the purchase – managers must carefully review reports provided by the card issuer. The aim is to detect any suspicious patterns of spending.

Accounting and payment exposures

5.15 A common risk faced by all organisations is that of financial fraud. There are many ways in which employees may divert organisational funds for their own purposes. Sometimes they may act on their own; sometimes the collude with a customer or supplier.

5.16 As Sadgrove points out (*The Complete Guide to Business Risk Management*), there are a number of preconditions to fraud.

- The fraudster must have a motive – a reason why he needs money, or feels he is entitled to defraud the organisation.

- There must be assets worth stealing – money is only the most obvious possibility. A fraudster may equally be tempted by tools, computer equipment etc.

- There must be opportunity – the fraudster must be able to steal the assets and (unless the theft is of money) and must be able to sell them on.

- Lack of control – this is where management may contribute to the fraud. If managers ensure that a good system of internal controls is in place, fraud is much less likely.

5.17 There are many different ways of committing fraud. Online fraud – ordering goods with stolen or fake credit cards – is increasingly a cost to UK businesses. Employees have been known to set up fake companies which then proceed to invoice the organisation for 'services' rendered. The employee ensures that he is the person with responsibility for approving invoices for that kind of service.

5.18 To avoid all this, organisations should begin by introducing a corporate fraud policy. The policy should make it plain that fraud is a form of theft. It should clarify what actions the organisation regards as fraud (eg 'borrowing' office stationery to take home). It should define methods for controlling and investigating fraud. And it should define who has responsibilities for the various control systems that should be in place.

5.19 Sadgrove suggests a number of specific steps for minimising this kind of fraud.

- Improve the recruitment process to ensure the honesty of staff recruited.
- Reduce the fraudster's motive.
- Reduce the number of assets worth stealing, or at least ensure that assets worth stealing are as inaccessible as possible consistent with operational efficiency.
- Minimise the opportunities to steal.
- Increase the level of supervision.
- Improve financial controls and management supervision.
- Improve detection.
- Improve record-keeping.

Chapter summary

- The large sums of money involved in capital projects, and the fact that cashflows will take place over an extended period, make it essential to adopt formal techniques of investment appraisal.

- Possible methods of investment appraisal include the payback method, the accounting rate of return method, and discounted cashflow.

- Investment appraisals are risky, because future cashflows cannot be guaranteed. Risk can be dealt with by, for example, adopting prudent assessment criteria; adopting an overriding maximum payback period; or calculating a range of outcomes based on different assumptions. Sensitivity analysis is a better developed form of this last technique.

- Buyers have an important role to play in capital purchases, in particular the management of a cross-functional team.

- Risk management is vital in capital projects because of the large sums involved, and also the possible reputational damage that may arise.

- IT projects have frequently failed to deliver what was required. For this reason, a careful, staged approach to implementation is essential.

- There are many differences between the public and private sectors. For example, the profit maximising objective does not usually apply in the public sector, and there is greater need for accountability in the public sector.

- EU procurement directives are a constraint on public sector buyers. Usually, such buyers are obliged to use a competitive tendering procedure.

- A modern trend in the financing of public projects is the involvement of private sector partners.

- Purchasing staff are obvious targets for attempted fraud and bribery. Professional codes of practice insist that purchasing staff should act entirely in the interests of the organisation employing them.

Self-test questions

The numbers in brackets refer to the paragraphs where you can check your answers.

1   Explain how the payback method works. (1.6ff)

2   Explain how the ARR method works. (1.10ff)

3   What is meant by the time value of money? (1.16)

4   Explain how sensitivity analysis works in capital investment appraisal. (1.31ff)

5   List distinguishing features of capital purchases. (2.4)

6   List the tasks a purchaser might have to carry out in dealing with a capital purchase. (Table 12.2)

7   List the considerations relevant in the procurement of funds for a capital purchase. (2.15)

8   List the four key elements in a successful implementation of new technology. (3.8)

9   List areas of difference between public sector and private sector purchasing. (Table 12.3)

10   Explain the impact of the EU procurement directives on the public sector buyer. (4.22ff)

11   What is meant by a public private partnership? (4.28)

12   Define 'fraud'. (5.1)

13   List signs that may indicate fraud or corruption in a purchasing department. (5.8)

CHAPTER 13

Reducing Risk through Negotiation

Learning objectives and indicative content

3.4   Analyse specific key risks and exposures in purchasing and supply and identify appropriate mitigating actions

- Appropriate negotiation strategies to reduce future contract risk and supply chain vulnerability to enhance long-term business value
- Key steps in negotiation planning for success
- Strategic approach and negotiation techniques
- Best practice methodology
- Tactics and standpoints
- Behaviour of successful negotiators
- Dispute resolution alternatives

Chapter headings

1   Planning for successful negotiations

2   Strategies for negotiation

3   Tactics and standpoints

4   Behaviours of successful negotiators

5   Dispute resolution alternatives

Introduction

Many supply chain relationships are established and maintained by a process of negotiation between buyers and suppliers. Effective negotiators can help to reduce the risks inherent in supply agreements.

1   Planning for successful negotiations

Segmentation tools revisited

1.1   Supply agreements typically arise either through competitive bidding or through negotiation with individual suppliers. The choice between the two is not a straightforward one, and is not one that can be taken once and for all and thereafter applied to every purchasing transaction. On the contrary, the variety of purchasing transactions suggests that different approaches will be necessary in different cases. This idea is formalised in the purchasing product portfolio devised by P Kraljic (which we looked at in an earlier chapter). Other segmentation tools may equally be illuminating.

1.2   The use of tools such as Kraljic's matrix implies that we are able to evaluate the supply risk relating to the different items we purchase. CIPS have outlined a detailed risk management process, consisting of five stages.

- Identify sources of potential risk
- For each possible risk event, determine its likelihood and its impact
- Assess the overall impact of all risk factors
- Investigate risk reduction
- Plan, control and reduce risk

1.3   **Sources of risk** may be predictable or unpredictable. For example, it should be possible to plan for staff shortages during peak holiday time because this is predictable. On the other hand, if two or three key personnel leave the organisation unexpectedly to pursue other opportunities we may be caught unawares.

1.4   The **likelihood and impact** of each possible risk should be determined. If a risk is judged to be of low likelihood, and low impact even if it occurs, then there is not much point in worrying about it. But where the risk is very likely, or could have a damaging impact even if it is unlikely to happen, it will be appropriate to take action in advance.

1.5   The **overall impact** of several risk factors may be greater than their individual impacts. To cater for this, the buyer should tabulate all possible risks and attach a weighting factor to each, based on their likelihood and potential impact. By adding up all the weightings the buyer can assess the overall risk.

1.6   To **investigate risk reduction** the buyer should consider the various possible things that could go wrong with a purchase and think of ways to reduce the risks. One possibility is to take direct action aimed at reducing the risk. Another is to transfer the risk to someone else by means of an appropriate term in the purchase contract. A final possibility is to take out appropriate insurance.

1.7   To **plan, control and reduce** risk is a task that should be assigned specifically to persons with appropriate responsibility. The task is carried out by careful monitoring of plans to ensure that actual outcomes are shaping up as they should. Use of technology is important in this area (eg in collating progress reports from suppliers, flagging when designated action is due to be taken etc).

Planning for a negotiation

1.8   In a case where negotiation is the preferred option, the above considerations should be taken into account at the planning stage. 'Negotiation is applicable where there is disagreement or potential disagreement between suppliers and buyers. A good buyer will be sensitive to potential areas of conflict and will seek to resolve these before they arise by ensuring that the terms and conditions applicable to the purchase provide for such contingencies.' (Lysons and Farrington, *Purchasing and Supply Chain Management*)

1.9   The terms subject to negotiation are of course very numerous. Price is the obvious matter: this includes the type of pricing agreement, discounts, terms of payment, contract price adjustment (CPA) clauses, transportation charges and so on.

1.10   Delivery and scheduling are also vital. The deadlines for delivery, the method of delivery, details of packaging and palleting are all relevant here. Remedies in the event of late delivery are also important.

1.11 Above all, negotiation must cover quality issues. This includes acceptable quality levels, methods and place of inspection, procedures in respect of rejected goods, site visits and so on. The relevance of all this to risk management is immediately obvious.

Setting objectives

1.12 A useful approach to setting objectives is given by the acronym MIL, originally coined by Gavin Kennedy. Kennedy distinguished between objectives we Must achieve, objectives we Intend to achieve (or which it is Important for us to achieve), and objectives we would Like to achieve. Must, Intend (or Important), and Like are the key words.

1.13 The MIL acronym identifies the relative importance of our objectives.

- The M objectives are show-stoppers. If we can't achieve these, the negotiation will fail.
- The L objectives are the icing on the cake. If we can achieve these we can feel that we have been very successful indeed.
- The I objectives occupy the middle position. While a failure to achieve one or more of these will not necessarily be disastrous, we will certainly be trying very hard to achieve them.

Collecting information

1.14 Another important factor to address in the preparation stage is exactly what information we are prepared to reveal to the other party and the information we will be seeking from him.

1.15 To prepare for a negotiation, and in particular to help in establishing objectives, the buyer must identify necessary information and take steps to assemble it. Where an existing supplier is concerned, the buyer must ensure that he is completely informed as to the terms of the current agreement and on the supplier's performance to date. Other types of information (such as cost analysis) are important whether a new supplier or an existing supplier is concerned.

1.16 Buyers sometimes use a checklist to ensure that their background information is sufficiently comprehensive. An example is given in Figure 13.1.

1.17 Notice in Figure 13.1 the reference to the relative strengths of the bargaining parties. The buyer will attempt to maximise the strengths of his own position. This can be weakened by any or all of the following factors.

- Few alternative sources available (perhaps because the supplier enjoys a monopoly position, or because he has the advantage of a premium branded product or specialised equipment)
- Suppliers indifferent about obtaining the business
- Urgent demand for the material
- Option to make the product internally is not available
- Lack of knowledge of the supplier's cost structure
- Insufficient background information on the supplier – personnel, levels of authority, position in the market
- Unexpected arguments advanced by the supplier
- Inappropriate conduct of the buyer (eg too much talking and not enough listening, speaking out of turn)

Figure 13.1 *Negotiation planning checklist*

Fictional plc		Negotiation planning checklist
MEETING WITH:	DATE:	
		Reference
General	What are our objectives?	
	What assumptions have been used in framing our objectives?	
	How may these assumptions be challenged?	
	What are their likely objectives and arguments?	
	What are our strengths and weaknesses? What are their strengths and weaknesses?	
	How have they performed under the current agreement?	
	By what date must we reach agreement?	
	Which of our staff will take part in the meeting? Who will be the team leader?	
	How much do we know about the personnel on their side? What level of authority do they have to conclude an agreement?	
Financial terms	What is the current price (if applicable)? What is the range of prices that we can accept or hope for?	
	What are the general terms of payment, including credit period?	
	Are stage payments applicable?	
	Are there discounts for bulk orders or for early pament?	
	Are foreign currencies involved, and if so which?	
Quality and delivery	Has the supplier been given a complete specification? What feedback if any have we had?	
	How is conformance with specification to be measured?	
	Are any variations permissible in the terms of the specification? Has the supplier suggested any such variations?	
	What delivery date(s) will apply?	
	What will be the delivery quantities?	
	What arrangements should be made for packaging, palleting and transportation?	
Contractual terms	Are the terms of the contract clear, and have they clearly been accepted?	
	By which country's law is the contract to be governed? In which country's courts are disputes to be resolved? Is there any provision for arbitration?	
	Who is responsible for the various elements of purchase cost? Who is responsible for insurance?	
	Are there clear administrative arrangements for implementing the contract once agreed?	

1.18 Nearly all of these weaknesses can be overcome by careful preparation, which again reinforces the importance of this phase in the process. Sometimes the buyer needs help in this from colleagues; for example, demand will not be urgent if requisitions are placed in good time by user departments. However, if the supplier has a dominant influence in the market by reason of a monopoly or near-monopoly position, then the buyer's position will be weak no matter how carefully he prepares.

Subdividing the planning phase

1.19   Several stages can be identified in the process of planning a negotiation.

- Defining the issues: these will usually include one or two major issues and several more minor issues

- Assembling issues and defining the bargaining mix: the MIL acronym may be helpful in determining which issues are negotiable and which ones less so

- Defining interests: which may include short-term price reductions, but could equally well include maintenance of a long-term relationship with the supplier

- Defining limits: the minimum acceptable outcomes in relation to each objective

- Defining objectives and opening bids: ensuring that the opening bids are not so ambitious as to frighten away the other party

- Defining one's constituents: the people that must be satisfied by the outcome, eg one's boss, one's shareholders

- Understanding the other party

- Selecting a strategy

- Planning the presentation and defence: with use of effective argument and substantiating detail

- Defining protocol: eg where the meeting is to take place and who is to attend

2   *Strategies for negotiation*

Two broad approaches

2.1   There are two basic orientations to negotiation.

- **Distributive bargaining** involves the distribution of limited resources, or 'dividing up a fixed pie'. One party's gain can only come at the expense of the other party: this is sometimes called a zero-sum game, or a win-loss outcome. If the buyer pushes the price down, for example, the supplier's profit margin will be eroded. If a trade union succeeds in securing a greater-than-budgeted wage increase for its members, the excess may have to be funded at the expense of shareholders (through reduced profits) or customers (through increased prices).

- **Integrative bargaining** involves collaborative problem-solving to increase the options available (or 'expanding the pie'), with the aim of exploring possibilities for both parties to find a mutually satisfying or win-win solution. This may also be called **added value negotiating** (AVN): the aim is to add value to the deal, rather than extracting value from or conceding value to the other party.

The distributive approach

2.2   The kind of tactics used in a distributive or transactional approach reflect a **push influencing style**.

- Presenting exaggerated initial positions/demands, in order to allow for expected movement and compromise

- Exaggerating the initial distance between the two parties' positions, and polarising conflicting viewpoints, in order to persuade opponents that their position is unrealistic

- Withholding information that might highlight areas of common ground or weakness in your bargaining position

- Using all available levers to coerce, pressure or manipulate the other party to make concessions

- Offering no concessions in return (unless forced to do so), even where they might be offered at low cost

The integrative approach

2.3 The integrative approach is now generally recognised as the most constructive, ethical (or principled) and sustainable approach. Negotiation gurus Fisher and Ury note that a 'wise agreement' is one that 'meets the legitimate interests of each side to the extent possible, resolves conflicting interests fairly, is durable and takes community interests into account'.

2.4 The foundation for win-win or integrative approaches in supply negotiations is the belief that cooperation along the supply chain can lead to elimination of waste at all stages, benefiting all parties. A buyer who focuses exclusively on one objective – say a 5 per cent price reduction – may miss opportunities to widen the discussion fruitfully. For example, by cooperating with the supplier in improved quality assurance measures the costs of assuring quality may fall for both sides. This may be enough in itself to achieve the desired improvement in profits without detriment to the supplier's margins.

2.5 Typical integrative tactics reflect a **pull influencing approach**.

- Being open about your own needs and concerns in the situation, and seeking to understand those of the other party: getting all cards on the table

- Collaboratively generating options (which may be more creative than either party could come up with on their own), seeking to find those with genuine mutual or trade-off benefits.

- Focusing on areas of common ground and mutual benefit, to keep a positive and collaborative atmosphere

- Supporting the other party in accepting your proposals, by emphasising joint problem-solving, offering additional information or help with follow-up etc

- Maintaining and modelling flexibility by making and inviting reasonable counter-offers and compromises

Selecting the appropriate approach

2.6 When it comes to negotiating in complex situations, the most appropriate style may be analysed on a grid (devised by KW Thomas) matching the negotiators' concern for the outcome (winning) against their concern for the long-term future of the relationship with the other party (relationship): Figure 13.2.

Figure 13.2 *Model of conflict-handling styles*

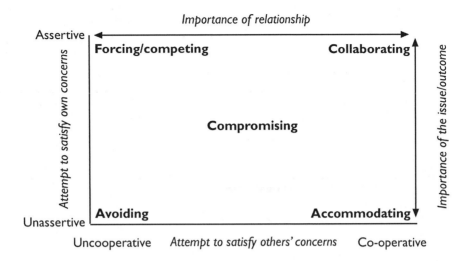

2.7   The diagram indicates the following possible approaches.

•   Avoidance may be used where the issue is unimportant to both parties: it may be left unresolved.

•   Competition/adversarialism may be used when a point is non-negotiable.

•   Accommodation may be used to give soft concessions, in order to earn reciprocal concessions in other areas.

•   Collaboration (integrative bargaining) may be used to explore win-win outcomes.

Using concessions effectively

2.8   Concessions are a cornerstone of the bargaining approach, enabling movement from polarised positions towards the middle ground. There are two basic orientations to making concessions.

2.9   An integrative approach uses concessions to build trust. Unilateral or unconditional concessions send the message that ongoing collaboration is a priority, and there is an underlying belief in the potential for mutual satisfaction and gains over time. However:

•   All concessions must be openly identified and acknowledged as concessions (ie of some cost to the offering party), so that the other party is placed under moral obligation to reciprocate.

•   Unilateral concessions must be relatively low-cost and low-risk to grant (while being valuable to the receiving party) in order to avoid exploitation.

•   The motives for making concessions (and demands) should be clearly explained where possible, in order to reduce suspicion: the more reasonable and justifiable your positions and expectations are, the less they will be perceived as purely political, adversarial or manipulative in nature.

2.10   A distributive, adversarial or transactional approach uses concessions as trading currency: they represent a cost to be tightly controlled, invested and leveraged for reciprocal gains. Such an approach leads to tactics such as the following.

- Avoiding being the first party to make a concession (a sign of weakness)

- Making concessions strictly contingent on gaining a concession of equal or greater value from the other party: no 'goodwill' concessions (which can simply be taken advantage of).

- Making concessions of least possible cost to you, while demanding concessions of greatest possible value to you (and/or cost to the other party)

- Giving the impression that every concession you make is a major concession: of great importance and cost (in order to earn greater reciprocal concessions from the other party)

- Making as few concessions as possible, in order to avoid creating an impression of weakness (or of excessive strength, raising the suspicion that the offer on the table is already biased in your favour)

- Getting the other party to make minor concessions in the early stages, in order to establish a pattern that can be applied to more important issues later.

Best practice methodology

2.11 The modern view of best practice in negotiations emphasises the superiority of a distributive approach when seeking a long-term supply relationship. This offers the best chance of minimising risk arising from a supplier's dissatisfaction with an agreement or his inability to fulfil it.

3 *Tactics and standpoints*

Distributive approaches

3.1 In the previous section of this chapter we outlined two contrasting approaches to negotiating: distributive and integrative. The distributive approach is based on the idea that there is a fixed 'pie' and our only objective is to maximise our share of it. We do so by obtaining concessions which reduce the supplier's share of the pie. By contrast, in an integrative negotiation we focus on joint problem solving in order to increase the size of the 'pie'.

3.2 In this section our focus is on tactical moves by buyer and supplier. Once again the distinction between distributive and integrative approaches is a useful one. We begin by discussing tactics associated with distributive bargaining.

3.3 A first step is to assess the other party's target (ie his hoped for outcome), his resistance point (ie his minimum acceptable outcome), and his costs of terminating the negotiation. The buyer may simply ask these questions directly, if he thinks this will elicit reliable answers. Or he may proceed by indirect means.

3.4 As an example of this, a buyer may check out his supplier's published financial accounts, or may take out a credit check via a company such as Dun & Bradstreet. The objective would be to analyse the financial strength of the supplier and possibly to obtain information about his normal profit margins.

3.5 Another tactical task for the buyer is to manage the other party's impressions. As we have seen, the buyer wants information about the supplier's target, resistance points etc. But he is equally keen to withhold the equivalent information about his own position. And it may go further than this: he may actively foster a misleading impression in the supplier's mind. For example, he may seek to convey an impression that any price above £X per unit is totally unacceptable, whereas in truth it might not be.

3.6 Of course there is an ethical dimension in this. A straight lie (eg about the volume of business the buyer wishes to place with the supplier, in order to induce a more favourable price) is simply unacceptable. But selective presentation (putting forward information that strengthens the buyer's case, while suppressing information that weakens it) is not regarded as unethical, at least by most buyers.

3.7 Another tactical task is to change the supplier's perceptions. This means putting the supplier's own objectives in a different light – making them seem less attractive or more costly than the supplier had originally thought. If the supplier can be made to think in this way, he will be more ready to move his position, hopefully in a direction favourable to the buyer.

3.8 This can be achieved by, for example, pointing out a consequence that the supplier has overlooked. Or, more controversially, it may be achieved by withholding information that the buyer is aware of but the supplier is not. Again, this is dubious ethically, and each case has to be judged on its individual merits.

3.9 Finally, negotiators may be able to manipulate the costs of delaying or terminating a negotiation. For example, a supplier may be under pressure to achieve a deal by a certain deadline in order to meet sales targets. If the buyer is free of time pressures, he can exploit the supplier's anxiety.

3.10 Notice that all of these tactics assume that buyer and supplier are on opposite sides. If we were collaborating, we might be more prepared to share information and the element of deviousness in the above tactics would be out of place. This leads us on to consider tactics in integrative negotiations.

Integrative approaches

3.11 In our earlier discussion of the integrative approach, we noted that one stage in the process is to generate alternative solutions. The tactical means by which such alternatives may be developed are explained in the paragraphs that follow.

3.12 One approach is simply to brainstorm the problem with a view to generating as many solutions as possible. Small groups of people throw out possible solutions without detailed examination of their pros and cons: that will come later. The objective is to think about the issue in a creative, freewheeling way, rather than being confined within the narrow limits in which the problem may originally have been framed.

3.13 Other techniques rely on redefining the problem. Five possibilities are suggested below: expanding the pie; logrolling; non-specific compensation; cutting the costs for compliance; and finding a bridge solution.

3.14 **Expanding the pie**. Instead of haggling over limited resources, the parties aim to find ways of increasing the resources available. For example, a buyer who can not obtain a satisfactory price from his supplier, but still wishes to do business with the supplier (eg because of his high quality), may consider ways in which he can increase the proposed volume of business. This may make the supplier more inclined to offer a keen price.

3.15 **Logrolling**. This means identifying different issues on which the parties have different priorities. A buyer who is not too concerned about Issue X may offer concessions on this point, in return for concessions from the Supplier on Issue Y (Issue Y being a low priority for the supplier).

3.16 **Non-specific compensation**. This means that a buyer may seek a concession from a supplier by offering some unrelated concession in return. For example, a supplier may be promoted to a 'preferred' list, increasing his chances of gaining future business.

3.17 **Cutting the costs for compliance**. For example, in return for a supplier's concession on price, the buyer may offer to bear all the legal costs of drawing up and agreeing the supply contract, both his own and the supplier's.

3.18 **Finding a bridge solution**. This implies a fundamental reformulation of the issues so that entirely new solutions may be devised. This is only likely to happen if buyer and supplier are strongly committed to working together.

3.19 With all these approaches, there is a need for information sharing so that each party truly understands the other's needs and interests. This is characteristic of the integrative approach to negotiation, but not of the distributive approach.

4 *Behaviours of successful negotiators*

Characteristics of a skilled negotiator

4.1 The individuals engaged in a negotiation will have different backgrounds, knowledge bases and skill sets. Their technical knowledge may cover different areas. But they have all presumably been chosen as negotiators because they exhibit characteristics which are thought to contribute to the likelihood of a successful outcome.

4.2 So what are the personal attributes that make a successful negotiator? Researchers have attempted to analyse this, and the list of characteristics identified by various different authors is a very long one indeed. The list includes such attributes as skill in preparation and planning, technical knowledge of the issue to be negotiated, clarity of thought under pressure, verbal expression, listening skills and numerous others.

The role of personality

4.3 When we talk about 'attributes' or 'characteristics' that negotiators (or people in general) have, we are partly talking about personality: a concept used by psychologists to identify, explain and describe the ways in which people differ. Personality may be defined as 'the psychological qualities that influence an individual's characteristic behaviour patterns, in a distinctive and consistent manner, across different situations and over time' (Huczynski and Buchanan).

4.4 Identified personality traits and types can be used to compare, explain and predict negotiation behaviour. A person who is extroverted, for example (sociable, assertive and talkative) may make a good sales negotiator, because of his or her natural ability to build rapport and relate to people. On the other hand, it should be remembered that:

- No one personality trait or type is 'better' than another: all have strengths and weaknesses that must be managed for desired outcomes. The extrovert might have to train himself to avoid impulsive decisions, for example, while an introvert may make a valuable contribution to the negotiating team by focusing on problem-solving and analysing the opposing position.

- Personality only reflects preferences or tendencies: skilled behaviours can still be learned and adopted, even if they are not 'natural' to us. Hence, when we talk about 'attributes of effective negotiators' we are talking both about personality (what they are 'like') and learned/skilled behaviours (what they actually 'do').

Interpersonal sensitivity

4.5 Researchers distinguish between two main social value orientations. Some individuals are **proself**; others are **prosocial**. The former are interested in personal outcomes and have little regard for outcomes obtained by the other party; the latter prefer outcomes that benefit both self and others with whom they are interdependent.

4.6 These two categories should remind you of the distinction between distributive and integrative approaches to negotiation. Proself individuals are likely to favour distributive negotiations; prosocial individuals are more likely to embrace an integrative approach.

4.7 A key issue in negotiation is the extent of interpersonal trust between the parties. Individuals differ in the amount of trust that they extend to others. 'High trusters' are disposed to expect others to be trustworthy and feel obliged to behave in the same way themselves. 'Low trusters' believe that the other party is likely to cheat, and may themselves be less ethical in their behaviour as a result.

4.8 There is a self-fulfilling aspect to this. If you approach your supplier with an attitude and style that communicates trust you are more likely to excite similar behaviour in the supplier. If instead you communicate suspicion and distrust, the result may be a less cooperative relationship.

The emotionally intelligent negotiator

4.9 Emotional intelligence is a current buzzword in the social sciences. It refers to an ability to perceive, assess and manage one's own emotions and those of others (eg the other party in a negotiation). It is often referred to as EI, and measured in terms of EQ (an emotional intelligence quotient – the term is modelled on the IQ score measuring general intelligence).

4.10 Investigations into the behaviour of negotiators have often assumed that they can be regarded as always acting rationally. The implication is that logical reasoning is the key driver of a negotiation.

4.11 This view has been challenged by researchers who emphasise the role of emotion in negotiations. A negotiator is a human being, not an automaton, and is affected more or less by non-rational, emotional considerations. A skilled negotiator must be able to exploit this in others, while being aware that he himself may be acted upon by non-rational factors. If he can achieve this, he can be described as an emotionally intelligent negotiator.

4.12 Negotiations create both positive and negative emotions. Positive emotions can arise from liking the other party and feeling good about progress in the negotiation. Negative emotions can arise from disliking the other party and from frustration at lack of progress.

4.13 Positive emotions generally have positive consequences for negotiations, while negative emotions have negative consequences. In particular, positive emotions are more likely to lead to integrative approaches, whereas negative emotions can lead to distributive approaches.

4.14 A final conclusion is that emotions can be used strategically as negotiation gambits. Manipulating emotions is generally regarded as more acceptable than manipulating information; in other words, it is regarded as more acceptable to feign exasperation at a supplier's price offer than to mislead the supplier about intended purchase volumes.

Effective questioning skills

4.15 Skilful questioning is a key technique for negotiators. Various authorities have attempted to classify the types of question that may be asked. As an example, consider the research of Gerard Nierenberg: Table 13.1.

Table 13.1 *Questions in negotiation*

Manageable questions	Examples
Open-ended questions – ones that cannot be answered with a simple yes or no. *Who, what, when, where,* and *why* questions.	'Why do you take that position in these deliberations?'
Open questions – invite the other's thinking.	'What do you think of our proposal?'
Leading questions – point toward an answer.	'Don't you think our proposal is a fair and reasonable offer?'
Cool questions – low emotionally.	'What is the additional rate that we will have to pay if you make the improvements on the property?'
Planned questions – part of an overall logical sequence of questions developed in advance.	'After you make the improvements to the property, when can we expect to take occupancy?'
Treat questions – flatter the opponent at the same time as you ask for information.	'Can you provide us with some of your excellent insight on this problem?'
Window questions – aid in looking into the other person's mind.	'Can you tell us how you came to that conclusion?'
Directive questions – focus on a specific point.	'How much is the rental rate per square foot with these improvements?'
Gauging questions – ascertain how the other person feels.	'How do you feel about our proposal?'

Unmanageable questions	Examples
Close-out questions – force the other party into seeing things your way.	'You wouldn't try to take advantage of us here, would you?'
Loaded questions – put the other party on the spot regardless of the answer.	'Do you mean to tell me that these are the only terms that you will accept?'
Heated questions – high emotionally, trigger emotional responses.	'Don't you think we've spent enough time discussing this ridiculous proposal of yours?'
Impulse questions – occur 'on the spur of the moment,' without planning, and tend to get conversation off the track.	'As long as we're discussing this, what do you think we ought to tell other grooups who have made similar demands on us?'
Trick questions – appear to require a frank answer, but really are 'loaded' in their meaning.	'What are you going to do – give in to our demands, or take this to arbitration?'
Reflective trick questions – reflects the other into agreeing with your point of view.	'Here's how I see the situation – don't you agree?'

Source: From Gerard Nierenberg, Fundamentals of Negotiation.

4.16 In a similar vein, Steele, Murphy and Russill (in *It's a Deal*) classify questions as follows.

- Open questions – when can you deliver?
- Closed questions – can you deliver by 20 October?
- Probing questions – what tests do you use to ensure consistent quality?
- Multiple questions – how can you ensure fixed prices, quality and delivery?
- Leading questions – these prices are fixed for a year, aren't they?
- Reflective questions – you seem a little unhappy about our proposal?
- Hypothetical questions – what if we extended the contract to two years?

4.17 With enough time on one's hands one could extend these analyses almost without limit, but this is probably enough to indicate that buyers use a wide range of questioning techniques throughout the negotiation process. Short of refusing to answer, the supplier is bound to contribute at least a limited amount of information in his reply, which means that the buyer has gained something.

Information seeking questions

4.18 A prime objective of asking questions is obviously to fill in the gaps in our information. This needs no further explanation. But it is worthwhile to consider the incidental effects of the information seeking process.

4.19 One aspect is that such questions may lead us to uncover deception on the part of the supplier. Another aspect is the use of questions in refocusing an integrative negotiation and generating win-win options. Earlier in this chapter we discussed five broad methods of doing so: expanding the pie; logrolling; non-specific compensation; cutting the costs for compliance; finding a bridge solution.

4.20 Each of these can be facilitated by asking appropriate questions. For example, in terms of logrolling, we can ask 'What issues are of higher and lower priority to each party?' In terms of non-specific compensation, we can ask 'What could I do that would make the supplier happy and simultaneously allow me to get my way on the key issue?'

4.21 Another incidental effect of questioning is that by promoting an exchange of information we may also be building trust. The literature emphasises the importance of a full exchange of information. This is characteristic of integrative negotiations and may lead to more profitable outcomes for both sides.

5 *Dispute resolution alternatives*

The role of EDR

5.1 EDR stands for effective dispute resolution. It describes a body of dispute resolution techniques which avoid the inflexibility of litigation and arbitration, and focus instead on enabling the parties to achieve a better or similar result, with the minimum of direct and indirect cost. These processes have become known in the UK as ADR (alternative dispute resolution), but this description is somewhat outdated, as mediation and other EDR techniques have become mainstream processes, alongside litigation and arbitration.

5.2 The most common form of EDR in commercial disputes is **mediation**. This is a flexible process conducted confidentially in which a neutral person actively assists parties in working towards a negotiated agreement of a dispute or difference, with the parties in ultimate control of the decision to settle and the terms of resolution.

5.3 It is possible to distinguish between facilitative mediation (where the mediator aids or assists the parties' own efforts to formulate a settlement) and evaluative mediation (where the mediator additionally helps the parties by introducing a third-party view over the merits of the case or of particular issues between the parties).

5.4 A suitable contractual clause should be sufficient to give the parties the opportunity to attempt to settle any dispute by mediation. The Centre for Effective Dispute Resolution (CEDR) Model Mediation Procedure provides clear guidelines on the conduct of the mediation and requires the parties to enter into an agreement based on the Model Mediation Agreement in relation to its conduct. This will deal with points such as the nature of the dispute, the identity of the mediator and where and when the mediation is to take place. If an ADR/mediation clause is sufficiently certain and clear as to the process to be used it should be enforceable.

5.5 To avoid the drawbacks of litigation, it is increasingly common for buyers and sellers to try other options first and to treat court proceedings as a last resort. Often they do so by including a provision in their contract to the effect that any dispute must be referred to **arbitration**. This allows the parties to choose an arbitrator in whom they both have confidence, and to explain their differences privately.

5.6 An important part of such an arrangement is that the parties agree to be bound by the decision of the arbitrator, which can be enforced as if it were the decision of a court. This of course makes it important to choose someone suitable. In some cases this means a person with legal experience, but often a specialised knowledge of the subject matter of the contract is more crucial.

5.7 General advantages of arbitration over litigation include the following.

- The proceedings are held in private, avoiding publicity of issues which parties may not wish to be broadcast.
- The parties can choose the individual or organisation to resolve any dispute.

- Arbitration is less confrontational than litigation. This is especially important if the parties wish to maintain good trading relations after the dispute is resolved.

- Aribitration is intended as a single 'one-stop' process, avoiding the endless appeals that may protract litigation.

- Arbitration should be speedier and less expensive than litigation.

5.8   However, the preference for arbitration is not entirely clear-cut in all circumstances.

- If the parties choose litigation, at least once the procedure is complete the outcome is final. Arbitration may be subject to intervention by the courts, although this should happen only exceptionally.

- The powers of arbitrators are less extensive than those of judges, which can mean a greater possibility of delay in arbitral proceedings.

5.9   From the perspective of risk management, the importance of all this is that buyers (and suppliers) should be concerned to avoid the trouble, expense and uncertainty of litigation. Appropriate contractual clauses can ensure that a less painful method of dispute resolution is used.

Chapter summary

- CIPS have outlined a detailed risk management process consisting of five stages: identify sources of possible risk; for each risk event, determine likelihood and impact; assess the overall impact of all risk factors; investigate risk reduction; plan, control and reduce risk.

- Planning for a negotiation should include determining objectives in advance. Kennedy's MIL framework (Must, Intend, Like) is a useful tool in this regard.

- Often a buyer will prepare for negotiation by completing a planning checklist.

- The two basic orientations to negotiation are distributive bargaining and integrative bargaining. The former is based on the idea that resources are fixed in amount, and the task of a negotiator is to obtain the largest possible share for himself, at the expense of his 'adversary'. The latter involves collaborative problem-solving with a view to 'expanding the pie'.

- The choice of a distributive or integrative approach will have a material effect on the tactics of negotiation and on the use of concessions.

- Five possible techniques in an integrative negotiation: expanding the pie; logrolling; non-specific compensation; cutting the costs for compliance; finding a bridge solution.

- The characteristics exhibited by skilled negotiators arise partly from inherent personality, but partly also from learned behaviours.

- Interpersonal sensitivity and emotional intelligence are among the characteristics of skilled negotiators. Effective use of questioning skills is another.

- Effective dispute resolution is a body of techniques that are designed to avoid the costs and inflexibility of arbitration and litigation.

Self-test questions

Numbers in brackets refer to the paragraphs where you can check your answers.

1 List five stages in a risk management process. (1.2)

2 List factors that may be subject to negotiation between a buyer and a supplier. (1.9ff)

3 Explain Kennedy's MIL framework for setting negotiation objectives. (1.13)

4 List factors that can weaken the negotiation position of a buyer. (1.17)

5 Explain the distinction between distributive bargaining and integrative bargaining. (2.1)

6 List the tactics used in a push influencing style. (2.2)

7 List the tactics used in a pull influencing style. (2.5)

8 How might a buyer seek information about a supplier's financial position? (3.4)

9 List five techniques for redefining the problem in an integrative negotiation. (3.14)

10 Distinguish between proself and prosocial individuals. (4.5)

11 Explain what is meant by emotional intelligence. (4.9ff)

12 In commercial disputes, what is the most common form of EDR? (5.2)

13 List advantages of arbitration over litigation.

CHAPTER 14

Monitoring and Control Techniques

Learning objectives and indicative content

3.2   Evaluate and apply monitoring and control techniques for testing risk on an ongoing basis.

- Internal audits
- Interdepartmental exchanges
- External experts: advisers, mystery shoppers, research companies and the police
- Use of benchmarking to assess and mitigate external risk
- Use of competitive intelligence

Chapter headings

1   Internal audits

2   The use of external experts

3   Benchmarking to mitigate risk

4   Competitive intelligence

5   Control models

1   Internal audits

Introduction

1.1   Once again, there is duplication in your syllabus here. The work of auditors (both internal and external) has been discussed already in Chapter 10, in the context of syllabus area 2.8. Both internal and external auditors are specified again in this syllabus area. In this section we briefly note a couple of points in relation to internal audit that would have been less relevant in the earlier context of risk identification and analysis.

1.2   The primary responsibility for identifying risk lies with line managers. Once risk has been identified, the internal audit department has a major role in controlling the risk. One way in which this is done is by means of systematic testing of internal controls. In the context of purchasing, these tests will cover all aspects of procurement, including supplier appraisal, tendering procedures, contract award, ongoing contract management, use of e-commerce and so on.

1.3   Apart from this ongoing work, internal audit also undertake project tasks. For example, if a large outsourcing contract is being considered, the internal audit department might contribute to a thorough review of how the activity is currently carried out in-house. This would help to shape the specification eventually to be agreed with the proposed external supplier.

1.4   Typically, the work of the internal auditors will be planned on a sampling basis. For example, the auditors might take a sample of items paid for with corporate purchasing cards and check to ensure that value has been received. If the sample of transactions is carefully chosen and reveals no problems, the internal audit team might conclude that controls are working effectively. On the other hand, if problems are detected, the team might decide to examine a larger number of transactions.

1.5   The internal audit function will report regularly to senior management and/or to the audit committee. Reports will cover both identified problems and suggestions for control improvements. This assists line managers in fulfilling their duty to implement and monitor a system of internal control.

Interdepartmental exchanges

1.6   This topic is specified in your syllabus at this point, but there is no explanation of what it means. The topic is not mentioned in the CIPS guidance for lecturers, nor in the recommended reading for the subject. If any clarification emerges as to what is meant, we will post additional study material on the CIPS website. In the meantime, it presumably cannot be examined.

2   The use of external experts

External auditors

2.1   As we have already seen in Chapter 10, a key factor in the work of an auditor is independence. Internal auditors attempt to achieve independence of top management by appropriate reporting lines (eg by reporting to the company's audit committee). However, it remains true that internal auditors are employees of the organisation they are auditing and this places limits on their independence.

2.2   The situation is different with external auditors. Auditors of private sector companies typically work for firms of accountants. They report directly to the shareholders, bypassing the directors. This is meant to enhance their independence. They are paid a fee to conduct their work, and their output is a report commenting on whether the company's accounts show a 'true and fair view' of the financial results for the year and financial position at the year end.

2.3   There are limits on the independence even of external auditors.

- Although in theory the auditors are appointed by the shareholders, in practice it is the directors who select the audit firm, and who sack them if they are dissatisfied with their work.

- Auditors are human beings with personalities. A director with a dominant personality may overawe an auditor of more timid disposition. The auditor may not press any concerns he has as forcefully as he might otherwise.

- Auditors invariably perform other, non-audit work, for their audit clients: tax advice, consultancy etc. They naturally wish to retain the income from such work and may therefore be reluctant to rock the boat with an unfavourable audit report. To avoid this problem, many countries have placed restrictions on the amount of non-audit work that the external auditor can perform for a client.

2.4 There is also the problem that for most companies in the UK, an external audit is not legally required. While there is nothing to stop small companies appointing external auditors voluntarily, few will do so. However, all large companies (with annual turnover above a defined threshold are required to undergo an annual external audit.

2.5 A final limitation on the usefulness of the external audit is sometimes referred to as the **expectations gap**. This is the gap between what the external auditor actually does and what the public believe he does. Most members of the public, if asked what an auditor does, would reply that he checks all the financial transactions of a company and attempts to detect any fraud or mistakes that have occurred.

2.6 The truth is very different. The auditor is required to report on whether the accounts show a 'true and fair view'. For this purpose, he is quite unconcerned about errors below a certain threshold (which will differ from company to company), because they are immaterial to the true and fair view. It is not part of his brief to detect fraud, unless the fraud leads to a material misstatement of the accounting figures. And in arriving at his conclusion, he will plan his work entirely on a sampling basis: it would be quite impractical to consider checking all transactions in a large company.

2.7 Despite all these reservations, the work of the external auditor is perceived as a useful check on the accuracy of the accounts. The auditor will also form conclusions on the company's systems of internal control, using the work of the internal audit department supplemented by his own investigations and testing. This can be useful in highlighting possible risk areas, though it is worth noting that the external auditor is not specifically required to report on risk, any more than on fraud.

2.8 The reason the external auditor is interested in internal controls is that he hopes to reduce the amount of audit work necessary in order to arrive at his audit opinion. If he concludes that internal control systems are effective, this gives him comfort that the accounting figures are reliable and reduces the amount of substantive testing he needs to carry out.

Risk consultants and security advisers

2.9 Appointment of an external auditor is not a discretionary task: it is obligatory for all companies above a certain size. (And audit of public sector organisations by such bodies as the National Audit Office and the Audit Commission is also usually a binding obligation.) The situation is different with external consultants, such as risk consultants and security advisers. A company will only contract such experts as these if they are expected to give value in excess of the cost of their services. The decision to appoint consultants, and the selection of a particular consultant, are subject to the same purchasing disciplines as any other external spend.

2.10 Often a consultancy firm will have a particular speciality. Here are some examples.

- International risks
- Kidnap and ransom
- Health and safety

- Premises security
- Fire and flood
- Environmental pollution

2.11 In many areas of this kind the **police force** is also a valuable, and generally under-used, resource.

2.12 Before spending money on external consultants, it is worthwhile to check whether any free assistance and advice is available. For example, there may be assistance from government bodies, trade associations or the company's own insurance firm.

2.13 There are obvious benefits that may emerge from appointment of external consultants.

- They bring a fresh and independent view of the company's situation.
- They have specialist skills and knowledge.
- Their prior experience may enable them to pinpoint risk areas more accurately and quickly than insiders could.

2.14 These benefits naturally must be weighed against the costs and potential disruption to everyday operations that may be incurred.

Mystery shoppers

2.15 Mystery shoppers are a specialised type of consultant. They are contracted by companies in the retail and service sectors and their purpose is to act as though they were genuine customers of the organisation. For example, a mystery shopper might telephone a college with an enquiry about a course. Their aim in such a case would be to record and report on the quality of the response they receive.

- Was the person who handled the call knowledgeable about the course?
- Did they announce themselves by name and make the 'customer' feel welcome?
- Did they take opportunities to sell additional courses or services?
- Did they follow up appropriately in order to convert the enquiry into a sale?

2.16 In the retail sector, mystery shoppers might be contracted to check on shopfloor prices for comparability, or might be asked to report on the level of customer service offered by the organisation or by its competitors.

Research companies

2.17 Finally in this section of the syllabus we mention the use of research companies. Numerous organisations exist with the purpose of scanning relevant information, summarising it, and making it available at a price. This can be a major aid in certain areas. For example, a company planning to expand into a new overseas market might commission dedicated research on market conditions, the local economy, the activities of competitors in the new market and so on.

2.18 Once again, it is worthwhile to consider free sources of information before rushing to spend money. In the example cited above, the UK exporter should first of all make full use of any assistance provided by the Department of Trade and Industry.

3   *Benchmarking to mitigate risk*

What is benchmarking?

3.1   Benchmarking is a business discipline that has been utilised over many years. It has gained widening appeal as technology has enabled performance measures to be compared, contrasted and evaluated within tight time-frames and with greater accuracy.

3.2   A dictionary definition gives the basic concept of a benchmark: 'A standard point of reference against which things can be assessed'. This suggests using an acceptable reference point to assess against.

3.3   A further definition serves to demonstrate that benchmarking can have a significant role in mitigating risk by identifying and learning from best practice in other organisations: 'The continuous process of measuring products, services, and practices, against the toughest competitors or those companies recognised as industry leaders' (Rank Xerox).

3.4   Benchmarking is about comparing an organisation with others to identify areas for improvement and putting in place systems and procedures to ensure effective delivery.

Interfirm comparison

3.5   'Benchmarking' as an improvement tool started in the UK in the 1960s as 'interfirm comparison'. Burman Associates for some years ran interfirm comparisons for several company groupings (including the major UK brewing groups) to compare various aspects of their respective distribution efficiencies. The many ratios compared showed each firm where attention was needed in its distribution structure and management. As this centered around one business area comparison of like with like could be immediately relevant.

3.6   Benchmarking is not necessarily a comparison between enterprises operating in the same business area but whatever benchmarking data and information is used it must be applicable to the benchmarking exercise being undertaken. Benchmarking can be most useful if it can be arranged between non-competitors, that is, enterprises that address different markets from their fellow benchmarking companies. This, of course, heightens the problem of comparing like with like. Delivering beer is not the same as delivering personal computers.

How to benchmark a function or process

3.7   Three types of benchmarking can be distinguished: internal benchmarking, competitive benchmarking and functional benchmarking.

3.8   **Internal benchmarking** means identifying best practice within a single organisation and sharing it. This type of benchmarking exercise will involve a structured approach using cross-functional and/or cross-site teams and developing measurement criteria of similar functions within an organisation with the aim of ensuring that the best practice within the company can be shared and realistic targets set to bring other internal areas in line with identified best practice.

3.9   **Competitive benchmarking** means comparing an organisation's performance with that of a similar competitor. Reliability and the direct comparability of data can often be a problem. Many organisations will keep data and information in house for competitive reasons; others make data and information readily available. Specialist organisations collect and collate data for comparison purposes or can carry out tailored research in specific business areas.

3.10 **Functional (or generic) benchmarking** compares specific industry functions such as storage and distribution. This area is possibly more advanced in using and applying benchmarking data than many others.

Benchmarking in practice

3.11 Benchmarking is at its most effective when looking at processes such as deliveries, downtime, idle time, and so on. The process triangle has been developed as a tool to help managers differentiate the type and importance of the various processes that may impact on customer service. The process triangle examines the three different bases for process requirement, and then uses these to highlight development areas.

- **Basic processes**: looks at processes such as receiving, administration and effective storage that underpin the service delivery.
- **Benchmark processes**: examines those processes that are important in delivering the required level of customer service and in consequence must be of a high standard.
- **Competitive processes**: examines those areas that may give a competitive advantage and help differentiate the organisation against its competitive market.

3.12 An assessment of these interlinked areas will evidence gaps where improvements can be made to efficiency, processes and customer service. Benchmarks that might be applicable to customer service could include:

- Correct and on-time delivery
- Speed of response
- Correct invoicing

3.13 Processes that may affect efficiency could be:

- Waste, rejects or errors
- Inventory levels
- Staff turnover

3.14 Martin Christopher proposed that when undertaking a benchmarking exercise organisations should start by asking themselves three basic questions.

- How relevant are our standards?
- How do we justify the way we do things?
- How competitive are we?

Benefits of benchmarking

3.15 Benchmarking brings a range of benefits. If developed as an integrated process, it becomes a tool for continuous improvement. Benefits quoted by the Public Sector Benchmarking Service include the following.

- Learning from others who have enjoyed success and gaining greater confidence in developing and delivering new approaches
- Greater involvement and motivation of staff engaged in benchmarking and change programmes
- Heightened awareness about performance levels
- Increased willingness to share solutions to common problems
- Wider understanding of the strategic implications
- Increased collaboration and enhanced working relationships

3.16 Benchmarking aids an organisation in its understanding of competitors and the methods by which they operate. They bring successful ideas from proven practice that can be adapted or built upon. With benchmarking more options become available as different approaches are introduced and these can help lead to superior performance over time.

3.17 Benchmarking is a pro-active approach that establishes credible goals and objectives enabling a considered understanding of real problems and issues supported by proven business responses.

Limitations of benchmarking

3.18 Benchmarking is complex and time-consuming to implement properly. To succeed requires a high level of consistent commitment over the long term. Clear systems and procedures must be put in place and followed.

3.19 Benchmarking is copying and adapting what other organisations have successfully achieved. Its limitation is that it can stifle creativity and original thought. You follow – you don't lead.

4 Competitive intelligence

Introduction

4.1 There is no indication in the guidance published by CIPS for this unit as to what this syllabus caption covers, but we assume it refers to what would usually be called competitor analysis. We begin by discussing competitor analysis, and then discuss competitive intelligence in the slightly more specific sense used by the Society of Competitive Intelligence Professionals (SCIP).

Competitor analysis

4.2 Competition is the existence of rival products or services within the same market. In addition to analysing all the company's critical components and resources, risk managers need to survey competition in its totality, including such critical strategic elements as competitors' R&D capabilities, sales, services, costs, manufacturing and procurement (including all the other businesses in which competitors may be engaged). Risk managers should put themselves mentally in the place of planners in rival companies to search out the key perceptions and assumptions on which the competitors' strategies are formulated.

4.3   The first problem in analysing competitors is to establish who exactly is the competition. This question is simple to understand but sometimes difficult to answer. Too often companies have focused on the wrong adversary, by being obsessed with old rivalries. Here are some examples.

- By concentrating its attention on its cross-town rival Kodak, and its new, and good, high-price copiers, Xerox effectively ignored the 'small timers' Savin and Canon who were operating in unimportant market segments. Then suddenly, or so it seemed, these mice turned into lions, and Xerox lost more than half its market share before it stemmed the tide.

- While the two Detroit giants of General Motors and Ford were looking over their shoulders at each other, Toyota stormed into both their markets.

4.4   So seeking an answer to the question is no easy task. Managers will need to check out:

- obvious majors in the market
- the next best competitors, region by region
- new, big companies, with troubles of their own likely to intrude into their market
- small domestic companies perhaps operating in small premium market niches
- foreign companies, with special emphasis on the first unobtrusive move into small domestic niches
- oddball forays from unexpected competitors.

4.5   A detailed profile should be built up on each major competitor. Some competitors span many industries whereas others are part of multinational organisations; some are concerned almost exclusively with the domestic market while others depend on exports for a high proportion of their sales.

4.6   Although it is tempting to evaluate a company's position solely on the basis of whether its products and services are superior to those offered by its competitors, there are a wide range of additional factors that determine competitive success. The objective features of a company's products and services, although important, often form a relatively small part of the competitive picture. In fact, all the elements making up consumer preference, such as product quality, service, price and location are only part of the competitive analysis.

4.7   The other part involves examining the internal strengths and weaknesses of each major competitor. In the long run a company possessing strong operational assets, with an organisation structure and industrial culture conducive to motivation and innovation, and having ownership of significant financial resources, will prove to be a tough, enduring competitor.

4.8   Competitive analysis should focus on four areas of concern.

- Identifying the company's major competitors
- Establishing on what basis competitive strengths are to be assessed
- Comparing the company with its major competitors
- Identifying potential new competitors

4.9 Data would need to be collected and analysed to enable the exercise detailed above to be carried out. Other comparative criteria would also be relevant. Examples are given below.

- Gross indicators used for both the company and its competitors: market share by segment, relative share, relative revenue etc.

- Technical traits: reverse engineering ('ripping apart their products'), comparative cost structures.

- Commonsense business queries. How do competitors organise for research and development? How is the organisation structured?

4.10 Competitive analysis should be everyone's business – design engineers, manufacturing managers, purchasing staff, service staff, sales force and so on. The fact is that everyone will hear things – from service and salespeople, from a customer, from a former employee and friend now working with a competitor, from a bank clerk, from a braggart at a professional institute meeting, from tit-bits here and there. Also of course, the benefit of getting every employee to think about competition is the positive effect it has on general readiness to accept change.

Competitive intelligence

4.11 A useful article in *Supply Management* (issue of 20 September 2007) makes the point that 'spying on competitors is surely a fact of life for business'. In the sense intended by the article, competitive intelligence is the process of obtaining information that competitors would regard as confidential. As long as such information is legally obtained, it can be a huge help for buyers.

4.12 The word 'legally' is of course very important here. Nobody is recommending the theft of product designs, customer mailing lists etc. But the *Supply Management* article emphasises that useful information can be obtained by an alert buyer without breaching legal or ethical principles.

4.13 Many large businesses employ staff dedicated to competitive intelligence, but until recently their activities have been directed to issues such as business strategy, new product development, mergers and acquisitions and so on. For purchasing, the same processes can be beneficial but are mostly under-developed.

4.14 For buyers, gathering competitive intelligence may be particularly appropriate during suppplier selection. This can help a buyer to validate any claims made by suppliers during the selection process. For example, information about a supplier's cost structures can help to indicate how viable their quoted prices will prove to be in the long term. The same techniques can help in supplier relationship management, for example in providing an early warning of potential difficulties a supplier may have.

4.15 There are a number of consultancies that specialise in gathering inside information. They use public news sources, often held on electronic databases; they talk to people who have recently worked for the target organisation; and where possible they talk to people still working for the organisation. Such practitioners must abide by legal and ethical principles, such as those laid down by SCIP's code of ethics.

5 Control models

Introduction

5.1 At this point the guidance published for this unit by CIPS includes a lengthy discussion of certain control models (COSO, CoCo and COBIT). There appears to be nothing in the syllabus referring to these, and if you are pressed for time this would be a good place to skip – the examiner should not be able to test knowledge that is not specified in the syllabus. However, to be on the safe side we are including brief coverage of the models, based mainly on the relevant article in the online *Encyclopaedia of Business and Finance*.

The COSO model

5.2 COSO stands for the Committee of Sponsoring Organizations of the Treadway Commission. This is the National Commission on Fraudulent Reporting, an independent private sector initiative in the United States which studied the causal factors that can lead to fraudulent financial reporting.

5.3 The COSO report was published by the Commision in 1992 and defines internal control as follows: 'a process, effected by an entity's board of directors, management and other personnel, designed to provide reasonable assurance regarding the achievement of objectives in the following categories – effectiveness and efficiency of operations; reliability of financial reporting; and compliance with applicable laws and regulations'.

5.4 According to the COSO model, internal control consists of five essential components.

- The control environment
- Risk assessment
- Control activities
- Information and communication
- Monitoring

5.5 The model can be illustrated diagrammatically, as in Figure 14.1.

Figure 14.1 *The COSO model*

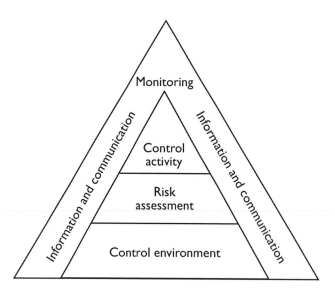

5.6   The importance of the control environment is apparently indicated by its position at the base of the pyramid. It refers to such factors as employee integrity, the organisation's commitment to competence, management's philosophy and operating style, and the attention and direction of the board of directors and the audit committee.

5.7   The next element – risk assessment – has been the subject of most of this text. That leaves just control activity to explain. Such activities include policies and procedures maintained within the organisation to address risk-prone areas.

5.8   The importance of information and communication is that staff who have timely, reliable information are better able to manage the organisation's operations. Monitoring activities provide information about potential and actual breakdowns in a control system.

5.9   According to the Encyclopaedia article, 'some users of the COSO report have found it difficult to read and understand'. We may well sympathise with them. In particular, we may question whether Figure 14.1 tells us anything that was not already obvious from our studies throughout this text. At any rate, help was soon on its way for puzzled readers of the report: enter the Canadian Institute of Chartered Accountants (CICA) and their CoCo model.

The CoCo model

5.10   CICA published their report *Guidance on Control* in 1995. It presented the CoCo model (Criteria of Control), which is said to build on COSO while being more concrete and user-friendly. According to CoCo, control comprises 'those elements of an organisation (including its resources, systems, processes, culture, structure and tasks) that, taken together, support people in the achievement of the organisation's objectives'.

5.11   The CoCo model recognises four interrelated elements of internal control: purpose; commitment; capability; and monitoring and learning. As usual, there is a diagram: Figure 14.2.

Figure 14.2 *The CoCo model of control*

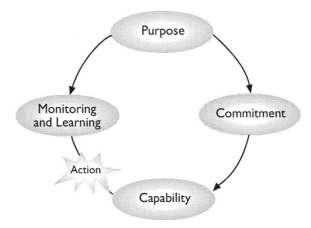

5.12 The meaning of the diagram appears to be as follows.

- To perform a task the organisation is guided by an understanding of the **purpose** of the task.

- The organisational **capability** is sufficient to accomplish the task.

- To perform the task well over time the organisation must demonstrate a sense of **commitment**.

- The organisation must **monitor** task performance in order to improve the task process.

5.13 If you have studied management topics, you may well have come across the distinction between the scientific school of management (pioneered by FW Taylor) and the human relations school (pioneered by Elton Mayo). Some commentators have seen a similar distinction between the COSO model (based on operations, processes and systems) and the CoCo model (based on characteristics of people – purpose, commitment and so on).

5.14 Readers of this text are training to be purchasing professionals and the Institute naturally encourage you to adopt a sceptical and critical attitude. The COSO and CoCo models seem like a good place to start.

The COBIT model

5.15 COBIT (Control Objectives for Information and Related Technology) was issued in 1996 by the Information Systems Audit and Control Foundation. As the name suggests, the model focuses on the efficient and effective monitoring of information systems. In relation to internal control, the model states: 'The policies, procedures, practices and organisational structures are designed to provide reasonable assurance that business objectives will be achieved and that undesired events will be prevented or detected and corrected'.

5.16 The model covers four main areas in relation to IT systems.

- Planning and organisation
- Acquisition and implementation
- Delivery and support
- Monitoring

Chapter summary

- The primary responsibility for identifying risk lies with line managers. Once risk has been identified, the internal audit department has a major role in controlling the risk.

- In principle, external auditors are entirely independent of internal management. In practice, complete independence is rarely or never achieved.

- The work of an external auditor is less comprehensive than most non-experts would expect. This is referred to as auditing's expectations gap.

- External consultants are contracted if they are expected to provide value for money. It is worthwhile first to check out any free sources of assistance.

- Benchmarking is a method of reducing risk by learning from best practice within other departments or other organisations.

- Competitors are an obvious source of risk. Managers should implement a systematic programme of competitor analysis.

- A number of formal risk control models have been developed. These include COSO, CoCo and COBIT.

Self-test questions

The numbers in brackets refer to the paragraphs where you can check your answers.

1   How can the internal audit function assist in controlling identified risks? (1.2)

2   Why in practice are external auditors rarely independent of internal management? (2.3)

3   What is the expectations gap in the context of auditing? (2.5)

4   What benefits may arise from the appointment of external risk consultants? (2.13)

5   Define 'benchmark'. (3.2)

6   Distinguish between internal benchmarking, competitive benchmarking and functional benchmarking. (3.7ff)

7   List benefits of benchmarking. (3.15)

8   What categories of organisation should managers check out as possible competitors? (4.4)

9   Describe the COSO control model. (5.2ff)

CHAPTER 15

Contingency Planning

Learning objectives and indicative content

3.3 Develop contingency plans designed to overcome risk situations.

- What is meant by a contingency plan
- The key components of a business continuity plan (BCP) and disaster recovery plan and how such plans are put into practice
- Key contingency measures used by a BCP: telephone cascades, emergency and fire wardens, use of IT systems to help coordinate activities, use of alternative accommodation and back-up information technology systems
- The benefits of business continuity planning from an operational, financial and reputational perspective

3.4 Analyse specific key risks and exposures in purchasing and supply and identify appropriate mitigating actions.

- Security of supply, contingency planning, stock holding and alternative sources of supply

Chapter headings

1 The nature of contingency planning

2 Business continuity management

3 Media management

1 *The nature of contingency planning*

Why we need contingency plans

1.1 All businesses can be affected by serious adverse events arising out of the ordinary run of business. Here are some of the possible crises that businesses should guard against.

- Natural disasters such as wind damage following storms or flooding following burst pipes
- Fire, which has an enormous potential to destroy premises and records
- IT system failure through power cuts, hackers, computer viruses etc
- Theft of computer equipment
- Vandalism to machinery and vehicles (which is not only costly but may also constitute a health and safety risk)
- Illness to key staff
- Outbreak of disease and infection
- Terrorist attack
- Crisis affecting suppliers' ability to supply
- A crisis affecting business reputation (eg the need for a product recall)

1.2   Contingency planning means putting plans in place to ensure business continuity in the event of such occurrences. Various 'contingency' or 'precautionary' measures are pre-planned and put in place to limit the effects of a disaster and to assist in restoring normal business operations, in accordance with a pre-determined schedule.

1.3   A contingency plan is a fallback position should anything go wrong. This differs from business continuity planning (which we will examine later in this chapter) in that the aim of business continuity planning is to minimise the risk of business failure by enabling the business to continue without interruption following a disaster.

1.4   Contingency planning has had a higher profile since the terrorist attacks of 11 September 2001. The most visible application of contingency planning is the number of drills and practice responses by the police and ambulance services in preparation for a potential terrorist attack.

1.5   Organisations that have taken steps to put in place considered contingency strategies will find themselves in a better position to respond than organisations where contingency planning has not taken place.

1.6   Kit Sadgrove (in *The Complete Guide to Business Risk Management*) gives a list of the most crisis-prone industries in the USA in 2003.

- Securities and commodities
- Supermarkets
- Gas/oil production
- Investment banking
- Restaurants
- Aerospace industry
- Telecommunications
- Accounting/audit services
- Discount/variety stores
- Electric power generation

1.7   Each industry can usually forecast the kind of crisis that may require a contingency plan. For example, airlines can suffer many extreme events such as terrorist attack, weather conditions closing airports, and aircraft crashes. In the airline example the need for contingency planning is obvious. In other business areas crises can come from a wide variety of sources that may not be as extreme or as easy to imagine.

Creating a contingency plan

1.8   There are several steps in creating a contingency plan.

- Do a risk assessment of the business.
- Determine the likelihood of the risks occurring and their impact if they do occur.
- Identify possible solutions to risks that are considered likely to happen or critical in their impact.
- Assess the costs and benefits of each solution identified.
- Identify and document the contingency response selected and how it will be implemented.

- Define and document what or who will trigger activation of the plans.
- Establish a trained team who know what to do in each circumstance.
- Ensure people know what to do if it happens.

1.9 Since businesses and projects involve uncertainty and risk it is likely that we will need to develop contingency plans for key areas of risk. This involves identifying risk scenarios, usually via scenario planning. The aim is to identify the risk of events which, if they actually occur, would have a significant impact on the ability of the organisation to carry out its business. Having identified the risks, we must then consider what options are available.

1.10 An example could be a new administrative system failing to go live on time. The contingency plan may be to carry on with the old system in which case we would have to think about issues such as the following.

- Is this feasible?
- What essential maintenance would be required?
- Do we have the necessary skills?
- When would be the next opportunity to switch systems?
- How will we transfer the data?
- What additional costs will we incur?
- How will this impact our clients?

1.11 Other alternatives may be to carry out the process manually or to contract it out to someone else, in which case many of the same questions would arise.

Scenario planning

1.12 A scenario is defined in the Chambers English Dictionary as 'an outline of future development which shows the operation of causes'. A scenario describes the possible future business environment but is not a prediction. It is a measured and considered account of a projected course of action.

1.13 'A scenario is an internally consistent view of what the future might turn out to be – not a forecast, but one possible future.' (Michael Porter)

1.14 A scenario describes a possible future business environment. It explores the extremes that may challenge or destabilise the existing business model. An important feature of scenario planning is the use of 'What if?' questions: What if the price of raw materials were to double? What if we were to lose our two biggest customers? What if the internet were to crash?

1.15 A scenario should be engaging, challenging and credible as well as being consistent with all known facts. A set of scenarios describes a range of future possibilities that are then refined to a workable number of those considered most likely. These are then developed further.

1.16 The scenarios are used to challenge existing business models and stimulate new ideas. They form the basis of a strategic debate that should be considered outside the traditional business planning cycle. Scenario planning creates a flexible plan for the business.

1.17 Scenario planning exercises involve identifying trends and exploring the implications of projecting them forward – probably as high, medium and low forecasts. These can include political, economic, social and technological factors. As different trends are chosen and different combinations of forecast levels are combined, a whole spectrum of possibilities can be identified.

Scenario planning methodology

1.18 A common approach to scenario planning is to use externally led workshop sessions where directors, managers and staff can contribute freely from their own perspective. Contrasting techniques are used in order to challenge established assumptions and stimulate creativity.

1.19 The workshop is likely to take place over two or three days, and should be residential in order to benefit from group dynamics and to allow informal evening work. Activities comprise a mix of small groups and plenary sessions.

1.20 It is generally accepted that people anticipate more change than actual over a period of two years, but significantly less change than actual over a period of ten years. One way of understanding the process of change and types of influence is to study the historical development in an area over the same period in the past as is intended for study in the future. An ideal period to consider is ten years.

1.21 Different political, economic, environmental and social environments, demographic and technological developments will be considered to identify those things that we cannot control – both those that we can forecast (the rules of the game) and those that we cannot. From these, participants will select those uncertainties judged to be key to the development of scenarios.

1.22 The route to each scenario will be mapped and leading indicators identified that will in future give an early insight into which path is developing.

1.23 Carrying out regular exercises does not necessarily mean that we will be prepared for an eventuality, but it does mean that we are more likely to be aware of the possibility and should be able to act very rapidly if a situation develops.

1.24 The external facilitator will manage a logical process, but will encourage creativity and lateral thinking. Wherever possible, small groups will adopt contrasting approaches to report back to plenary sessions for discussion and integration. To stimulate thinking and maximise the wealth of information generated the facilitator will repeatedly ask participants to propose a wild card: 'What could happen that nobody was expecting?'

Procurement and contingency planning

1.25 The 'What if?' question, now common across many business areas, is highly relevant to contingency planning. It stimulates discussion in a more informal manner than the externally led process described above. The objectives are the same: think the unthinkable, rationalise to the more relevant and then develop contingency plans for those selected.

1.26 The particular risks facing supply chains were highlighted in a *Supply Management* article of 23 October 2006: Figure 15.1.

Figure 15.1 *Supply chains vulnerable, says survey*

A large number of companies still have no contingency plan to deal with disruption to their supply chain, a survey has revealed.

According to *The Fourth Annual Global Survey of Supply Chain Progress*, published last week by Computer Sciences Corporation, 44 per cent of firms have no written contingency plan. Only 37 per cent thought their company paid enough attention to supply chain security.

The report asked why senior management is not more demanding in this area, given recent global issues such as terrorism and natural disasters.

It also identified a 'disturbing trend' – that the number of companies reviewing their supply chain annually had fallen by 13 per cent, from 56 per cent in 2005 to 43 per cent in 2006.

European companies were more likely to review their supply chains every year (56 per cent), compared with only 41 per cent of North American businesses. The survey said the lack of review would lead to 'ultimately poor results'.

The research incorporated interviews with supply chain staff from 134 companies in Europe, North America, Asia and Australia.

1.27 An earlier article ('Preparing for supply meltdown', *Supply Management* 25 May 2006) focused on how few companies have contingency plans in place. Research from the Chartered Management Institute suggests that 49 per cent of companies do not have any plans in place to ensure they will be able to keep running if disaster strikes.

1.28 The article quotes Rene de Sousa, senior procurement specialist at CIPS, who says it is part of procurement's responsibility to ensure continuity of supply – and for that it has to draft contingency plans. 'It is really vital. You must identify where the constraints are and put procedures in place whether you are in the private or public sector. The consequences of not doing it can undo a lot of good work in your business, especially if you look at your reputation as well – your customers expect you to manage this.'

1.29 Procurement faces many challenges in regard to contingency planning. The increase in global sourcing and offshoring introduces geographical, political and cultural risks into the supply chain. Issues such as earthquakes, bird flu, severe acute respiratory syndrome (SARS) all seem remote at a local level but when viewed globally become far more relevant to the continuation of the supply chain.

1.30 The impact of SARS on supply chains was examined in a further in an earlier article, *Supply Management* 8 May 2003. 'Globalisation means that the 'here' now includes every corner of the globe where a company or its supply chain operates'. Reliance on Asia for half the world's silicon chips, outsourced manufacture that would be hit by increased absenteeism, and possible disruption to shipping were all considerations.

1.31 To date the threat has not materialised significantly, but this is not the point. Supply chain contingency planning is about considering the issues and the possible ramifications. The role of purchasing is fundamentally about securing supply and that is particularly relevant when things go wrong.

2 *Business continuity management*

Introduction

2.1 Business continuity is a management process that provides a framework to ensure the resilience of a business to any eventuality, to help ensure continuity of service to key customers and to protect brand and reputation. It provides a basis for planning to ensure long-term survivability following a disruptive event.

2.2 Business continuity management (BCM) is a generic management framework that is valid across the public, private and voluntary sectors. It is about maintaining the essential business deliverables of an organisation during a disruption and forms part of the government's wider resilience policy.

2.3 Figure 15.2 is an article by Wanja Eric Naef that appeared in *Infocon* magazine (October 2003 issue).

Figure 15.2 *Business continuity planning – a safety net for businesses*

> The events of 11 September 2001 were a drastic reminder to all companies that business contingency planning (BCP) should not be disregarded. According to the *Information Security News* magazine (2000), an effective BCP and disaster recovery plan can reduce losses by 90% in the event of an incident. According to another study 81% of CEOs indicated their company plans would not be able to cope with a catastrophic event like the 9/11 attacks.
>
> There are numerous examples of companies suffering because of poor business contingency planning. In the 1993 World Trade Center bombing, 150 companies went out of business (out of 350 affected) – scarcely an encouraging statistic. But an incident does not need to be a dramatic terrorist attack to have a massive impact on an organisation. For instance, in the case of fires, 44% of businesses fail to reopen and 33% of those that do fail to survive beyond three years. The examples could be continued endlessly. The bottom line is that businesses need to have plans in place to cope with incidents (whether they be major terrorist attacks or a minor hardware problem) and thereby avoid major business interruptions.

2.4 Business continuity is not to be confused with either contingency planning or disaster recovery. A contingency plan is a fallback position should anything go wrong, enabling the business to recover over time. Contingency planning is often about 'unlikely' events. This differs from business continuity in that the aim of BCP is to minimise the risk of business failure by enabling the business to continue without interruption following a 'disaster'.

2.5 It is also not be confused with disaster recovery which concentrates on the restoration of facilities after a major incident (eg loss of IT systems, recovery after a fire or flood etc). In general disaster recovery plans are written on the basis of recovery after an event. BCM examines the entire business.

2.6 BCP involves the processes and procedures for the development, testing and maintenance of a plan (or a series of plans) that will enable an organisation to continue operating during and after a disaster. Plans are typically designed to cope with incidents affecting all the organisation's business-critical processes and activities, from failure of a single server, or server room, all the way through to complete loss of a major facility. BCP is a response to an enterprise level risk assessment.

2.7 Disaster recovery planning (DRP) usually takes place within the BCP framework. Disaster recovery plans are usually relatively technical and will focus on the recovery of specific operations, functions, sites, services or applications. A single BCP might contain or refer to a number of DRPs.

The BCM process

2.8 Before even starting to create a BCP it is important to get the full support of the management and governance of your organisation. Without this it will be very difficult to push BCP plans through the entire company. Directors should be involved in the strategic design of the BCP as this will help to create a realistic plan that will be focused on the business interests of the company.

2.9 A BCP team should then be formed. The team will be responsible for designing the BCP and for initiating the BCM process. The team will serve as a central focus point during the entire process. It is also important to set a timescale for the BCP delivery and to create a budget for the process.

2.10 The BCP team must identify threats and conduct a risk assessment, which will help to design the areas on which the plan should focus; it is impossible to avoid or mitigate all risk. The team will have to prioritise depending on likelihood of the risk and business impact. It is very important to analyse all risks and threats: technical, economic, internal, external, human or natural.

2.11 Once the risk assessment has been done the risk must be managed. Preventive, detective and reactive means must be put in place in order to protect the company. For example, it might be possible to migrate risks by using insurance, contracting out some services, implementing safeguards and controls and so on. Risks with high potential impact, but low probability, and which cannot be mitigated, are prime candidates for BCP.

Business impact analysis

2.12 A business impact analysis identifies, quantifies and qualifies the business impact to an organisation of a loss, interruption or disruption of business processes. It provides the data from which appropriate continuity strategies can be determined.

2.13 A business impact analysis will help to define critical business processes. This is useful because once a major incident happens all efforts must be invested to return the primary business functions to a predetermined level during the critical business resumption phase and to establish the time span to achieve these objectives.

2.14 The objectives must be determined by management beforehand. Data must be collected in order to decide which are the primary business processes and which are secondary. As a company has limited resources it is critical to understand where it needs to focus in order to recover in case of an incident.

Planning

2.15 Once that has been done the team can design the BCP(s). It is important to make the plan simple enough so that it can be executed without any problems during a crisis and it needs to be based on steps previously described.

2.16 The threshold for every incident should be defined so that appropriate measures can be taken depending on the incident. Once the BCP has been designed and approved it should be tested under realistic conditions. Untested BCPs are likely to fail.

2.17 David Spinks, Director of Information Assurance EDS, stresses that, 'we see far too many business continuity plans and/or disaster recovery plans that have been tested in unrealistic ideal conditions and thus we do not truly recognise what really happens in a crisis.'

2.18 BCPs should be clear, concise and tailored to the needs of the business. Unplanned events can have catastrophic effects and the disruptive incidents can come from accidents, criminal activity or natural disasters. Business continuity should become part of the way we perform business.

2.19 BCP improves an organisation's ability to react to such disruptions. The plan describes how to restart operations in order to meet business-critical objectives.

2.20 Effective continuity management is built on the 'seven Ps'.

- People – roles and responsibilities, awareness and education
- Programme – proactively managing the process
- Processes – all organisational processes, including ICT
- Premises – buildings and facilities
- Providers – supply chain, including outsourcing
- Profile – brand, image and reputation
- Performance – benchmarking, evaluation and audit

2.21 These issues must be fully considered when developing continuity plans, Procurement has a role to play in ensuring continuity of the supply chain in the event of disruption so will focus on the providers' role. Marketing and Public Relations will focus more on the profile aspect.

Crisis management

2.22 The starting point for developing any form of crisis management is to understand the business: its vulnerabilities, how long it can function without its key activities, and the response of individual departments.

2.23 **Understanding the vulnerabilities of the business**. What are the activities of the organisation that, if they were stopped for any reason, would cause the greatest impact on business?

2.24 Here are some key questions to ask.

- Who in the organisation is essential?
- What equipment, IT, telecommunications and other systems, does the organisation need to be able to function appropriately?
- Who does the organisation depend on to carry out key activities?
- Who depends on the organisation?
- Are there any service level agreements, legal or regulatory obligations on the organisation?

- Do disaster recovery, business continuity and emergency plans already exist and do they cover the key activities?

- Are there any natural fluctuations of operational activity (eg month-end for payroll, or end of year for accounts)?

2.25 How long can the business manage without key activities? The impact may be felt immediately or it may escalate over time. Prioritise according to the analysis.

2.26 Consider the response of individual departments. How essential are they in the immediate aftermath? Can personnel be redirected to other tasks? Is their role essential to the overall performance of the organisation in the short term?

Defining the business continuity strategy

2.27 From this point the need is to develop a continuity plan to enable the organisation to be resilient to the event. The BCP is designed as an emergency response to a problem that allows the business to continue to produce a minimum acceptable output.

2.28 Once the key activities and resources have been identified, together with the associated risks, it is now important to determine how the risks can be managed.

2.29 The following strategies are those most commonly applied.

- Accept the risks and change nothing.
- Attempt to reduce the risks.
- Attempt to reduce the risks and make plans to restore key activities as soon as possible.
- Cease the activity altogether.

2.30 One essential decision is how to respond to risks that cannot be reduced.

Developing the plan

2.31 The BCP should contain the key areas as listed in Table 15.1. This is not an exhaustive list and other key pieces of information may be required as part of the strategy.

Table 15.1 *Key areas of the BCP*

Roles and responsibilities	Identify who needs to take responsibility for each action, including deputies to cover key roles. Identify a recovery team and a coordinator.
Incident checklists for key staff	Use checklists that readers can easily follow.
First stage	Include clear, direct instructions or a checklist for the crucial first hour following an incident.
Following stages	Include a checklist of things that can wait until after the first hour.
Document review	Agree how often, when and how you will check your plan to make sure it is current. Update your plan to reflect changes in your organisation and in the risks you might face.

2.32 It is essential to have top-level support. Gaining management and staff support comes from education and training, increased awareness and embedding the crisis management ethos within the organisation.

Rehearsing the plan

2.33 Testing and rehearsing the plan is an important part of contingency planning. It gives an opportunity to test the arrangements and principles of the plan in a 'safe' environment, without risk to the business. There are various levels of rehearsal or evaluation that can be used. They will obviously vary with cost and value, but a planning lifecycle should allow for periodic tests of different types: see Table 15.2

Table 15.2 *Methods of rehearsing the contingency plan*

Table top exercise	Test the plan using a 'what if' written scenario. New pieces of information can be added as the scenario unfolds, in the same way that more details would become clear in a real incident.
Communications test	With or without warning, a test message is sent out to everyone at the top of the call cascade lists in the plan(s). An audit can then determine how well the information was communicated through the organisation.
Full rehearsal	A full rehearsal will show how well different elements in the plan work together, which may not have become clear when testing the individual parts. However, this can be an expensive way to test the plan.

2.34 The main advantages of a planned response are as follows.

- Identification of critical systems and information in advance of an event, so that an informed decision can be taken on the extent to which such systems should be protected
- Definition of the roles of individual officers
- Determination of the resources required to maintain a minimum level of service to the community/customers

2.35 It is important always to relate aims during the BCM process to the business needs. For example, it is not the function of an information security plan to protect all information; it just needs to protect the information that the business needs to have protected.

2.36 BCM aims to ensure that crises don't occur, but should the worst come to the worst, effective crisis management can make the difference between business-as-usual or disaster.

2.37 Once the plan has been tested and designed, it is important to evaluate the plan periodically and retest it as business processes change. This is because the requirements of a business change constantly; for example, a company may buy new equipment on which it is heavily dependent and which was not included in the BCP. Thus a BCP should be revised after purchases and upgrades of equipment and so on. The BCP is a living document, which must be changed and adjusted if business requirements change.

2.38 It is equally important to educate everyone in the company about the BCP. Since it will be the employees who are there to react to (or in some cases prevent) an incident, a BCP's success or failure depends largely on the way it is implemented by the employees. If they are not properly trained regarding the BCP, its likelihood of success is seriously diminished.

The Business Continuity Institute

2.39 The Business Continuity Institute (BCI) defines BCM as 'a holistic management process that identifies potential impacts that threaten an organisation and provides a framework for building resilience with the capability for an effective response that safeguards the interests of its key stakeholders, reputation, brand and value-creating activities'.

2.40 The Business Continuity Institute was founded in 1994 and defines the professional competencies expected of business continuity professionals. These are encompassed in the ten disciplines detailed in Table 15.3.

2.41 The Business Continuity Institute considers that these ten disciplines are essential to any BCM process but there should be no particular significance attributed to the order in which these disciplines are presented.

BCM methodology

2.42 The BCI has developed a five-stage process that has become widely accepted. This model provides a generic framework that is applicable across industry and the service sector. Work is presently underway to integrate the methodology into a British Standard.

2.43 The business continuity process follows the BCM lifecycle containing five stages. Part 1 of the lifecycle outlines the requirement for a business impact analysis (BIA) and a business risk assessment (BRA).

2.44 The BCM lifecycle usually includes a series of steps.

- Risk assessment and BIA
- Plan development
- Document
- Test
- Maintain

2.45 The BRA looks at the probability and impact of a variety of specific threats that could cause a business disruption. The risk assessment should focus on the most urgent business functions.

2.46 This should in turn be followed by developing and writing a full BCP. Table 15.4 contains an outline.

2.47 In conclusion businesses should have both contingency planning and BCP in place in order to resume functionality, and procedures in case of an incident which affects the company. This will enable them to recover far more quickly and with less losses than a company who disregards such plans, thinking 'it could never happen to us'.

Table 15.3 *Ten disciplines of business continuity*

1	**Project initiation and management**	To establish the need for a BCP. This includes obtaining management support and organising and managing the BCP project to completion within agreed time and budget limits
2	**Risk evaluation and control**	To determine the events and environmental surroundings that can adversely affect the organisation with disruption as well as disaster, the damage such events may cause and the controls needed to prevent or minimise loss
3	**Business impact analysis**	To identify the impacts resulting from disruptions and disaster scenarios that can affect the organisation; to apply techniques that can be used to quantify these impacts; to establish critical functions, their recovery priorities and inter-dependencies in order that recovery time objectives can be set
4	**Developing business continuity strategies**	To determine and guide the selection of alternative business recovery operating strategies within the recovery time objective, while maintaining the organisation's critical functions
5	**Emergency response and operation**	Develop and implement procedures for responding to and stabilising the situation following an event
6	**Developing and implementing business continuity plans**	To design, develop and implement the business continuity plan that provides recovery within the recovery time objective
7	**Awareness and training programmes**	To prepare a progamme to create corporate awareness and enhance the skills required to develop, implement, maintain, and execute the business continuity plan
8	**Maintaining and exercising business continuity plans**	To pre-plan and coordinate plan exercises, and evaluate and document plan exercise results; to develop processes to maintain business continuity planning within the organisation
9	**Public relations and crisis coordination**	To develop, coordinate and evaluate exercise plans to handle the media during crisis situations; to develop, coordinate, evaluate and exercise plans to communicate with and, as appropriate, provide trauma counseling for employees and their families, key customers, critical suppliers and corporate management during crises; to ensure all stakeholders are kept informed
10	**Coordination with public authorities**	To establish applicable procedures and policies for coordinating continuity and restoration activities with local authorities while ensuring compliance with applicable statutes or regulations

2.48 Business continuity should be seen as a safety net for businesses. Even though there are costs involved, it is well worth having such plans as it will save the business during an incident and help it to react in an ordered and timely matter.

2.49 Manufacturers are highly dependent on their suppliers. It is important to work together with major suppliers (at least the ones that support the primary business functions) and make sure that partners and suppliers have good BCP plans in place. It is of little use to have effective BCP plans in place whilst the main suppliers have none.

Table 15.4 *Steps in developing a BCP*

1	**Commence log**	It is vital to commence a record of timings, decisions (by whom) and actions taken from the onset of any disruption. The record/log keeper must also sign each entry. The log is likely to be required at any subsequent inquiry, Tribunal or Court hearing.
2	**Emergency services**	If the emergency services are involved it may be necessary to appoint a Liaison Officer.
3	**Record of damage**	Carry out a damage assessment and document: • Injury to staff/visitors/members of the public • Damage to property/loss of stock/services • Damage to contents of buildings (machinery, equipment, vehicles) Assess extent of disruption (business completely/partially disrupted).
4	**Assemble business recovery team**	The business recovery team members and alternates should be listed, with contact telephone numbers, in the BCP.
5	**Look after and brief staff**	• It is vital to ensure that staff are properly cared for. Should anyone need medical treatment they should be escorted to hospital and their next of kin informed. If necessary, provision should be made to get next of kin to the hospital also and appropriate welfare provision should be put in place as required. • Keep all staff fully briefed (emails, text messages, letter, telephone, local media, set up a help line etc) • Should they remain at work, should they report for work – when/where? • If the workplace is destroyed what does the future hold? • If they are re-deployed consider transport, childcare etc. • Maintain a record and copies of all briefings.
6	**Inform**	Customers, suppliers, contractors; maintain a record of all communications.
7	**Public information**	• Ideally there should be a trained media representative who is capable of dealing confidently with all media. Ensure that what is given to the media is factual and honest. In return you should receive sympathetic and helpful coverage. • Consider a prepared holding statement.
8	**Debrief**	Arrange a full debrief following the disruption. Invite all those involved and disseminate the lessons learnt to all concerned. Assign responsibility, actions and timelines for corrective activities.
9	**Review BCP**	The board of directors should be accountable for ensuring that the organisation has developed and tested business continuity and disaster recovery plans that deal with all the likely risks that face the organisation. BS 25999 is the international best practice standard for business continuity plans. BS 25999 will be a two-part standard that contains both a specification for, and best practice guidance on, business continuity planning.

3   *Media management*

Introduction

3.1   One aspect of BCP that deserves special attention is media management. It is important to have good media management during this process. This is because an organisation that recovers after an incident, but does not communicate with its customers, suppliers, stakeholders, shareholders, employees, or affected public will have lost the trust of these groups.

3.2   This will have an adverse impact on the company's public perception, leading to a deterioration of faith in the company. In the end it will translate itself into revenue losses. So BCP should also focus on what the military like to call 'hearts and minds' operations, where the company tries to maintain its public standing. Businesses should prepare public statements beforehand as it would be very bad to have no comments during a crisis. In the absence of such prepared comments, journalists will still write about the crisis, but possibly in an ill-informed way. This can be seriously damaging in terms of public relations.

Public relations

3.3   Public relations (PR) is the management of an organisation's corporate image through the management of relationships with the organisation's stakeholders (publics).

3.4   A definition of public relations was given by Roger Hayward (1998): 'Those efforts used by management to identify and close any gap between how the organisation is seen by its key publics and how it would like to be seen'.

3.5   The role of public relations is brought to the fore at times of crisis. Public relations actions and responses are an integral part of the BCP process.

3.6   Public relations will form a cross-functional team, usually no more than four or five people as this aids communication. A typical team may include a PR officer, the safety manager, the factory/office manager and a board member. The team should meet regularly to review risks identified in the overall risk management process as well as those highlighted in contingency planning and BCP.

3.7   The team should be trained in presentation techniques, especially TV interviews. Nominated deputies should be appointed and trained. A number of responses should be considered and prioritised.

3.8   An issue that must be considered in crisis management is that many crises are newsworthy. An organisation should prepare for this in advance with effective planning and, where possible, having established a good rapport with the press over time. Preparation is important and as soon as the crisis breaks the crisis team should be ready to organise a press conference, if possible on the company's premises.

3.9   The PR team must not exacerbate the situation. Care must be given to statements made. Insurance and legal liability may be affected by what is said – not to mention the potential damage to the company's reputation.

3.10 Crisis management should not be left until the crisis happens. Integrating public relations into the wider risk management framework ensures that responses are considered and appropriate. Public relations brings a degree of professionalism to communications with the media that can answer questions appropriately and minimise the impact to an organisation.

Chapter summary

- Contingency planning means putting plans in place to ensure business continuity in the event of adverse occurrences.

- A contingency plan is a fallback position should anything go wrong.

- A scenario describes a possible future business environment but is not a prediction. Scenario planning is not about predicting the future. It is about exploring the future.

- The 'What if?' question now common across many business areas is highly relevant to contingency planning.

- Supply chain contingency planning is about considering the contingency issues and the possible ramifications.

- Business continuity is a management process that provides a framework to ensure the resilience of a business to any eventuality, to help ensure continuity of service to key customers and the protection of brand and reputation.

- Business continuity plans should be clear, concise and tailored to the needs of the business.

- The business continuity plan is designed as an emergency solution to a problem that allows the business to continue to produce a minimum acceptable output.

- Make sure that partners and suppliers have good BCP plans in place as it is of little use to have effective BCP plans in place whilst the main suppliers have none.

- An issue that must be considered in crisis management is that many crises are newsworthy.

- Public relations actions and responses are an integral part of the business continuity planning process.

Self-test questions

The numbers in brackets refer to the paragraphs where you can check your answers.

1   Give five examples of possible events that might constitute a crisis. (1.1)

2   Outline the steps in creating a contingency plan. (1.8)

3   Define scenario planning. (1.12)

4   According to the Chartered Management Institute, what percentage of companies do not have any plans in place to ensure they will be able to keep running if disaster happens? (1.27)

5   How does business continuity planning differ from contingency planning and disaster recovery? (2.4, 2.5)

6   What is the purpose of a business impact analysis? (2.13)

7   List methods of rehearsing the contingency plan. (2.33)

8   How does the Business Continuity Institute define business continuity management? (2.39)

Further reading

*   Kit Sadgrove, *The Complete Guide to Business Risk Management*, Chapters 16
*   Business *Continuity Management*, Confederation of British Industries

CHAPTER 16

Mock Exam

THE EXEMPLAR PAPER

The exam paper below was published by CIPS as an illustration of what might be expected under the new syllabus. If you are able to make a good attempt at the paper below you should be very well prepared for the live examination.

Instructions for Candidates:

This examination is in two sections.

Section A has **two** compulsory questions, worth 25 marks each.

Section B has **four** questions: answer **two**. Each question is worth 25 marks.

Time allowed: **THREE** hours.

SECTION A

You are strongly advised to spend approximately 30 minutes reading and analysing the following case study.

QuickTime Telecoms

QuickTime Telecoms produces an extensive range of products used in the telecommunications sector, focusing on optical communication equipment and components, including transmitters and receivers. The managing director has turned his attention to the supply chain management of the company to help boost the profitability of the firm. He decided to source laser transmitters and optical receivers from China in an effort significantly to reduce costs. The materials and parts for this equipment were currently being bought from UK suppliers, and then the finished products were assembled at QuickTime's UK manufacturing centre.

QuickTime needed assistance with its procurement project to source laser transmitters and optical receivers from Chinese suppliers. The company used the services of an agent Offshore Sourcing and Select (OSS) to develop sources of supply from China. OSS promised to achieve greater control of import costs as well as to ensure general reliability of supply arrangements made with Chinese suppliers.

OSS introduced QuickTime to a manufacturer of laser transmitters and optical receivers, Shahida Industries (SI). The company boasted investment in manufacturing equipment of over $80 million and had approval to ISO 9001: 2000 series as well as accreditation to various Chinese quality assurance standards. With staffing of in excess of 150 personnel, and a plant in excess of 3,500 square metres, Shahida Industries appeared to have the necessary resource and capacity to meet QuickTime's requirements. Jim Hunt, the manufacturing manager of QuickTime, received samples of laser transmitters and optical receivers produced by SI.

These were subject to rigorous testing to analyse their reliability. QuickTime designers prepared detailed specifications with tolerances as well as materials composition. These specifications were then sent to SI's research and development facility. Equipment used on the QuickTime production lines for laser transmitters and optical receivers was despatched under a separate contract made with a specialist shipping and logistics company, InterFreight. The equipment was then set up at SI's plant and so once the line had been commissioned, the supplier was in a position to trial prototypes for production.

SI confirmed its ability to produce volume quantities of the products specified. In November, initial purchase orders were placed via OSS for the first batches of production for both laser transmitters and optical receivers. The first orders were received with the absence of any defects in the products supplied or delays. Further orders were then sent in December for February delivery.

In March, there were the first signs of trouble. The February shipments due were not delivered, causing lost sales for QuickTime as its customers decided to cancel their orders and use other suppliers instead. SI's marketing manager was most apologetic, and blamed the delays on congestion at a Chinese port. The February deliveries were eventually delivered in the third week of April. The inventory planning section of QuickTime decided to reschedule all deliveries.

The next consignment delivered in May was not only late, but the stock supplied was damaged. QuickTime's managing director, procurement manager and manufacturing manager decided to make an impromptu visit to SI. The QuickTime delegation were shocked at what they saw. Of the greatest concern was the working conditions that the supplier's personnel worked under, as well as the age of the female workers employed, as many appeared to be of school age. Meanwhile, during a walk through to the finished product area, they saw packages marked to be sent to both Quintec and AB Telecoms, QuickTime's competitors. A look at the stores revealed boxes of optical receivers produced by another Chinese firm, Tellus Group.

The team went away to think about the day's events. They realised that they had been too reliant on OSS and were now asking questions about how the situation could be resolved. QuickTime had orders from its customers to meet, but no longer had any in-house capability to meet this demand. Solutions needed to be found, and fast.

The information in this case study is purely fictitious and has been prepared for assessment purposes only.

Any resemblance to any organisation or person is purely coincidental.

QUESTIONS

You are strongly advised to read the questions carefully and it is recommended that you spend approximately 35 minutes answering each question.

Question 1

(a) Describe the risk assessment processes QuickTime could have used to analyse the risks in adopting the sourcing strategy. **(12 marks)**

(b) Using the processes identified above, analyse the risks that were experienced by QuickTime when entering into the contract with SI. **(13 marks)**

Question 2

(a) Summarise the actions that QuickTIme could have taken to manage this sourcing project more proactively. **(13 marks)**

(b) Suggest the actions QuickTime should now take to resolve the current problems with SI. **(12 marks)**

SECTION B

You are strongly advised to spend 10 minutes carefully reading the questions in Section B before selecting **TWO** questions to answer. It is recommended that you spend approximately 35 minutes answering each question from this section.

Question 3

Discuss how the Kraljic matrix can be used to manage supply chain risks. **(25 marks)**

Question 4

In order to assess the risks of particular events that can impact on the performance of contracts with suppliers, it can be productive to use probability theory to estimate the likelihood of events.

(a) Explain the different types of probability theory. **(15 marks)**

(b) Explain how probability theory can be used to assess risk in the supply chain. **(10 marks)**

Question 5

Explain how a risk register can be applied to the procurement process. Illustrate your answer with examples. **(25 marks)**

Question 6

(a) Analyse the technological risks that may be present with the use of e-procurement systems. **(15 marks)**

(b) Suggest the possible means of mitigating the risks you have identified. **(10 marks)**

CHAPTER 17

MOCK EXAM:
SUGGESTED SOLUTIONS

Solution 1

This open-ended question lends itself to discussion of many different techniques covering a wide scope of the syllabus.

Part (a)

Business risk can be defined as the level of uncertainty associated with the possible operational outcomes of a business venture. This venture by QuickTime certainly has a high level of risk exposure that could easily have an adverse impact on continuity of supply to customers and therefore ultimately on the market reputation of QuickTime. A range of appropriate risk management tools and techniques could have been deployed to mitigate this level of risk exposure.

QuickTime management could have developed a structured approach to managing the risk associated with this outsourcing venture. This could have commenced with senior management defining the level of risk appetite they considered appropriate for the QuickTime supply chain and then ensuring that any associated activities were aligned and managed accordingly.

A structured approach to managing risk could have been further enhanced by the introduction of a risk register. This would have ensured that a systematic approach to assessing and managing risk was undertaken by QuickTime. Indeed the risk register provides the organisational focus and responsibility that supports the necessary culture for managing business risk.

In terms of supply chain management at the operational level purchasing could have used a range of segmentation tools such as the Kraljic matrix, supplier preference modelling etc to analyse the QuickTime supply chain vulnerability.

In addition, purchasing could have used market research facilities to provide the QuickTime management with market status information relating to the supply of optical components.

Finally, audit mechanisms could have been used in an attempt to mitigate supply risk. Prior to supplier selection, audit techniques might have included in-depth organisational analysis or supplier site visits.

Part (b)

QuickTime's focus on supply chain activity to increase the profitability of the organisation appears to be a logical initiative. Indeed, within most organisations there is often a significant potential for cost reduction along the supply chain, especially given the increasingly global nature of supply markets.

Alternative supply solutions (such as outsourcing to low-labour cost countries) appear to present an attractive proposition. However, this type of solution will often expose organisations to increased levels of business risk. This is especially probable where organisations such as QuickTime have no, or little, previous experience of managing global supply chains that can span many thousands of miles and that present problems not previously encountered within UK inbound supply.

The level of risk from choosing an international unproven single source of supply must be regarded as significant. A more prudent approach might have been to consider a dual sourcing alternative. This could have involved QuickTime producing in parallel up to the point where the Chinese supplier was a proven and trusted supply source. Once this was proven, the QuickTime production could then be progressively phased out over a period of time.

The use of segmentation analysis would have clearly highlighted the critical nature of this intended supply source. Other segmentation models such as supplier preferencing might have supplied a different market perspective as seen from the supplier's point of view.

In addition, the use of market research databases would have provided an invaluable source of organisational data including that of benchmarking SI as a prospective supplier.

If a single supplier was to be selected then a more penetrating examination of the supplier would have been recommended, including both financial and commercial analysis. In addition it would have been essential to supplement this examination by on-site audits for such a critical category supply source.

It was imperative that the QuickTime management encouraged and supported a structured risk awareness approach when managing such ventures. It is essential that all personnel understand their roles and responsibilities in managing the risks involved.

A critical tool in supporting a structured approach to managing risk is the formulation and subsequent maintenance of a risk register. A key component of the risk register is the risk assessment and impact analysis of all identified risks associated with the QuickTime venture. This might have included using techniques such as scenario planning where a range of potential possibilities for project eventualities could have been considered.

Another key component of a risk register is the mitigation of risk. QuickTime should have developed proposals and indeed contingency plans to reduce the level of risk exposure. For example, the risk associated with single sourcing its optical components could have been thoroughly examined and discussed from all organisational viewpoints. Alternative, and lower-risk, options could have been developed (such as dual sourcing) that would have significantly mitigated the level of risk for QuickTime.

Organisations such as QuickTime who are engaging in international sourcing of this significance need to be very proactive in their management of such ventures. They opted for the easy option of using an intermediary to manage their affairs. This actually increased the level of risk exposure for the project. Whilst it is eminently sensible to take advantage of local expertise the central role of responsibility should have remained with the QuickTime management.

If such a level of trust was to be bestowed upon SI then at the very least QuickTime should have negotiated some level of insurance or use of indemnities from the agent.

A more proactive QuickTime role would have significantly reduced the risk exposure from this international supply source. Far more robust and penetrating attempts to establish supplier credentials were needed from the outset of the venture. For example, a supplier selection process that involved QuickTime personnel visiting prospective suppliers would have highlighted both production and ethical concerns about the SI organisation.

Solution 2

Part (a)

The overall approach by QuickTime to managing this project appears to be somewhat sloppy in nature. They should have been far more proactive in managing this venture.

Far too much reliance and trust was placed upon the OSS organisation in appraising, selecting and managing this key supply source.

Audits of prospective suppliers could have been undertaken. This could also have included data gathering exercises related to existing customers of these potential suppliers, covering operational considerations such as reliability, quality, communications etc. Indeed other third-party personnel could be involved in this exercise where appropriate specialisms were required.

Having identified prospective suppliers using appropriate market research the QuickTime management could have visited a range of potential suppliers and therefore have been far more proactive in supplier selection.

Having made a decision as to future supplier(s) QuickTime really needed some of their own staff seconded to the nominated supplier to reduce the risk level related to misunderstanding of the QuickTime needs.

This need for some level of QuickTime presence is further evidenced by the concern that the pre-production samples provided by SI may have been produced by a third party. This in itself is of concern as the involvement of an unknown third party further increases the potential risk of the supply.

The role of the purchaser in this QuickTime venture also needed to be far more thorough. Using appropriate analysis techniques and market research the purchaser could have provided much valuable information to assist in reducing the risk exposure of the project. For example, environmental analysis techniques would have provided a more balanced consideration of the project implications. It appears that minimal consideration has been given to ethical or environmental considerations involved in this sourcing supply.

Supply chain modelling and mapping analysis would have provided QuickTime with a more comprehensive understanding of where value was being generated within the supply chain together with any associated vulnerabilities. This is particularly important in understanding the total risk and costs associated with this potential supply source. Too often organisations fail to see the total implications of such outsourcing initiatives. As a consequence many are forced to reverse the outsourcing decision later on.

QuickTime should have given significantly more attention to securing business continuity. The prime reason for this initiative appears to be profit orientated with little regard being given to the risks involved in sustaining and improving the level of customer service. QuickTime would be well served by reminding themselves that if their customers become dissatisfied then business profitability will be significantly jeopardised.

Part (b)

The current QuickTime dilemma clearly does not present any prospect of an immediate solution. The focus of any potential recovery actions must therefore be based on damage limitation. The company is in danger of losing market credibility and, in the short term, contingency actions must be developed that protect their market position as best they can.

There are a number of possible considerations that are focused on retaining market credibility and securing continuity of ongoing optical supply.

Proactive customer service campaign

It is essential that QuickTime limits any damage to both its customer base and its market reputation. This will clearly be a sensitive operation until assurances of supply continuity are in place. Nevertheless QuickTime must seize the initiative with its customers by means of a proactive and positive communication initiative. In liaison with its customers QuickTime needs to establish a realistic priority list of forthcoming customer needs. This will ensure optimum use of limited optical stocks in the short term.

What can be salvaged from SI?

There are clearly major commercial doubts about continuing any business relationships with SI. Apart from their delivery capability there are also serious ethical concerns emerging from the impromptu visit of QuickTime representatives.

The commercial reality is that the QuickTime representation will probably not change the cultural and ethical stance of SI with regard to the issue of child labour. However, the QuickTime representation might be able to salvage some level of WIP supply from SI before a veil is drawn over the unhappy venture. If successful this would provide some level of optical supply that could meet immediate customer demand.

Negotiate direct supply from Tellus Group

It is apparent that SI are using the third party Tellus Group to supplement the supply of optical components (or indeed may have outsourced the complete provision to this Chinese organisation).

The QuickTime representation could open negotiations with the Tellus Group and quickly explore the possibility of commencing direct supply. Visits can be made by the QuickTime representatives to ensure that their supply needs are capable of being met by the Tellus Group. At the same time ethical considerations important to QuickTime can be assessed and discussed accordingly.

Alternative global supply considerations

Using appropriate market research alternative optical supply sources could also be considered. Specialised market research databases could be utilised to accelerate this process.

If successful in this search QuickTime could consider, at least in the short term, using multiple supply sources to overcome the current commercial problem. Supplier performance could then be appraised as to the development of a future supply strategy.

Other short-term considerations

Owing to the nature of the short-term situation QuickTime could also revisit previously rejected optical stocks with a view to assessing the viability of rectification work.

Another emergency consideration might be to explore the possibility of using alternative products that could be re-badged with QuickTime logos. These could be offered to customers as a cut-price alternative in the short-term absence of the genuine products.

Finally, depending on the commercial relationships with its competitors, QuickTime could attempt to negotiate supplies of optical stocks from them as a short-term contingency measure.

Solution 3

The recommended response structure for this open-ended question is as follows.

- *General introduction to Kraljic*

- *Main body*

  - *Explain the mechanics of the Kraljic matrix*
  - *Discuss how Kraljic can be used to manage supply risk exposure*
  - *Outline potential weaknesses of the technique*

- *Summary conclusions*

The Kraljic matrix is essentially a supplier segmentation technique that categorises procurements on the basis of their risk versus expenditure (or impact on organisational profitability). In general terms supply chain risk can be assessed along the following two dimensions.

1. Complexity of the supply market

2. Supply impact on business operations and profitability

The following paragraphs describe the principles of the Kraljic matrix together with its application in managing inherent supply chain risk.

The Kraljic matrix, or procurement positioning grid, was developed by Peter Kraljic in 1973. It is a tool of analysis that seeks to map the importance to the organisation of the item being purchased against the complexity of the market that supplies it. The vertical axis (measuring the importance of the item) is usually related to the amount of the organisation's annual spend on the item in question: high spend implies high importance – see the figure below.

Complexity of the supply market

	Low	High
Low	**Routine or non-critical items** Require systems contract approach to purchasing	**Bottleneck items** Require continuity of supply
High	**Leverage items** Require competitive bidding	**Strategic items** Require a 'partnership and alliance' approach

Importance of item to the organisation

The approach that the organisation should then take to sourcing an item is decided by where the item is positioned on the grid.

- If an item falls within the low spend/low risk category as a routine item the approach may be to use IT management of the spend. This may be achieved by permitting the supplier to manage the inventory and re-stocking against an annually negotiated agreement, eg as with stationery supplies. Purchasing management is achieved by monitoring spend against regular reports provided, as agreed with the supplier.

- If an item falls within the high-dependency bottleneck section the objective is one of strategic security. Approaches could be carrying a higher level of stock than would otherwise be the case or developing a closer relationship with suppliers than the value of the item would otherwise indicate. The purchasing objective is to ensure continuity of supply.

- The leverage section indicates a more traditional approach where a number of suppliers exist in a market and can be judged by commercial criteria such as price, quality and delivery. The objective is to secure supply but it is not one where a long-term relationship of importance is envisaged.

- The strategic section of the grid examines the implications of high-risk and high-value items where the approach could be a more long-term sustainable relationship that will bring benefits through closer supply chain, IT and management processes.

The horizontal axis demonstrates the risk an organisation is exposing itself to in terms of the degree of difficulty in sourcing a particular product or component or the vulnerability of the supplier to fulfil their obligations. The vertical axis examines profit potential and is used to indicate the extent to which the potential of supply can contribute to profitability.

Profit potential may be realised by cost reductions or efficiency gains. For items in the strategic quadrant we can consider supplier relationships over the longer term by developing supply chain solutions to areas of cost and waste. This can add to profit potential by joint product/service development opportunities and a more integrated approach to information technology and knowledge management.

Any supply market is potentially a dynamic and volatile entity. The application of the matrix might therefore yield different results for different organisations, and even for the same organisation over time. For instance, the sourcing of steel has moved from an adversarial relationship for many organisations when there was a situation of global over supply to a more strategic relationship as organisations react to the impact of Chinese demand on the supply market. In other words, for many organisations steel has moved from being a leverage item to being a strategic item.

Applying Kraljic's matrix to a particular context is a fairly straightforward process that can prove highly effective. However, it does have some weaknesses.

- It ignores the fact that not all the risk of the supply comes from within the relationship between customer and supplier. External environmental factors, especially competition and the PESTLE factors, can impact greatly.

- It applies to products/services rather than to suppliers. A supplier of non-critical items may also be the supplier of strategic ones, for instance. Applying the grid to suppliers rather than goods or services is often used when contemplating a supplier reduction programme. Treating a strategic supplier as a non-critical one, for instance, simply because it supplies both types of product would be a clear mistake.

- While the buyer may perceive an item to be a leverage one, this is only perceived on the other side of the relationship by the supplier if the buyer's spend is significant. In other words, the relative sizes and perceptions of the parties should also be taken into account.

In summary, the Kraljic matrix can provide a relatively user-friendly segmentation mechanism that enables supply chain risk exposure to be logically identified and subsequently managed. However, any organisational supply profile is a dynamic entity and therefore its relative risk exposure is ever-changing in today's global supply markets.

Whilst the Kraljic matrix brings an ordered approach to managing supply risk it also has weaknesses as previously discussed. It should be viewed as one technique amongst several that can be deployed in the overall assessment of supply risk. Other tools and techniques (such as the supplier preferencing model, PESTLE analysis, and Pareto analysis) can also be used to supplement the overall assessment of supply chain risk.

Solution 4

Part (a)

This was a very difficult question to interpret. The phrase 'different types of probability theory' in Part (a) has no obvious meaning. It appears from the examiner's report that it refers to different types of probability distribution.

Probability as a quantitative tool aims to add a numerical scale of measurement to ideas such as 'very unlikely' or 'quite likely'. By convention, the measurement scale ranges from 0 (impossible) to 1 (certainty): 0.5 therefore represents an even or 50:50 chance.

If there are **m** equally likely outcomes to a trial, **n** of which result in a given outcome **x**, the probability of that outcome – symbolised as P(x) – is n/m.

For example, if an unbiased die is thrown in an unbiased way, each of the scores 1 to 6 is equally likely. The probability of an even number being thrown can be calculated as follows:

P(even) = 3/6 = 0.5; ie three of the possible six outcomes are even numbers (2, 4 and 6).

There are three main different types of probability distribution used in statistical analysis: the binomial distribution, the Poisson distribution, and the normal distribution.

The **binomial distribution** is applicable for discrete events with only two outcomes (**p** or **q**: eg success or failure; has or doesn't have a particular attribute; answer is yes or no; event will or won't happen). Mathematically, this relationship can be represented by:

$P(p + q) = 1$.
So if $p = \frac{1}{2}$, $q = 1 - \frac{1}{2} = \frac{1}{2}$.

Typical applications for the binomial distribution include the following.

- Probability of a batch containing defects or non-defects; x or more/less-than-x defects

- Customers buying or not buying a brand.

- Success or failure of a project; delivery on time or late

The Poisson probability applies when the chance of an occurrence is unknown and small. So for example, Poisson can be used when there is a **small** probability of the event occurring in a single test, and in a very **large** number of tests.

Typical Poisson applications include the following.

- Quality control: defects (or non-defects) within, for example, a length of cable or time period

- Risk assessment: problems occurring, or success/failure within a given time period

The **normal distribution** (also referred to as the Gaussian distribution) applies to other random events not covered by the binomial and Poisson applications. It is one of the most commonly applied tools for predicting the behaviour of many natural processes. The normal distribution frequency is represented by a 'bell curve' shape that orientates around the central mean value of the process.

The application of the normal distribution is the foundation for predicting the probability of likely occurrences based on continuous historical data that is formed into a frequency distribution and often presented as a histogram.

Typical applications include predicting the probability of defects. For example, if a process is behaving 'normally' then any process defects are normally distributed around the mean and it is therefore possible to calculate the probability of, for example, a steel rod output from a manufacturing process having a diameter between 1.2 and 1.3 centimetres.

Part (b)

Probability theory can be used to predict the likelihood of any individual event, including events within a business supply chain.

For example, by analysing the historical data of suppliers' delivery achievements it is possible to predict the probability of late deliveries. Typically, this probability data can be represented on the following simplistic risk scale.

Risk probability	Interpretation	Risk rating
> 0 – < 0.30	Not very likely to occur	Low
> 0.30 – < 0.70	Reasonable chance of occurrence	Medium
> 0.70 – < 1.0	Likely to occur	High

Analysis of the above risk exposure can influence supply chain decisions such as:

*   Levels of safety stock needed to support supply chain continuity

*   Need for supplier development

*   Market research for alternative suppliers

The same probability logic can be used to assess the risks of many supply chain activities (eg quality of delivered product). The only requirement to enable this statistical analysis to be performed is the availability of historical data.

Historical data can be used to assess the arithmetic mean (or average) values of past performance. This in turn enables the standard deviation of the process to be calculated which can then be used to support continuous improvement initiatives.

If samples of data are used then it is important to ensure that the samples are representative of the entire data population. If this is not the case then clearly this may lead to misrepresentation of the potential risk exposure.

Solution 5

The recommended structure for answering this question is as follows.

- *Introduce the concept and context of a risk register*

- *Describe the essential components of a risk register including illustrative procurement applications, where applicable*

- *Reflective summary on the benefits of using risk registers*

The concept of risk management can be developed at any level within the organisation. This therefore embraces strategic, tactical and operational considerations, although the focus and direction of managing risk within the business needs to be shaped at the highest level.

An important tool for managing business risk is known as the 'risk register'. This is a formal record of identified risks related to a business activity. The register contains information listing all the risks identified for the activity. In addition the register includes information that explains the nature of each risk and information relevant to its assessment and management.

In accord with the overall organisational management of risk, risk registers can be drawn up at different levels within the organisation. They therefore embrace a continuum that includes everything from strategic considerations to individual supply contracts. For example corporate and strategic planning objectives can be broken down into a number of subheadings that include procurement initiatives for the forthcoming financial year. Typically, this might include the development of strategic supply partnerships which exposes the business to increased levels of risk. In managing this risk exposure a risk register would be developed accordingly.

The completed risk register related to the development of strategic supply partners should be brief and to the point, so that it quickly conveys the essential information. It should be updated on a regular basis, at least monthly. The description of the risk should include the associated consequences where these are not obvious. These consequences can be useful in identifying appropriate mitigation actions.

This specific risk register should contain the following information.

- Reference number: this should be a unique reference code for the risk. This will be essential to ensure that no risks are missed and will act as a key where risks are escalated.

- Description: this should describe the nature of the risks related to the development of supply partnerships and how the risk will impact on the organisation. For example, the development of supply partnerships might involve moving to single sourcing of key supplies. The potential impact of lack of supply can have rapid consequences on production continuity. The implications of this possibility in terms of customer supply, profitability etc must be clearly understood within the organisation.

- Probability: this is the likelihood of the risk happening, measured in high, medium and low ratings depending on the organisation's preference. A high rating (H) would suggest that the risk is highly likely to be realised, whilst a low rating (L) would suggest that the risk is unlikely to be realised. It may sometimes be helpful to show intermediate assessments, e.g. H+. It can also be helpful to show a range for the risk, e.g. M–H (medium to high), particularly when the risk is first identified and further analysis is required to fully assess the risk.

- Impact: this is a rating defining the effect that the risk will have on the ability to achieve objectives, measured in high, medium and low ratings. A high rating would suggest that an incidence would severely impact on the ability of the organisation to deliver its objectives, or where the side effects of achieving the objective are considered undesirable. A low rating would suggest that there would be little impact on the ability to achieve objectives or that any side effects are minor. The impact of losing key purchasing skills can be particularly damaging especially where specialised skills are involved (eg commodity negotiations). Equally, the loss of supply for a period of more than 24 hours might present severe trading limitations and would logically deserve a high risk rating.

- Mitigation: this is a description of the action to be taken to reduce the probability of the risk occurring, or to reduce its impact. For each counter-measure indicate whether it reduces probability, impact or both. It is also helpful, especially where there are a number of counter-measures, to indicate the overall level of probability. Where both probability and impact are low, it may be appropriate to accept the risk and not take any mitigating action. In such cases it is still necessary to monitor the risk to ensure that the characteristics have not changed. For example, the impact of interrupted supply might be mitigated by holding safety stocks at appropriate points within the supply chain. In contrast the risk of losing key purchasing skills might be mitigated via the introduction of a multi-skilling programme within the purchasing function.

- Contingency: where a risk is considered to be severe, for example those marked as high probability and high impact, consideration should be given to a contingency plan. The cost of a proposed contingency, and the level of certainty that the counter-measures will prevent the risk occurring, should be considered when deciding whether to spend effort on developing a contingency plan. Contingency plans can be drafted and recorded separately from the risk register but the register should show the document name or other link to the relevant document. The contingency plan related to single sourcing might include the provisional certification and approval of alternative supply sources. Clearly this is a delicate negotiation situation. On one hand you will not wish to undermine the confidence of the main supply partner. On the other hand engaging an alternative supplier without placing any actual orders is not an easy task either.

- Owner: this is the person who carries the responsibility for ensuring that the risk is monitored and, where appropriate, effectively managed. It might not be the person who has to actually do the necessary tasks but they must be continuously aware of the risk status.

- Status: this is a description of the current position for the risk. Include whether the counter-measures are in place and whether they are effective. The status should be reviewed regularly.

In summary, the development of a risk register provides a focal point for managing organisational risk. The potential organisational benefits from the development and use of risk registers include the following.

- Provide a useful tool for managing and reducing the risks identified before and during the year

- Provide the project sponsor, Board or senior management with a documented framework from which risk status can be reported

- Ensure the communication of risk management issues to key stakeholders. For example in the development of strategic supply partnerships this might include both internal and external considerations

- Provide a mechanism for seeking and acting on feedback to encourage the involvement of the key stakeholders, eg regular focus meetings, e-mail newsletter etc

- Identify the mitigation actions required for implementation of the risk management plan and associated costings

Solution 6

Part (a)

Increasingly organisations are using e-business solutions to either attain or sustain competitive advantage. Specifically, the procurement function has evolved numerous e-procurement applications to continuously improve the purchasing functionality of the organisation.

These e-procurement systems are reliant on both hardware and software technology, and specifically on web or internet based technologies. Whilst this technological advancement has yielded many business advantages it has also meant that e-procurement systems have been exposed to increasing levels of risk from both internal and external sources. These business risks can be generally categorised as follows.

- Functional risk, eg internal system malfunction including speed and reliability; this also embraces internet issues such as peak loading operational problems

- Risk of physical theft

- Electronic theft of data/malicious damage

As regards functional risk, the effective application of information technology lies at the heart of organisational management and operations. Increasingly organisations are reliant on their IT systems and infrastructure. This dependence may also expose an organisation to risk.

Computer failure can often be attributed to a small number of causes: breakdown, mainframe issues, hardware problems and electrical failure are perhaps the most common.

As regards physical theft, computers are an attractive proposition to a thief as there is a ready market for the stolen goods.

As regards electronic theft of data and malicious damage, organisations can also be subjected to malicious hacking when attempts are made to either disable the organisation's system completely or to find out security details such as passwords and accounts so that fraudulent transactions can be made. The security of such systems is a significant issue, and there can be internal fraud too as the procurement system can be used for personal gain.

Hacking means seeking unauthorised access to the system and this can take two forms.

- A member of staff trying to access confidential areas

- An external hacker trying to access company data and information

The hacking of data can often involve the use of virus and spyware applications.

A virus is a self-replicating program, usually intended to cause damage to a computer system.

Spyware, although not as invasive as viruses and related programs, involves collating information about the user's internet activities. Spyware programs capture financial and other details and send them back. All computers are vulnerable.

Government survey data indicates that two thirds of businesses surveyed had suffered a system incident in the last twelve months where they had to restore a significant amount of data from backup.

Any organisation with a high degree of reliance on IT systems can be brought to a total standstill if computer failure occurs. Organisations that have a high reliance on real-time processing (organisations such as Amazon, eBay, British Airways etc) are at serious risk in terms of lost business and reputational damage. Other impacts could include: resulting cashflow problems, inability to pay staff, backlog of work and service and quality reduction issues. Computer failure will have different risk ramifications for different organisations but the increasing reliance places IT risk high on the priority list for most organisations.

Part (b)

In relation to functional risk, management of the technological infrastructure of an organisation is critical. Any decisions made relating to the supplying company, possible outsourcing, maintenance agreements etc, should be rigorously assessed as part of the risk management process.

The organisation's ability to use information technology effectively is dependent on the installed computer system, communications, telecommunications and other support systems that comprise the information network. The strategic decisions relating to information systems have long-term ramifications for organisations. They should be considered thoroughly and the potential risks discussed and evaluated.

As mentioned previously, computer failure can often be attributed to a small number of causes. The application of a risk management process will consider each of these and the impact the failure will have on the business, and will develop disaster recovery and contingency planning scenarios that can be implemented to minimise or mitigate the impact.

To counter physical theft, organisations should put security procedures in place (eg marking, securing or installing an alarm) but should also be aware that if computers are stolen there is an increased risk of the thief returning when new computers have been installed.

To counter electronic theft and hacking, organisations may use a firewall, but this should not be relied on completely. Firewalls are a combination of hardware and software located between the parts of an organisation's computer system requiring screening and those accessible from outside. Firewalls enable the restriction of access to selected systems and data through a single gateway, enabling password protected access to authorised users.

If the system detects a hacker they should be locked out by severing links immediately because when discovered the hacker may take extreme action such as deleting company information.

Internal and external access should be password protected with passwords changed regularly. Passwords should be unique to the individual and not obvious. Software programs can go through an entire dictionary using all possible words in an attempt to discover a password. The system should allow only a certain number of attempts at password entry before locking the person out of the system. Similarly, the system should insist that a password contains a mix of alphabetical and numerical characters.

An integral part of protecting against infection by viruses is the use of anti-virus scanning software that will particularly focus on the interface where emails and the internet enter the system.

Anti-virus software should also be placed on each individual computer. Many viruses enter the system when employees download programs from the internet or bring in their own CDs or memory sticks. Official organisational policy should discourage this but can be difficult to enforce as staff increasingly work from home, or at least take work home with them in the evenings.

All computers should also have anti-spyware software which is as important as anti-virus software. Both software types require constant updating as the threats change over time.

Finally, organisations can use ISO 17799, an international standard that can be applied by companies seeking to manage their IT systems.

Amongst other requirements ISO 17799 involves putting in place the following actions designed to minimise the impact of IT risk issues.

*   Define the organisation's information security policy

*   Define the scope of the system

*   Assess the risk; identify the threats and vulnerabilities and assess the impacts on the organisation

*   Identify the risk management areas

*   Select and put in place the controls that will be used

*   Document the selected controls

Subject Index